BANKERS' SAFETY
Methods and Techniques

About the Author

Dr. James Vadackumchery is an eminent criminologist whose achievements are honoured within the pages of the DICTIONARY OF INTERNATIONAL BIOGRAPHY, 24th edition of the International Biographical Centre, Cambridge, England. As an author of [illegible] authentic and authoritative books on police, crime and justice, an author of hundreds of articles and study reports published in national dailies and professional journals of repute, a sought after speaker and an expert [illegible] institutions and media on criminological issues, he [illegible] in T.V. networks both national and international. He is a visiting member on the faculty of many Staff Training Colleges of nationalised and scheduled banks all over the Country. He is presently working on the Faculty of the State Police Training College, Thiruvananthapuram.

Dr. Vadackumchery is B.A. (Criminology), M.A. (Criminology), LL.B. (Law) and Ph.D. (Criminal Justice). He is married to Mary and has two daughters, [illegible] and Neethu.

About the Author

Dr. James Vadackumchery is an eminent criminologist whose achievements are honoured within the pages of the DICTIONARY OF INTERNATIONAL BIOGRAPHY, 28th edition of the International Biographical Centre, Cambridge, England. As an author of 45 authentic and authoritative books on police, crime and justice; an author of hundreds of articles and study reports published in national dailies and professional journals of repute; a sought after speaker and an expert for institutions and media on criminological issues, he telecasts in T.V. networks--both national and international. He is a visiting member on the Faculty of many Staff Training Colleges of nationalized and scheduled banks all over the Country. He is presently working on the Faculty of the State Police Training College, Thiruvananthapuram.

Dr. Vadackumchery is B.A. (Criminology), M.A. (Criminology), LL.B. (Law) and Ph.D (Criminal Justice). He is married to Mary and has two daughters, Neethu and Neethie.

BANKERS' SAFETY

Methods and Techniques

JAMES VADACKUMCHERY

CONCEPT PUBLISHING COMPANY, NEW DELHI - 110059

ISBN 81-7022-937-5

First Published 1985
Second Edition 2002

Published and Printed by

Ashok Kumar Mittal
Concept Publishing Company
A/15-16, Commercial Block, Mohan Garden,
NEW DELHI -110059 (India)

Phones : 5351460, 5351794
Fax : 091-11-5357103
Email : publishing@conceptpub.com

DEDICATED

TO

MARY, MY WIFE

PREFACE TO THE SECOND EDITION

This is the second edition of my book **Bankers' Safety in Money Transactions** which received enviable acceptance all over the Country. The reviews of the book show the appreciation which the book received from the bakers' community. Many banks asked me to bring out a second edition of the book immediately as the frauds and forgeries are rampant everywhere. The Concept Publishing Company, New Delhi came forward to bring out the second edition in print. Staff Training Colleges of nationalised and scheduled banks give instructions to their officers basing on the contents of this book and many of them have invited me to enlighten their staff on the detection of frauds, forgeries, counterfeiting of money, alterations, additions, erasures, obliterations etc. on bank cheques, drafts etc. I could understand that most of them required badly scientific information on the detective aspects of functional banking. The theory explained in the book on each topic and the ways the theories would be applied to practical areas of Indian banking could certainly help the bankers to detect frauds and forgeries without resorting to expert consultations which might be time consuming, expensive and labourious. The availability of trained experts in each branch of the bank would deter criminals and potential criminals to withdraw from their nefarious activities.

I hope that the methods and techniques discussed in this edition will ensure bankers to do their business with more self-confidence and pleasure.

July, 2001
Thiruvananthapuram

James Vadackumchery

PREFACE TO THE FIRST EDITION

This book is designed to serve as a reference tool for bank officers and others who, in the normal course of their professional activities, invariably, come into contact with problems for which expert advice may not be available at arm's length. Though commercial banks have been transacting business with lakhs of people daily, it seems that they have not attempted to give adequate professional skills to their employees in their functional safety measures in banking transactions. The result has been that the people with criminal tendencies approach the banks with fraudulent claims, forged currency notes, false documents, erased or obliterated cheques, etc.

The incidence of banking frauds has shown a steady and alarming increase in the recent past. It is roughly estimated that one hundred crore of rupees is lost to banks every year by various methods of frauds—by cheating, personation, forgery, theft, criminal misappropriation, false claims, misrepresentation, etc. During a period of twenty-six months, taken on random basis, from 1980 to 1985, 370 series of hundred-rupee notes, 64 series of fifty-rupee notes, 56 series of twenty-rupee notes, 209 series of ten-rupee notes, 38 series of five rupee notes, 73 series of two-rupee notes were forged and circulated. Some of the employees in banks are found to indulge themselves in various kinds of criminal activities which cause colossal loss to banking organisations. Lack of knowledge and academic training for bankers' and bank employees in safety measures contribute largely to this state of affairs.

The banker should have the ability to compare the signature of the customers with those kept in the specimen cards; but unfortunately very little scientific knowledge is available to the banker in the comparison of signatures. The Reserve Bank of India, in a circular to the commercial banks, has asked the employees of the banks to compare the signature on the cheque with the specimen on record, by turning both of them upside down. It is believed that this type of examination of signatures can reveal major differences between the signature on the cheques and that on the specimen card. But, what are these differences? Few bankers know them clearly and the result has been that they perform their tasks with a total lack of self-confidence and with a genuine doubt regarding the correctness of their judgements. This book deals extensively with the writing characteristics which, it is hoped, will make the banker to be fully equipped with professional skills needed in banking transactions.

The psychology of the signatory while he signs on a cheque and the characteristics of genuine signature have been elaborately discussed. Detection of traced and free-hand forgeries, erasures, additions, alterations, obliterations, overwritings on cheques, drafts, etc. is still unknown to a good number of bank employees. Clever forgers are quite competent to forge the signatures so skillfully that a banker, unless he is well-informed of the methods of detecting such forgeries, can cause heavy loss to the bank, to the customers or to both.

Bankers are likely to be defrauded by the counterfeiters unless they know the techniques of detecting forged currency and bank notes. Quite often, floating forged money find its way into the banks. Whenever newspaper reports about counterfeit currency notes appear, it is learnt that some banks reject even genuine notes. This causes a lot of problems to both the bank and the customers. The methods of identifying genuine and fake currency and bank-notes are elaborately dealt with in this book.

The finger-prints of illeterate or semi-literate people taken in banks reveal the crude method of taking finger impressions. Litigations in courts fail owing to the crude method of finger-printing resorted to in some of the banks. Ignorance about the proper techniques of finger-printing and the incapacity to appreciate the fine ridge characteristics have been mainly responsible for this state of affairs. This book furnishes literature—theoretical and practical—on finger-printing of customers for banking transactions.

There are a number of professional criminals who have developed their own *modus operandi* to commit crimes in banks. Some of them work in collaboration with unscrupulous bank employees. Knowledge about the methods of operation of these professional criminals and adequate preventive methods to check the rising trend of crimes in banks will surely equip the banker to have a surveillance over the antisocial elements who make a living by committing crimes in banks. This book discusses it in detail.

Knowledge of psychology, behavioural patterns, defence mechanisms, etc. of people is very essential today to ensure security in banking. When a counterfeiter is detected, a forgery is noticed, and an erasure is found out, the *modus operandi* of the criminal is identified, the banker has to question him, i.e., to induce him to admit his guilt. This is not an easy task to do. The book discusses the finer points in interrogation-psychology as well. If the police are contacted, a vivid description of the criminal/suspect must be given and the methods of describing people in such instances are provided with.

When a crime is committed in a bank, the banker has to set the criminal law in motion. He has to guard the scene of crime and should aid the police in their investigation. The book discusses at length all these aspects together with case laws to make the banker to do full justice when situations so demand. When a crime has been registered by the police, the prosecution procedures follow. The banker will have to appear before the Court to give testimony. The banker needs information relating to how best he can perform his duty in a court of law.

In chapter 6 of this book, a number of new safety methods have been suggested. Introduction of these new safety methods, it seems, is the need of the hour. Innovations in any organisation is likely to be resented. Doubtlessly, they call for more man-power, expenditure and labour. Here one has to choose between safety and more expenditure, man-power, etc. If safety is what the banks desire, other things are only secondary.

I must place on record the invaluable help offered by Prof. K.T. Varkey, Principal and Mr. O.J. Thomas, Lecturer, Staff Training College, Catholic Syrian Bank Ltd. They were very enthusiastic from the very outset and devoted several hours for discussion on various points that needed clarification.

Mary, my wife, to whom this book is dedicated has been an inspiration for me, without which this work would not have seen the light of day. I express my eternal gratitude to my devoted wife. Neethu and Neethie, my sweet little daughters have always been very helpful to me in various ways. They are gratefully remembered here.

It must be finally stated that the contents of this book do not represent the views or opinions of the Government, the Home or Police Departments. These are the views of the author and he takes the responsibility for any shortcomings in this book.

JAMES VADACKUMCHERY

CONTENTS

Preface to the Second Edition vii
Preface to the First Edition viii

1. Personal Identification in Banks 1
2. Handwriting Characteristics 23
3. Genuine Signature 52
4. Forgery of Signature 72
5. Erasures and Alterations 94
6. New Safety Methods 109
7. Forgery of Indian Money 137
8. *Modus Operandi* and Criminals in Banks 158
9. Customers : Their Psychology and Safety 191
10. Crimes in Banks : Investigation and Prosecution 209

Bibliography 227
Index 232

1

PERSONAL IDENTIFICATION IN BANKS

Finger-Prints

Banks always insist on *personal identification* of their customers. The identification of customers is done in many ways and the banks generally require the identity of customers to be established by the introduction by someone known to the bank. If the customer is literate, he is asked to put his *signature* : otherwise, his ***thumb impression***. The officers employed in the bank take the ***finger impressions*** of their customers with little or no knowledge of dactylography. As a result of this, they often take the finger impressions in a crude manner with the help of a stamp-pad readily available with them. This crude method of taking finger impressions does not make the finger-prints clear and one finds it difficult to read the ridge characteristics for establishing the identity of the customers. A basic understanding of the science of finger-prints becomes therefore necessary for all officers working in banks.

Dactylography

Dactylography is a branch of science which concerns with the study of finger-prints. Eversince organised banking has come into existence, finger-printing also bas been used by the banks to establish the identity of the customers—perhaps more in the past than in the present; more in the rural areas than in the urban areas; more among the illeterates than among the semi-literates and literates. Even before the banks have started taking of finger-prints, people in various walks of life knew the science of finger-printing, although nobody knew for certain where or when the science had originated. The Indians, the Chinese and the Japanese claimed the credit for the first use of finger-prints for personal indentification. It is in 1897 that the first Finger-Print Bureau in the world was established in Calcutta. The whole science of personal identification is based on certain specialities that are seen on finger impressions.

Finger-prints are nothing but the impressions left by the pappillary ridges that are present on the fingers and palms of a person (and also on the soles of the feet) when they come in contact with a surface or an article. The pappillary ridges are the raised nipple-shaped skin-lines that are seen on the fingers, the palms and soles of the feet. The depressed ones are called *furrows*. These lines which appear three months before the birth of a child remain without any alteration until the decomposition of human body. This *persistence* is one of the characteristics which helps for making personal identity of an individual. The dimensions of the finger-print may change a little with time, but their characteristics remain permanent. In other words, no change takes place in the number and arrangement of these friction-ridges during the growth and development of a person.

The second speciality of finger impressions lies in their *individuality* : no two finger-prints are ever identical. The pictorial effect of two finger impressions may appear to be alike but a close examination will prove that they exhibit formidable unlikeness. This implies that the ridge characteristics are different in all finger impressions. The banker should know these ridge characteristics and should be familiar with the terminology in dactylography.

Ridge Characteristics

1. Bifurcation or Fork : If the banker examines a finger impression, he will find that all the skin-lines in a print are not seen to be continuous. In other words when a ridge branches off into two directions, it is called a *bifurcation* or *a fork*. (Fig. 1.1).

2. Island : If a skin-line in a finger impression branches off and then rejoins the parent ridge to form an enclosure, it is called an *island.* It is also called an eye or enclosure. (Fig. 1.2).

3. Termination : If a skin-line in a finger impression abruptly ends, it is called *termination*. Termination in dactylography is also known as *free-end, ridge-ending,* etc. (Fig. 1.3).

4. Cross-over : If an intervening ridge in a finger-print connects any two ridges that run almost parallel to each other, it is called a *cross-over.* (Fig. 1.4).

5. Short Ridge : When a skin-line in a finger-print starts and ends abruptly it becomes short in length, and it is called a *short ridge* (Fig. 1.5).

6. Dot : A *dot* in a finger-print is a short ridge so small as a dot. (Fig. 1.6).

7. Hook : When a skin-line in a finger impression branches off or splits into another in such a way that one of the bifurcated ridges is very small in length, it is called a *hook* or a *spur.* (Fig. 1.7).

8. Recurving Ridge : When a ridge at a certain point in its course curves back in the direction of its starting point, it is known as a *recurving ridge.* (Fig. 1.8).

9. Converging Ridges : If two skin-lines in a finger impression abruptly tend to approach each other at one point, perhaps meeting there and continuing as a single ridge, they are named *converging ridges.* (Fig. 1.9).

10. Divergence : If two ridges spread apart in such a way that they, after running parallel to each other, abruptly separate and spread apart and then cease to be parallel, it is called a *divergence.* (Fig. 1.10).

11. Patterns : The ridges in a finger impression form definite designs. This, in dactylography, is called *patterns*. The various patterns of fingerprints are discussed at length elsewhere in this chapter. *Bifurcations* and *ridge-endings* appear more frequently

Fig. 1.1 : Bifurcation

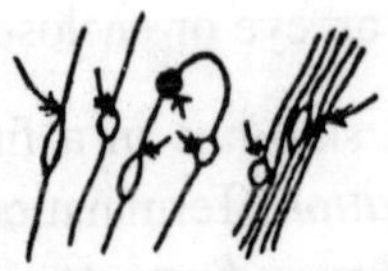

Fig. 1.2 : Island

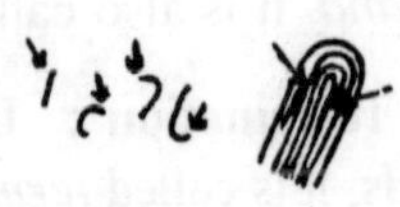

Fig. 1.3 : Termination

Fig. 1.4 : Cross Over

Fig. 1.5 : Short Ridge

Fig. 1.6 : Dot

Fig. 1.7 : Hook

Fig.1.8: Recurving Ridge

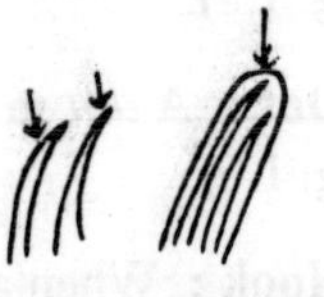

Fig.1.9: Converging Ridge

Fig. 1.10 : Divergence

Fig. 1.11 : Core, Delta Type Lines

Ridge Characteristics

than *islands*, *dots*, *spurs*, *cross-overs*, *short ridges*, etc. In fact, these two are the main ridge characteristics in a finger-print pattern. The pattern area, where the ridge characteristics are seen, is the only portion of the finger impression with which the banker should be concerned when he examines the print after taking the impression of the customer (Figs. 1.11 & 1.12).

12. Core : The finger-print patterns may have some fixed points and they can be the *core*, the *type-line* and the *delta*. The core is the inner terminus located or seen at the approximate centre of the pattern. (Figs. 1.11 & 1.12).

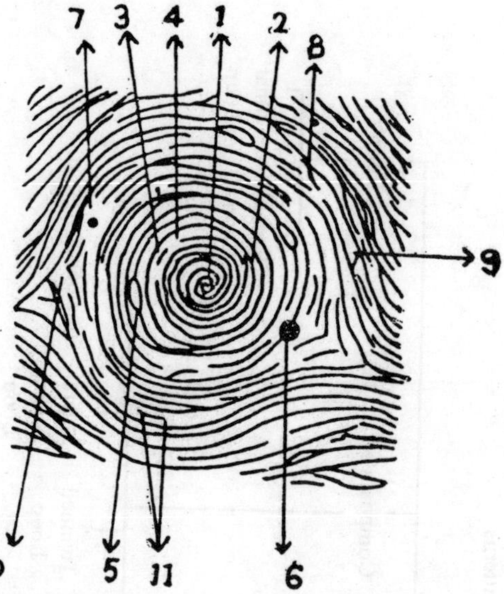

1. Core
2. Bifurcation
3. Short ridge
4. Ridge-ending
5. Enclosure
6. Island
7. Dot
8. Hook
9. Cross-over
10. Delta
11. Short ridge

(See the Ridge Characteristics)

Fig. 1.12 : Model of a Whorl Pattern

13. Type-lines : *Type-lines* are the ridges that surround the pattern area of a finger impression. Here the ridges go parallel and then separate. *Delta* and its location are determined from these type lines. (Figs. 1.11. & 1.12).

14. Delta : The *delta* is otherwise called the *outer terminus*. It is a bifurcation of a single ridge in such a way that it accommodates the finger-print pattern inside it. It can also be the sudden divergence of two ridges that run parallel to each other. The delta is located at the close of the divergence of the *type-lines.* Delta is seen in all finger-print patterns, except in *Plain Arch* and *Tented Arch.* (Figs. 1.11 & 1.12).

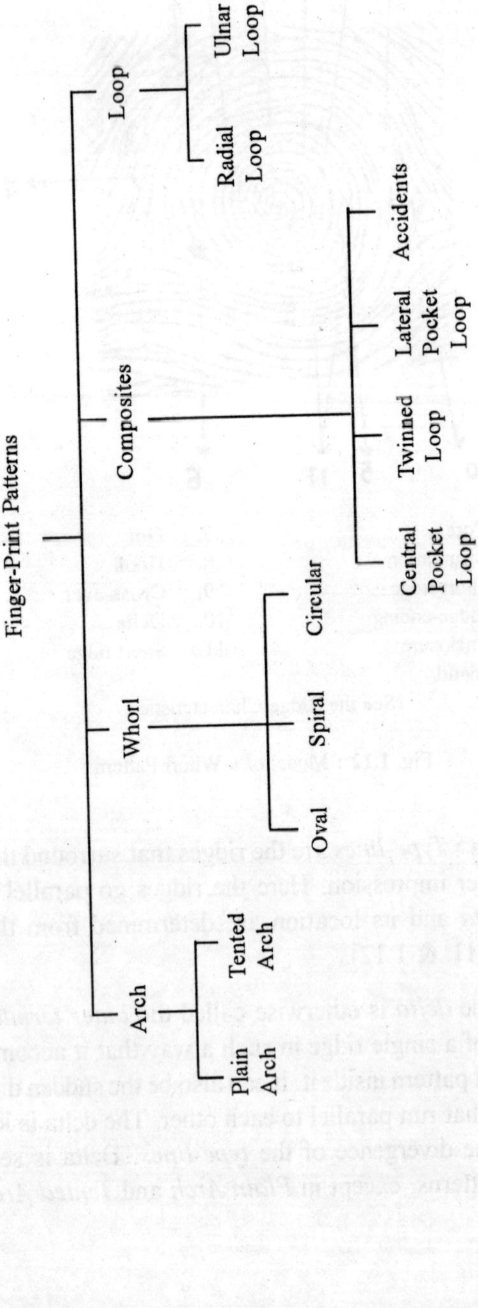

Chart 1.1 : Finger-Print Patterns

Finger-Print Patterns

Principally, there are only four types of finger-print patterns and they are further subdivided into eleven categories :(see Chart 1.1).

(a) *Plain Arch (Arch Pattern)*

The *Plain Arch pattern* is one in which the ridges run from one end of the impression to the other without making any backward turn, the ridges rising slightly in the middle of the pattern. In this type, there is no delta and core. Approximately 5 to 6 per cent finger-prints will have Arch Patterns in them.

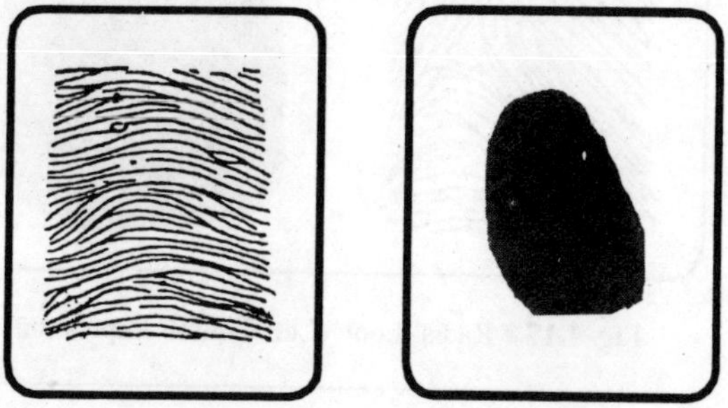

Fig. 1.13 : Plain Arch

(b) *Tented Arch*

A Plain Arch having the appearance of a tent in the central portion is called *Tented Arch.*

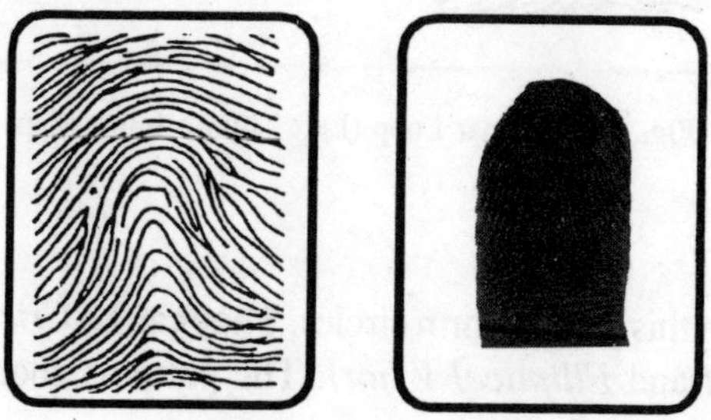

Fig. 1.14 : Tented Arch

(c) *Loop*

In this pattern the skin-lines about the centre of the pattern form a hairpin thus turning back and terminating on the same side from which they started. Delta and core are available in a loop pattern. Nearly 58-62 per cent of the finger-print patterns will have loops in them.

The loop patterns are of two kinds : *Radial* and *Ulnar*. If the slope of the loop is towards the little finger, it is called *Ulnar Loop* and to the thumb is called *Radial Loop*.

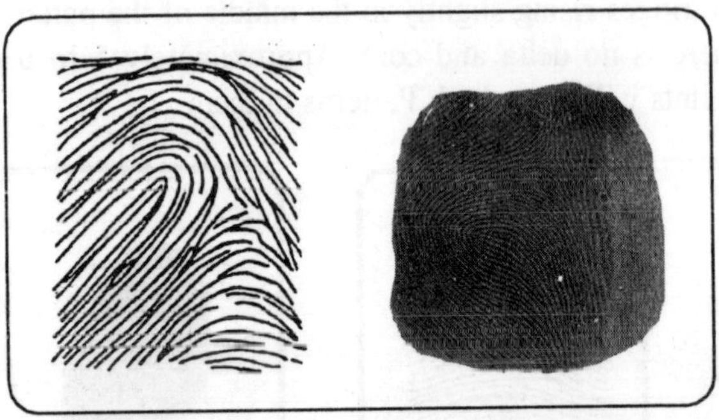

Fig. 1.15 : Radial Loop (Left Thumb Impression)

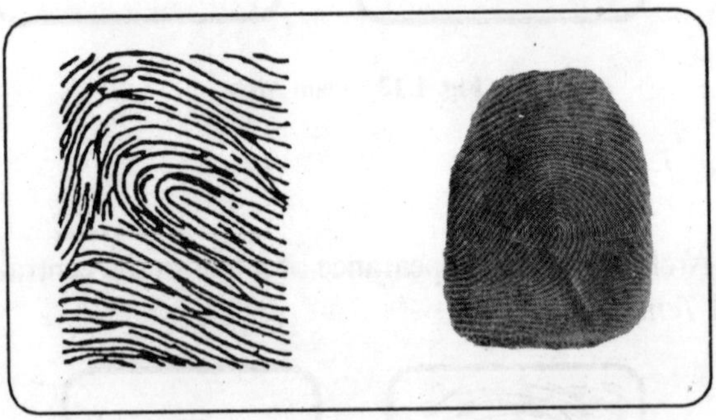

Fig. 1.16 : Ulnar Loop (Left Thumb Impression)

(d) *Whorl*

The ridges in this pattern form circles. They can be *Crircular Whorl, Oval Whorl* and *Elliptical Whorl*. The patterns should have two deltas. It is estimated that about 28-30 per cent of the finger-print patterns will have whorls (including the composites) in them.

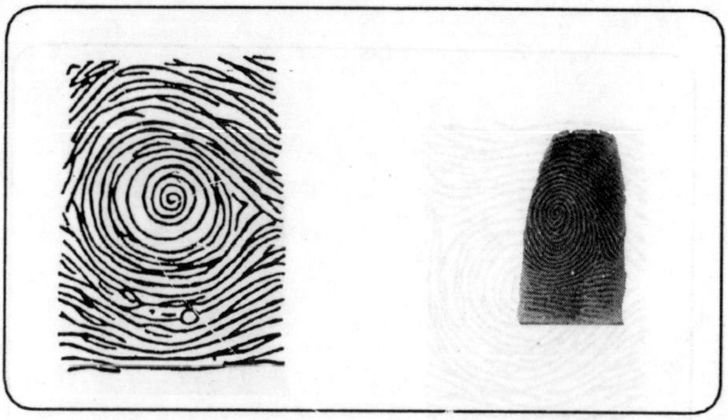

Fig. 1.17 : Spiral Whorl

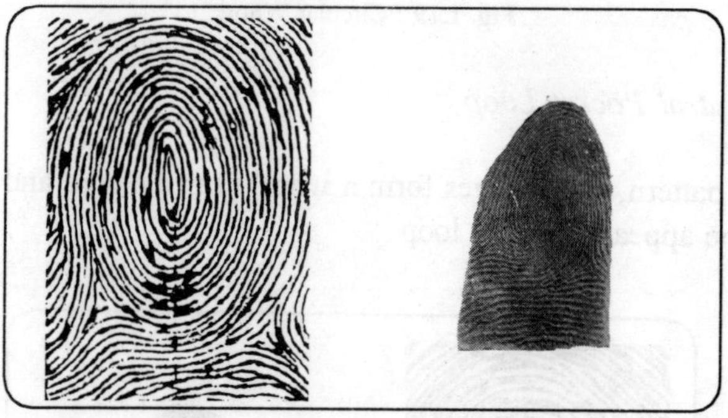

Fig. 1.18 : Elliptical Whorl

There will be a core in every whorl and it is at the centre of the first ridge.

(e) *Composites*

The composites are of four kinds :

(i) Central Pocket Loop;
(ii) Twinned Loop;

(iii) Lateral Pocket Loop; and

(iv) Accidentals.

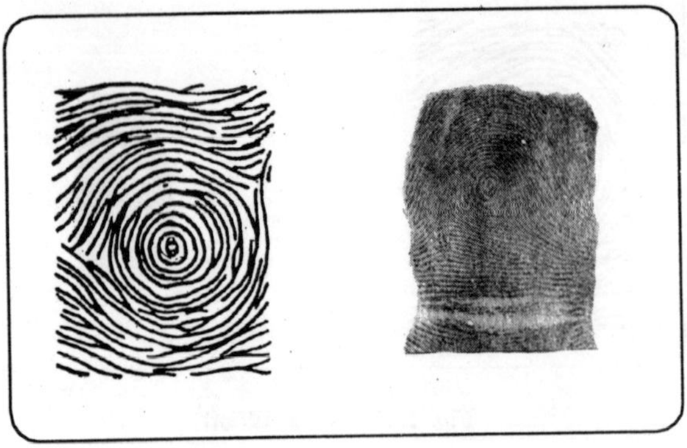

Fig. 1.19 : Circular Whorl

(i) *Central Pocket Loop*

In this pattern, some ridges form a whorl near the core and others have the appearance of a loop.

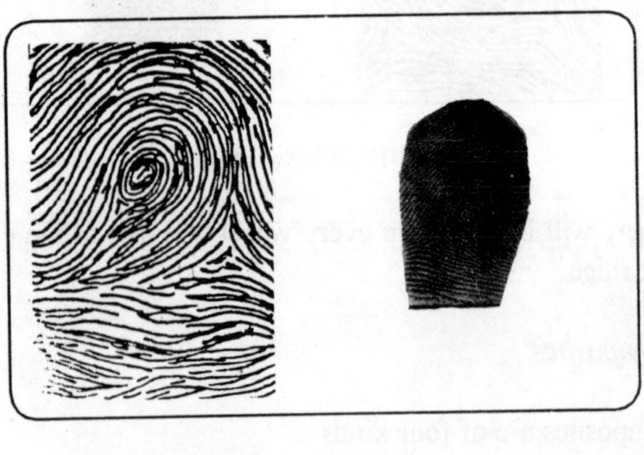

Fig. 1.20 : Central Pocket Loop

(ii) *Twinned Loop*

They have two cores and two deltas.

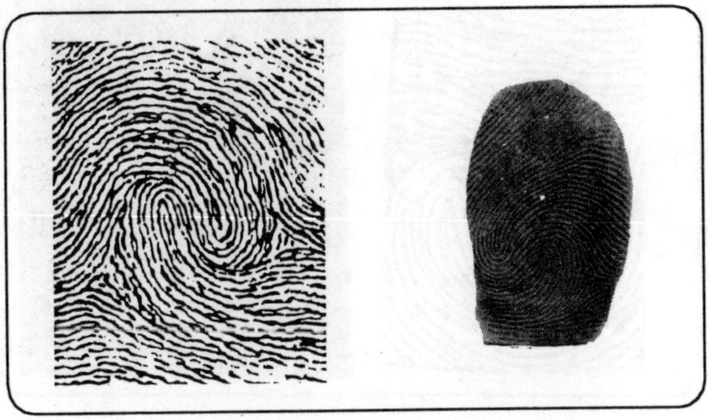

Fig. 1.21 : Twinned Loop

(iii) *Lateral Pocket Loop*

In this pattern there are two loops and two deltas. The ridges bend on one side before they recurve and on that side a pocket is formed by the ridges.

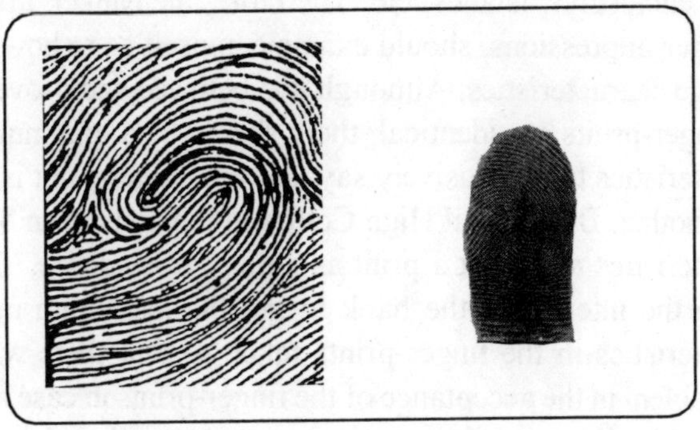

Fig. 1.22 : Lateral Pocket Loop

(iv) *Accidentals*

They have the appearance of two or more patterns—usually with three deltas and sometimes more. They appear rarely in finger-print patterns.

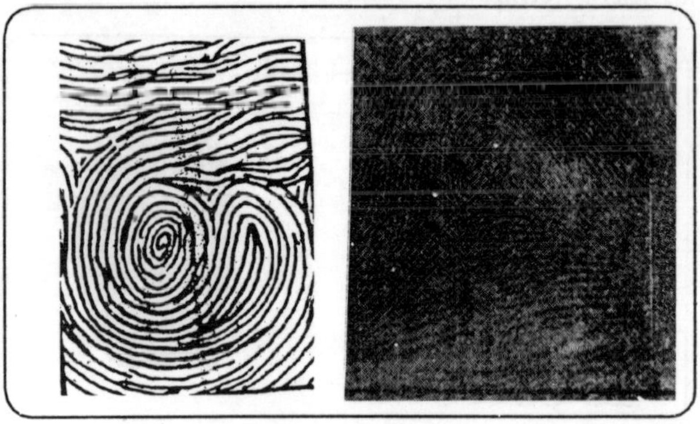

Fig. 1.23 : Accidental

Identification of Thumb Impressions

The bankers should have a thorough understanding about how the thumb impressions of their customers are identified. As has been indicated earlier, the identification of finger impressions is always made by the help of ridge characteristics, e.g., forks, dots, short ridges, enclosures, islands, etc. Therefore, the banker, after taking the finger impressions, should examine himself as to how clear are the ridge characteristics. Although it is believed and proved that no two finger-prints are identical, there should be a minimum of four characteristics to conclusively say that one finger-print is different from another. But several High Courts in India insist on 8-12 ridge characteristics to accept a print as a piece of evidence. Therefore, it is to the interest of the bank to get the maximum number of characteristics in the finger-prints taken so that there will not be any problem in the acceptance of the finger-prints in case litigations arise and in which the finger-prints are to be produced to prove the identity of the customers. The author has personally examined a number of finger-prints taken by the banks and it is most unfortunate that he could not identify even two or three characteristics in the impressions taken by the banks.

The banker should remember that by just producing only the finger-print patterns, i.e., Arch, Loop; Whorl or Composites, no identification is possible. The ridge characteristics occur in all patterns, but the order or the sequence in which they occur are different in different finger-print patterns.

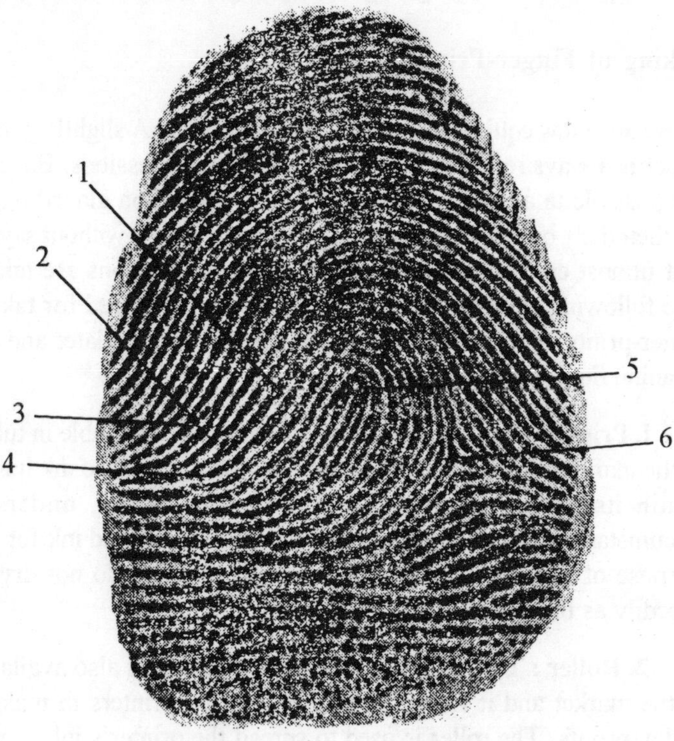

1. Ridge
2. Dot
3. Hook
4. Bifurcation
5. Core
6. Delta

Fig. 1.24 : Thumb Impression

The bankers have little or no knowledge about how best should they take the finger-prints. As a result, they take a stamp-pad readily available and ask the customers to affix their impression in such a manner that the impressions taken are simply smudges or just the tip of the thumb-even the patterns are not clear, let alone the ridge characteristics. One should remember that such impressions do not serve any useful purpose. The thumb should never be twisted nor should it be pressed over and again while impression are taken. Such impressions do not give generally finger-print characteristics.

Taking of Finger-Prints

There are a few equipments used in finger-printing. A slightly glazed paper is always recommended for taking fine impressions. But it is not possible in a bank to have such forms printed on glazed paper for their daily business transactions. Therefore, it goes without saying that utmost care should be given when the impressions are taken. The following equipments and materials should be used for taking finger-prints : (1) printer's ink; (2) roller; (3) inking plate; and (4) cleaning fluid.

1. Printer's Ink : The printer's ink is readily available in tubes in the market. It must be kept at room temperature if the ink has to retain its proper consistency. The banker should, under no circumstances, use the ordinary, coloured or stamp-pad ink for the purpose of finger-printing as they are too thin and do not dry as speedily as the printer's ink.

2. Roller : The roller used for finger-printing is also available in the market and it is similar to that used by printers in making galley proofs. The roller is used to spread the printer's ink evenly and thinly on the plate.

3. Inking Plate : Aluminum, steel or copper plate etc. may be used as inking plate. But the best is a glass plate-one fourth of an inch thick with reinforcement from a wooden base.

4. Cleaning Fluid : Cleaning fluid is used to clean the plate, roller and the thumb of the customer before the print is taken. Gasoline, benzine, alcohol etc., can be used as the cleaning fluid.

Any commercial firm which supplies equipments to the Finger-Print Bureaus, the Forensic Science Laboratories, to the Police, to the Sub-Registrar of the Registration Department, etc. can give a

Finger-Print Kit suitable for use in the banks. The kit is not very costly.

How to Obtain Clear Impressions?

The inking plate should be placed at a height sufficient enough to permit the customer's forearm to assume a horizontal position when the thumb is being inked. Usually, the left thumb can be inked as he does not use it afterwards for taking his food etc. The customer should then be asked to stand directly in front of the inking plate and at the forearm's length from it. Such a position is good to eliminate the accidental strains and pressures on the thumb and will enable him to get a fine and uniform impression. When his left thumb is being printed, his other hand should hang alongside his body. The customer should be warned not to assist the banker in the taking of his impression. He must be permitted to relax. For this purpose, he must be asked to look at an object kept on the opposite wall. If he does not relax himself, the rolling of the thumb becomes difficult.

How to Prepare the Inking Plate?

The inking plate and the roller should be cleaned thoroughly by the cleaning fluid. Failure to clean thoroughly these equipments may cause false marking or distortions. Gasoline, benzine, alcohol etc. can be used as cleaning fluids. Then the printer's ink should be evenly and finely spread over the plate by using the roller. When the ink is nicely spread over the inking plate, the bulb of the thumb is inked evenly by rolling it on the inked plate from tip to below the first joint and from one side of the nail to the other. The pressure exerted on the thumb, while rolling, should be light and even. Uneven pressure causes distortion of the thumb print.

After the thumb is evenly inked, the thumb should be affixed with an even pressure without twisting the thumb over again. A rolled impression is taken by rolling the thumb from one end to the other without any twisting. When the thumb is completely rolled, it is lifted quickly upward from the paper. A slow or dragging movement causes distortion of prints. Once the rolling of the thumb is over, never should it be rolled back. The left thumb is rolled from left to right and the right thumb from right to left.

Reasons for Poor Impressions

The following errors in taking a thumb impression can cause poor printing:

1. **Poor Ink :** Stamp-pad ink, think ink, etc. can cause pale or smudged printing. If printer's ink is not available, then pad-ink, preferably black pad-ink, may be reluctantly used.
2. **Improper Cleaning :** Improper cleaning of the thumb, plate and roller can cause distortion of the ridges in the prints, false markings and loss of ridge characteristics. The thumb should be wiped dry of perspiration.
3. **Improper Rolling :** Failure to roll the thumb fully from one side to the other can cause poor impressions.
4. **Incomplete Inking :** Failure to spread the ink evenly, finely and lightly over the plate as well as on the entire bulb of the thumb from joint to tip and from side to side of nails can result in the loss of important ridge characteristics.
5. **Insufficient Inking :** Insufficient inking will not make ridge characteristics clear.
6. **Slippage :** If the thumb is permitted to slip or twist during its rolling it can result in blurs and false patterns.

Precautions

After the printing is complete, write down *right thumb* or *left thumb* under the impression. If the left thumb is injured and has a sore, a bruise or an open cut etc. such a thumb should not be printed. In such cases, take the print of the right thumb. If the customer has some skin diseases on the thumb/fingers, it is advisable not to take finger-prints of such a customer until his disease is cured completely. If the customer is a person whose profession or occupation causes partial effacement or destruction øf the ridges, his thumb should be printed with utmost care and caution. Care should be taken to the proper inking and correct pressure. The ridge characteristics should be examined by the help of a magnifying glass as to its clarity. If the customer has a dry skin, then gently apply the thumb with oil or vaseline. After removing the excess substance, the printing can be done in the normal way. In the case of aged people, since their ridges are usually faint and ill-defined from wear, a thin coating of vaseline or oil can help obtain better impressions. So, is the case with infants whose ridges are very fine, faint and close together or ill-defined in characteristics.

Examination of Characteristics

After Finger-printing

After taking the finger impression the banker should examine the print by the help of a magnifying glass to identify the ridge characteristics. He should examine :

(1) the pattern,
(2) the ridge formation,
(3) the number of ridges,
(4) specific ridge characteristics, and
(5) the location of the characteristics etc.

If he is satisfied with 12 characteristics, he needs not bother about anything further. Hence, every bank should give theoretical and practical training to their officers and clerks regarding the taking of finger impressions and appreciation of ridge characteristics during their induction as well as in-service training courses. If the print is taken by a peon or clerk in the bank, it should invariably be verified by an officer and should affix his signature under the print as the verifying authority. Remember that the science of identification with the help of finger-prints or thumb impressions is an exact science and the evidence is accepted in any court of law as conclusive evidence for proving the identity of the person whose prints are submitted for the Court's perusal.

Use of Finger-Prints in Banks

The full utility of finger-prints is yet to be explored by banks. Many banks satisfy with the taking of finger-prints only in cases where the customer is illiterate or incapable of signing. The banks can utilize the finger prints in many other fields if they so prefer to do so. Some such uses are as under :

Finger-printing of all customers is the best method of personal identification.

The finger-prints of all the officers of a bank can be used in cases where demand drafts or mail transfers for huge amounts are issued i.e., in case a demand draft worth Rs. 50,000/- or more is to be issued, the print of the left thumb of the issuing officer is taken at the back of the said draft. The officer at the paying bank, if he knows the identification technique of ridge characteristics, (this can be taught within 10 hours of training in the identification of finger prints) can easily know that the demand draft has been issued by so and so in such and such branch. Now, the signature of all officers in the bank are circulated. Likewise the banks can provide a book containing the blocks of the left thumb impressions of all officers empowered to issue demand drafts worth Rs. 50,000/- or more and it can be used as the reference material for comparison of finger-prints when demand drafts are issued. The same can be used when mail transfers are sent.

When cheques for huge amounts are discounted, the finger-prints of the customer can help to fix the identity of the payee. Sometimes, it so happens that some of them put their signature in such a way that later if a litigation comes, they would prefer to dispute and plead innocent. Many rulings by the Supreme Court of India are in their favour if disputes come in the case of signatures/ handwritings. In Bhagwan Kau *vs.* M. K. Sharma (A.I.R. 1973 S.C. 1346, 1973 Cr. L. J. 1143) and in Ramnarain *vs.* State (A.I.R. 1973 S.C. 2200; 1973 Cr. L.J. 1187), it has been held by the Supreme

Court that "The evidence of a handwriting expert is generally of a frail character and its fallibilities have been quite often noticed. The Courts should therefore be wary to give too much weight to the evidence of handwriting expert". The banks should remember that the handwriting expert has to examine the disputed writing/signature from very many angles and from several points of view such as pen-pressure, line quality, pen-position, skill, speed etc. which are dealt with extensively in the next chapter. In the case of thumb impressions the expert can arrive at a conclusive opinion just by examining the pattern and ridge characteristics. And his evidence is believed by the Courts as to the identity of the person giving the finger-prints. At the same time the banks should recognise the fact that blurred impressions become a subject of dispute. Identification of blurred impressions is very difficult if not impossiblc. Similar is the case with incomplete impressions. For, if an impression is so blurred or so incomplete, then an expert more often than not cannot establish the pattern and the formation of the ridges. In such cases no opinion of any kind is possible.

EXAMINATION OF THE FINGER IMPRESSION TAKEN BY THE BANKER

Ask the following questions and try to answer them :

1. Can you identify the pattern of the finger impression?
2. Do you see any ridge characteristics in the pattern? If so enumerate them below :

   1........................ 2........................ 3........................

   4........................5........................6........................

   7........................8........................9........................

   10........................

3. Can you locate the delta (if there is), the core etc. in the impression?
4. Have you marked left thumb under the impression (If right thumb impression is taken, write down that fact).

CASE–LAW : FINGER-PRINTS

In Govind Reddy *vs.* State of Mysore it was held that the opinion of the expert based on a careful comparison of the enlarged photographs when not shattered by the lengthy cross-examination is admissible (See A.I.R. 1958 Mys. 150; I.L.R. (1957) Mys. 177).

Personal Identification by Introduction

As stated earlier in this chapter, banks allow personal identification by introducing the new customer by an account holder. Though this method is found to be quite successful in good number of cases, the fact remains that this privilege has been misused by some account holders. As the introducer has no criminal liability over the acts done by the new customer, the former takes it only as a formality in banks. Cases have been reported that some account holders introduce demand-draft and cheque stealers to banks. The usual '*modus operandi*' is to introduce the new comer as the person whose name has been written on the demand draft/cheque-leaf. After opening the new account in the bank with the false name and signature, the cheque/draft stealer gets the demand draft/cheque encashed from the bank. Later, when the cheating is located, the introducer gets shocked and the cheque/draft stealer is not located.

While the personal identification by trustworthy introducers is good, it should be made *pukka* by other more reliable methods. Chapter 6 deals with this aspect extensively.

Personal Identification by Signature of the Customers

Another method by which banks make personal identification is through the signature of the customers. It has been observed that some income-tax evaders and those having black money have four or five signatures. They open accounts in many banks with different signatures and transact business without being caught by the law-enforcement authority.

Signatures are said to be not a very reliable means of personal identification. Nevertheless, they are relied heavily by banks. Minor variations in signatures of one and the same person always occur. Bank officers make identification of their customers from signatures with little or no academic training about the comparison techniques. They compare the signature of the customer kept in the specimen signature card tray with the one presented before them. While doing so, they have 'JUST A LOOK' on both signatures and get an 'IMPRESSION' which is not suspicious. Providence also helps here to arrive at this conclusion. Of course many of the officers in banks are well experienced persons so much so that their judgements, though not scientific and well based, often become true. One reason is that the vast majority of the customers are not criminals. Comparison of signatures in a scientific way is discussed in the next chapters.

Personal Identification by Sight and Acquaintance

Luckily enough, a good number of customers belonging to a bank are known to the bank employees through their frequent contacts with them. As a result, the bank employees, generally, do not bother about even varifying the signature presented to the signature kept in the specimen signature card tray. The rule—the bank should compare the signature of the customer every time when he presents a cheque with the specimen signature kept in the bank is very often difficult to be followed. In busy hours of banking transactions, the comparison of signatures is difficult and not practicable—that is what many bank employees complain. They are forced to pass the cheques knowing fully well that they are taking a risk. But they cannot help it. A new method in transacting cheques is discussed in chapter 6. Along with the new method, if the bankers know the scientific method of comparing the signatures, no doubt, they can pass the cheques with a lot of self-confidence in all suspicious circumstances.

References

Battley, H., *Single Finger Prints*, London, Her Majesty's Stationary Office, 1930.

Bose, H.C., Rai Bahadur, *Finger Print Companion*, Culcutta, Finger Print Bureau, 1927.

Brewester, F., *Finger Prints*, Calcutta, The Eastern Law House, 1936.

Bridges, B.C., *Practical Finger Printing*, New York, Funk & Wagnalls Co., 1942.

Browne, D. G. and Alan Brock, *Finger Prints*, London, George G. Harrap & Co. Ltd., 1953.

Chapel, C.E., *Finger Printing : A Manual of Identification*, London, Chapman & Hall Ltd., 1946.

Cummins H., and Charles Midlow, *Finger Prints, Palms and Soles*, Philadelphia, 1943.

Duncan, J.H., *An Introduction to Finger Prints*, London, Butterworth & Co., (Publishers) Ltd., 1942.

Faulds, H., *Guide to Finger Print Identification*, Hanley : Wood, Mitchell & Co., Ltd., 1905.

Field A.J., *Finger Print Handbook*, Springfield, Charles C. Thomas, 1959.

Hardless, H. R., *Handwriting and Thumb- Print Identification and Forensic Science*, Allahabad Law Book Co., 1970.

Malik, B., *Field's Expert Evidence*, Allahabad, Delhi Law House, 1980.

Mehta, M.K. *The Identification of Thumb Impressions and the Cross Examination of Finger Print Experts*, Bombay, N. M. Tripathi Private Ltd., 1963.

Wilton, G. W., *Fingerprints : History, Law and Romance*, London, William Hodge & Co., Ltd., 1938.

2

HANDWRITING CHARACTERISTICS

In transacting business, banks have to deal with a number of documents. It may include documents with suspicious signatures on cheques, notes, receipts, contracts, wills, deeds, agreements and similar instruments. There may be cases in which the entire document itself may be a false one. Again, there may be instances in which the bank may see fraudulent alterations or changes such as change in the date or adding or changing figures or altering any other part of the text of the document. There may be documents with ganuine signature and fraudulent text. In all such situations the banks are supposed to examine the documents with meticulous care and to do so the banker should be acquainted with many facts which can aid him to recognize whether a document is valid or fraudulent and to help him to discover facts leading to prove the authenticity of the document. Serious examination of document submitted for getting a heavy loan sanctioned should not be examined by an amateur banker in his office. Such documents should be examined in the bank's central or regional laboratories. Nevertheless cheques and similar documents for which the response time from the bank is considerably limited, the banker should know how to examine them and detect fraudulent writings, alteration, additions or changes etc. For this, he must know the *characteristics* of handwriting and signatures. Such an understanding will surely help him to detect forgery in banking transactions.

All handwritings have some identifying characteristics which may fall into two categories : (1) *Style Characteristics;* (2) *Personal*

Characteristics. The former refers to the general style of an individual's writings and the latter to those features introduced into the handwriting by the writer either consciously or unconsciously. The *style characteristics* are not of any considerable importance to identification of handwriting except in a limited way. Perhaps, it may help decide the nationality of the writer as people in different countries develop their own national characteristic features in their handwriting. The Americans, the Africans, the Indians and so on can be recognized well by looking into the style characteristics.

A banker is more concerned with the personal characteristics of handwriting/signature. He has with him a signature-card tray where the specimen signatures of all his customers are kept and it is with the help of these signatures that he makes comparison of the customer's signature seen on a cheque, bill, receipts, etc. He should remember here that his customer's signature/handwriting suffers from some change owing to the nature of the pen, paper, ink position, health, psychological mood, etc. Nevertheless; all these changes are only superficial. Certainly, there are many common characteristics in every customer's signature/handwriting. They are more or less permanent and unchangeable. And it is these personal characteristics that distinguish one signature from another.

While comparing the signature or handwriting of the customers, it should be borne in mind that one signature will not be exactly identical with another in all respects. There will be variations; and these variations can be in the length, breadth, size, etc. But such differences will be *minor* in nature and therefore they are called *natural* differences. In spite of these natural differences the banker can see a number of *personal characteristics* peculiar to a particular customer's signature or handwriting and in fact they form the basis for identification of signatures in banks.

While an individual commits forgery of signature, the offender assumes the personality of another person whose signature the forger intends to imitate. More often than not, the offender himself does not/cannot know what the personal characteristics of his own signature as well as the same of the signature of the person whose signature he tries to forge. For instance, while forging a signature, the offender has to look at the model and there will surely be hasitations. As a result, his pen will halt now and then. The line may not be smooth. There will be pen-lifts. About the movement in genuine signature, Wilson R. Harrison writes : 'The novice will slowly lower his pen on to the paper and allow the point to rest momentarily before beginning to trace out the line. This is not the practice of the fluent writer whose pen-point is in motion before touching down on the paper. This forward motion of the pen-point is continued when the word has been completed and the pen is being lifted from the paper. A similar state of affairs applies to the writing of a fluent signature, possibly more so, for a signature is generally written with a dash and flourish absent from the normal handwriting.'[1]

Writing Characteristics

A basic understanding into the major and minor characteristics of handwriting is necessary for the personnel employed in banks. Writing characteristics are understood to mean the peculiar/special qualities or idiosyncrasies in a person's writing which enable an individual to examine the handwriting to prove that a particular signature is of a specific individual. The major characteristics include those habits in writing which are difficult to change or modify and minor characteristics mean the features that can be modified without difficulty. The speed, movement, manner of holding pen, pen-pressure, degree of muscular coordination, style or design of writing, size of the comparative size of letters in relation to each other, direction of slope of strokes and curves, relative positioning of letters, alignment, etc., are said to be handwriting characteristics.

The banker can resort to qualitative or quantitative tests to decide upon the characteristics. Those characteristics which are judged come under qualitative features and those which are measured come under quantitative characteristics. Accordingly, the speed, movement, pen-pressure, shading, style, position of letters etc. are put under the first category, and alignment, slope, direction of strokes, size of letters, spacing, etc. are enlisted under the second

---

1. Wilson, R. Harrison, *Suspect Documents : Their Scientific Examination*, Sweet & Maxwell Limited, London, 1966.

category. It should be remembered that a person can modify, either intentionally or otherwise, his characteristics of writing. At the same time, he cannot modify all his writing characteristics simultaneously because they are very many and too complex in nature.

Movement

When a person writes or puts his signature, there is movement which is owing to the muscular action of the hand.

This movement in writing can be :

(1) finger movement;
(2) wrist movement;
(3) arm movement;
(4) forearm movement; and
(5) combination of all the above movements.

When children and illiterate people write, one generally sees the finger movement wherein only the fingers are said to be in action. As the pen is held by the thumb, the index and the middle finger, the wrist functions as the fulcrum. Such writings suffer from irregular alignment and connections. The writing will not have generally smooth and clear-cut strokes and there will be round and broad curves. Inconsistency in sizing and spacing of the letters takes place. In the wrist movement, the writer holds the pen firmly by the fingers and the wrist moves. Instead of the wrist, the forearm acts here as the fulcrum. As a result, there will be a tendency to develop angular movement and the alignment may assume arch type. The strokes will be clear-cut and as a rule the wrist movement is faster than finger movement. In forearm movement, it is the elbow that functions as the fulcrum. The forearm as a whole acts here. The fulcrum in this writing rests on the table and the forearm moves. The letters, usually, are bigger in size and the spacing is wider than in finger or wrist movements. The speed is found to be faster. There will be clear-cut and smooth strokes and straight alignment with a tendency to go up or down. In arm movement, the entire arm moves and other parts remain without any movement. People write on black boards by this sort of movements. In some cases, instead of one single movement there will be a combination of movements.

When an individual writes on a cheque or paper, his fingers and the thumb together help him to form letters in the signature/ words. The hand moves in a lateral way across the width of the cheque /paper. Here, therefore, the signatory's/writer's hand helps him to form outward and inward strokes and curves which are elongated and this is particularly the case with final strokes and curves of the last letter in a word if the movement is really high.

The movement of the fingers and hands of a person when he puts the signature on a document/cheque is a natural and fixed habit to him. This habit of the writer can be judged from the design of letters, slant of strokes and curves, special nature of connecting strokes and curves between letters, spacing of letters etc.

Movement of an individual is specific and to that extent individualistic. Upon judging the movement, the banker should take special care to understand the type of pen used, quality of the ink and paper. See whether the ink has good consistency; the paper is smooth; and the pen has narrow or broad points. All these factors affect the writing and particularly the movement of the writer.

Impulse Action of an individual affects his movement while writing. Some have '*Stroke Impulse*, others have *Word Impulse* or *Letter Impulse* and yet others have *Whole Sentence Impulse*. The affinity to a particular *Impulse Action* decides how he writes with simple finger movement; with advanced finger movement; combined finger and wrist movement etc. Novices and those who are unaccustomed to write often, usually, have simple finger movement and there will be disconnections in every letter that they write. Nevertheless their letters are not ill formed or badly shaped. One who has affinity to *Letter Impulse Action* shows advanced finger movements. Resultingly, two or more letters are formed and connected with single pen operation. Naturally, there will be, in such writings, close spacing between letters and between words. The one who has *Word Impulse Action* resorts to combined finger and wrist movement. As a result, he connects the letters in a word by one pen-operation. Of course he may not do so if he is doubtful of the spelling of a word or if the letter is unusually long. There will be extended spacing between letters in words as well as between words. Here the speed will be very high. Finally, in a person who has the *Whole Sentence Impulse Action* has the combined wrist and forearm movement. Here one can notice wide spacing between letters in a word. There will also be connecting strokes and curves between two words particularly if the words are having only few letters. Flourishes with a tapering points are seen in the final strokes of the last letter in the word. There is high speed in such writings.

The Size of Handwriting

The variation in the relative sizes of letters and parts of letters, i.e., measurement of the height and width of letters are of importance in the comparison of handwriting or signatures.

For example, consider the name Prakash and then measure the height of the capital P and the width the oval in P. Likewise, the height and width of 'r' also may be measured. The sizing of letters is of considerable importance in traced forgeries. It is well recognized that no two signatures put by the same individual will be exactly alike, i.e., with regard to forms of letters, size of letters, space between them and the position of letters. A metal scale (one foot) in the bank can be used for measuring purposes.

Speed

Speed is defined as the degree of fastness or slowness of the motion of hand and fingers while writing. As the speed can only be judged and not measured, it has to be understood from the style or design of a writing and particularly by seeing the quality of the strokes, curves and the slant of strokes, and the roundness of curves, design and quality of connecting strokes, and curves between latters in words. The banker should study the shaded and unshaded strokes, curves, pen-tracks or furrow-tracks (marks). Pen-track or furrow-mark is the white line to be seen in a stroke or curve. This is made by the divergence of the two points of the nib during the process of writing.

The speed can be slow, medium and fast and it is jugged from :

1. style of letters;
2. the degree of slant in strokes of letters;
3. the degree of pressure applied on the pen—this can be seen in the furrow-marks;
4. the roundness or angularity of curves;
5. the firmness or shakiness of strokes and curves;
6. the continuity or brokeness of strokes and curves;
7. the quality of terminals of strokes and curves;
8. the quality and shape of dots;
9. the cross-bar of letters; and
10. the *matra* signs in Indian languages etc.

The slow speed is judged from pen-pauses and pen-lifts. Many pen-pauses and pen-lifts indicate very slow speed. Likewise, heavy pressure on the pen while writing, tremors or shakiness in the quality of strokes and curves and the letters and interconnected strokes and curves made in a disjointed manner, etc. are indicative of slow speed. Likewise, the fast speed is judged from light pen-pressure, good quality of the strokes and curves, terminals of curves and strokes coming to a point, dearth of pen-lifts and pen-pauses, appearance of half-formed (sometimes illegible) letters and a flourish at the terminal of a final letter in a word etc.

Line Quality

The condition or quality of strokes/curves etc. can be of use to say whether or not the writing is an imitation. The line quality is judged and not measured and depends very much on the quality of ink, the kind of pen used, and the paper. Many forgeries will be defective in line quality—especially with respect to curves, elongated terminal strokes and the connection between letters. The genuine signature is put without paying any attention to the letter designs and line quality. At the same time in traced forgeries, a lot of attention is paid to the letter designs and it is executed in a slow manner with the result that there will be poor line quality. As the movement of the pen is slow, there will be pen-pauses, pen-lifts and hesitations.

It gives a laboured appearance on the whole. The line quality of the signature put by illiterate persons will not be usually smooth.

Pen-pressure

Pen-pressure is the weight or the force which is brought to bear on the pen while it is in movement. If pressure is not exerted on the pen, no writing is possible. The pressure given to the pen during the process of writing is an unconscious act and it is individualistic to every writer as the degree of pressure exerted becomes a habit with every individual.

Pen-pressure is judged qualitatively and not measured. It is appreciated well in a writing instrument which has two points as in a nib which during the process of writing ploughs into the surface of the paper creating two tracks that appear to have been merged into a single track. When downward strokes are written, the two tracks become more distinct, as the points of the nib open out, if great pressure is exerted on the right or left point of the nib as the case may be. The pen-pressure can be (1) light, (2) heavy, (3) regular/ uniform, (4) uneven, (5) lateral, (6) initial, and (7) graduated. If the pen-pressure is light, the writing will be rapid. The width of the strokes will be usually thin. On the contrary, if there is heavy pen-pressure, there will be only slow writing and the edges of the strokes will be generally rugged and width of the strokes broad. In graudated pen-pressure, the writing will be rapid and skillful. Also, there will be sharp edges for the strokes and even flow of the ink. In a normal handwriting the pen-pressure will be symmetrical. Some people employ heavy pen-pressure, while others employ light or medium pen-pressure. If one writes and his writing shows that the pen-pressure is even with freedom of movement, speed and skill, it shows that the writing is genuine. In disguised writings, the pen-pressure will be usually heavy and there may be irregularity. A forged writing or signature will have inconsistent pen-pressure. This may be due to the fact that the forger then concentrates more on the model to be forged than many other things. Hence, if a signature shows irregularity in varying pen-pressure (hesitating type), it indicates that the signature is a forged one. Some of the cheap quality ballpoint pens when used for writing may show inconsistent type of pen-pressure. Owing to the irregular flow of ink, it may appear that there are hesitations in the writing. Therefore, the pen-pressure exerted with a ballpoint pen cannot be usually judged with accuracy.

The signature put by an illiterate person may show heavy pen-pressure. If the nib of the pen is of a poor quality it may affect the pen-pressure. Likewise, cheap quality papers with rough surface may show, when written, inequality in pen-pressure.

Style

Mental and physical, i.e., urge and action, components are seen in any signature/writing of a person. In other words, a person first desires mentally to write and the physical action produces the writing on the paper. It is therefore rightly said that writing is the action of an impulse in man. While writing, the mental urge and the physical action work together. Sometimes, the physical and mental forces do not work in co-ordination. This lack of co-ordination between the mental and physical forces, at times, affects the quality of writing. It has been observed that for some people, the mental force is superior to the physical force while in others the reverse is found to be at work. This is the reason why a highly intellectual person produces generally bad quality writings. As he is more concerned with what he writes, he does not usually pay much attention to what is called the quality of penmanship. Quite contrary is seen among semi-literate people who, as a rule, take special care to write in a very legible way. Of course, exceptions are seen in both categories.

When a person is conversant with writing he may write a complete letter or a complete word in one pen-operation. Most of the people write their signature in one pen-operation. One pen-operation means complete the letter/word without lifting the pen once one starts writing. When an individual has the capacity to write a complete word/letter in one pen operation, he is said to have developed cursive writing/running style of writing. In the running hand, the letters in word are connected with curves and strokes.

It is often found that the style (design) of writing influences the quality of writing. Usually, an individual develops a particular style depending upon the convenience he has when he writes. As stated earlier, the style of writing is the product of mental urge. The brain has no doubt a mental picture of the letter/word before it is executed.

The quality of the paper, strangeness in using a particular pen, the nature of the ink, the space available for writing/putting the signature, the actual posture of the writer at the time of writing, physical corditions etc. do affect and influence the style/quality of writing/signature. Nevertheless, it does not mean that at a given time, an individual's writing/signature is entirely different from how he writes in a normal condition. This is the reason why people have to make strenuous endeavours to disguise their own writings/ signatures if they want to do so. Thus, one may see letters in a disjoined (broken) manner with a number of apparent pen-pauses and lifts and with shaky or tremulous strokes and curves in a disguised writing/signature.

In a forged signature, if the forger is capable of producing the letter designs/styles, he may be successful in giving a pictorial effect to the signature. But, this is easier said than done; for, the forger usually cannot overcome the impulse action of the original signatory in the signature. Hence, if the signature is firm and has good quality strokes, curves of letters etc. the forger feels it extremely difficult to reproduce them as they are seen in the original signature. Likewise if poor penmanship (letters seen are produced in an awkward manner) with ill-formed letters, bad connections between letters, blunted terminals of letters, pen-lifts/pauses etc. the forger has to imitate the signature in that manner.

Shading

Shading means a forceful and rather a very conspicuous pen-pressure. When a curve is drawn in a speedy manner, shading can be clearly seen. There will be some portions in such curves where wider pen-lines are noticed. When there is shading, the two sides of the nib split in such a way that one can easily see that there is more pen-pressure there. These wider pen-lines in handwriting generally occur on the downward strokes. The manner of holding pen by the writer decides considerably the shading in handwriting. It is found that the shading owing to pen-position is always unconscious, i.e., it is owing to the writer's personal habits. If one resorts to conscious shading, it means that he specially applied force while he was writing and that he had good command of the pen when he was writing.

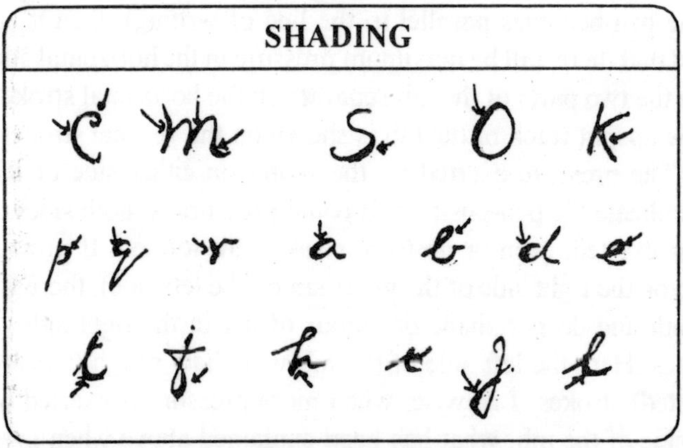

Fig. 2.1 : See the shading in letters. The part of letters where shading is likely to be seen are thickened by retouching to make the shading clearer.

Shading in handwriting is important for detecting forgeries. A wrongly placed shading is indicative of forged writing.

Pen-position

Pen-position is otherwise called the manner of holding the pen when one writes. Pen-position cannot be easily disguised by an individual. Some people like to write with their own pen as their pen makes them happy when they write. They may refuse to write with another's pen and also may not like to give their pen to others to write. For, they are afraid that others will damage their pen even to the extent of disturbing their habitual method of holding.

The angle of the pen to the line of writing and also to the surface of the paper decide the pen-position or the manner of holding the pen. This angle can be determined in an almost accurate way. For this, one has to examine the points where the two parts of the nib separate or the location of the shading. For instance, when a pen is devoid of good flow of ink and is used for writing, the two parts of the nib separate when downward strokes are written. Likewise, the horizontal strokes would show a single upsplit tract of the nib. On the contrary, reverse the position of the pen (the concavity of the pen becomes parallel to the line of writing), then it can be noted that there will be maximum pressure in the horizontal strokes. Here the two parts of the nib separate on the horizontal strokes and single upsplit track of the nib is shown on the vertical strokes.

The pressure exerted by the writer on either side of the nib can indicate the pen-position. If equal pressure on both sides of the nib is exerted, even or uniform strokes are formed. If pressure is more on the right side of the nib (than on the left side), there will be smooth and deeper shade or colour of ink in the right side of the strokes. Here the left side of the nib will show rough (indented or serrated) strokes. Likewise, when more pressure is exerted on the left side of the nib, what has been explained above when pressure is exerted on the right side of the nib will be noticed on the left side of the strokes.

Alignment

Alignment means the relation of individual letters, words or signature or a writing to an imaginary or actual baseline. The alignment can be straight, irregular or arc-like. It may be ascending or descending. Some of the letters in a word or signature will not be resting at all on the base-line. First of all, therefore, the alignment of letters of a particular signature to the base-line should be examined. This will help the banker to appreciate which particular letter or part of a letter, part of a curve or a stroke is habitually out of the overall alignment. It can also bring out the extent of variation in relation to other letters in the signature.

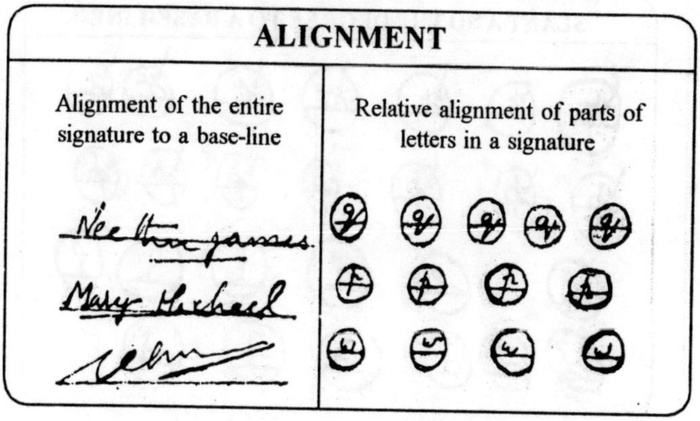

Fig. 2.2 : On the left hand side, the alignment of the whole signature to a base-line is given. And on the right hand side, the relative alignment of parts of letters to a base-line is shown.

The relative alignment of the letters in a signature is of considerable importance to the banker. The variations—particularly malalignment —in alignment of a particular word/signature remains generally constant or permanent. The greater the speed of writing, the straighter will be the overall alignment of the writing, and the slower the speed, the more irregular will be the alignment.

Slope or Slant

The slope or slant denotes the angles formed by the letters to a base line. This is a permanent or fixed habit of many writers. Quantitatively the slant can be measured. This is very valuable for a banker when he wants to decide upon the genuineness of a signature. The irregular slope can be consciously created and such alterations take place in disguised handwriting. However, the writer who makes disguised writing cannot maintain the consistency in the slant/slope. Hence, when there is no disguise, the slant of an individual writer is appreciably constant. Slant has no importance in forged signatures by means of tracing methods. But in simulated forgery, the slant is of great importance.

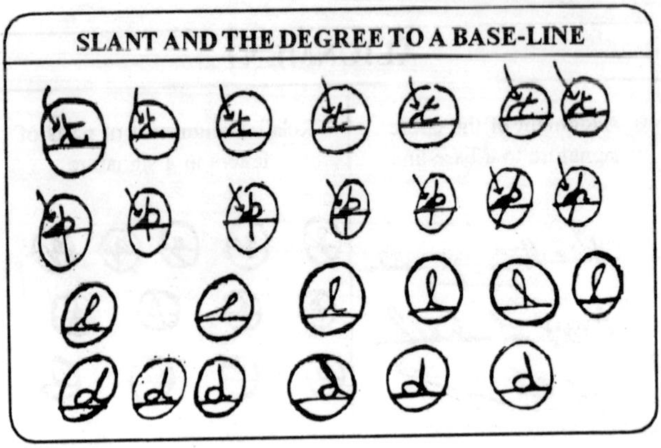

Fig. 2.3 : The slant and degree of t, p, l, d to a base-line are shown

Spacing

Spacing means the distance between the letters, words or lines in writing. Once spacing habits are developed, the habits thus formed remain fairly permanent or constant. But, the spacing in a signature is affected by the space available to put the signature. The writer can reduce the spacing if he wants to accomodate the signature in a limited space. Therefore, when the specimen signature card is given by the bank, it is better if the individual is asked to give six signatures with varying space-length so that the bank will know how he adjusts the spacing of letters in different spaces given for signatures. While the provision to put six signatures is given, see that the area given for two signatures (one by a fountain pen and the other by a ballpoint pen) is equal and thus three categories of two signatures each are received at three varying spaces. For example,

1 ______________________

2 ______________________

3 ____________________

4 ___________________

5 _______________

6 _______________

Straight lines given should not be in the specimen signature card, for straight lines given affect the writing habits.

Under normal circumstances, people maintain uniformity in spacing although some may give adequate spacing while others may give narrow or irregular spacing between letters, words or lines. In simulated forgery, spacing assumes importance. In such cases, the forger often does not pay much attention to the peculiarities in the spacing of the letters *interse*. His concern there is to imitate the model by giving a pictorial effect in the signature rather than maintaning the spacing of letters.

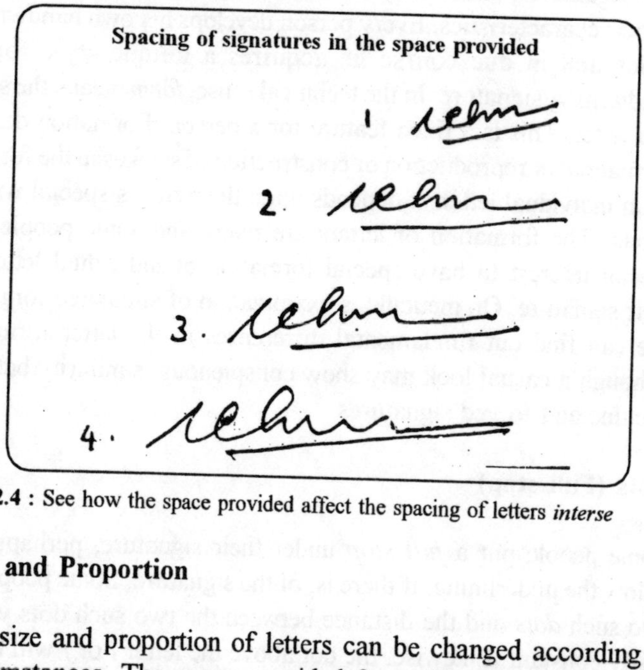

Fig. 2.4 : See how the space provided affect the spacing of letters *interse*

Size and Proportion

The size and proportion of letters can be changed according to circumstances. The space provided for writing decides how the size and the proportion should be. A hasty writer, if the area for writing is large, may increase the size of letters and conversely enough if the area is small, he may reduce the size particularly when he writes slowly. Although the size of the letters can be consciously altered, one cannot keep the consistency if he has to write several pages. After writing a few lines or pages he comes back to his normal writing. In a signature, the banker may remember that the height of short letters in relation to long letters of a good majority of people remains appreciably constant and has, therefore, a greater significance, particularly when free-hand forgeries are examined. Here size and proportion of letters should be carefully examined to draw conclusions.

Form and Formation

The form and formation of letters are individual characteristics. Two signatures, unless they are traced forgeries, are bound to differ in their characteristics. Every person develops his own handwriting styles and in due course he acquires a unique style for his handwriting/signature. In the technical sense, *form* means the shape of a letter. This is a fixed feature for a person. Formation denotes the manner or reproduction or construction of strokes in the forming of an individual letter. It depends upon the writer's special writing habits. The formation of letters are many and some people take special interest to have special formation of individual letters in their signature. On meticulous examination of simulated forgeries, one can find out fundamental differences in the letter formation although a casual look may show conspicuous similarity between genuine and forged signatures.

Dots (Full stop)

Some people put a *full stop* under their signature, perhaps, just below the underlining, if there is, of the signature. Some people put two such *dots* and the distance between the two such dots will be fairly constant. Likewise, the dot above the letter *i* or *j* will be put almost at a constant distance from either letter. This distance can be measured. In an altered or disguised signature the forger may not take due care and caution to put the dot above *i* or *j* exactly at the same distance as seen in the genuine signature. Another example is the diacritic in *t*. Some people put it behind; others *on*; and yet others *after* the letter.

Dots in Signatures

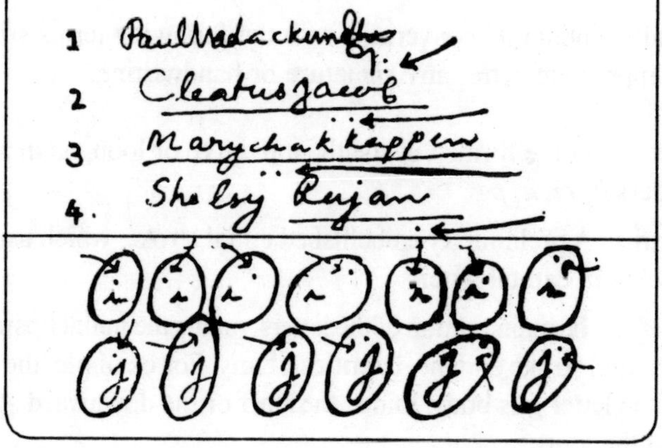

Fig. 2.5 : The dots are found to occupy fairly at a constant distance from a particular point in the signature/letters having dots.

Arrangement

Arrangement is the word used to mean the manner in which a writing is placed on paper. Particularly when signatures are put on cheques, each individual, if he is not keen about the arrangement, has his own special position on the cheque-leaf to sign. Coupled with other writing characteristics, arrangement assumes importance in the identification of forged signatures. Therefore, along with the specimen signature card, the account holder should be asked to sign a cheque-leaf (cancelled) so that the arrangement of his signature in a special position on the cheque -leaf can be appreciated.

General Execution

The general execution of the genuine signature or a writing means the overall visual impression a signature or writing makes at the first sight. The general execution helps invariably estimate the identity of signatures, particularly during the busy hours of transactions in a bank.

TERMINOLOGY*

The banker should be conversant with the following terms so that he can appreciate better any signature or handwriting.

(a) *Arc* : A curve formed inside the top curve or loop, as in small letters *h, m, n, p*.

(b) *Beard* : A preliminary embellished initial stroke, which usually occurs in capital letters.

(c) *Body* : The main portion of the letters, minus the initial upstroke, terminal stroke and the diacritics, if any. For example, the oval of the letter *g* is body, minus the staff or the downward stroke and the loop.

(d) *Buckle* . A loop made as a flourish which is added to the letters, as in the small letter *k* or in capital *A, K, F*.

(e) *Connections* : A stroke which connects two strokes or letters.

(f) *Diacritics* : Crossing in *t* and the dots in *i* and *j* are known diacritic signs. The *matras* in the Indian scripts are also called diacritic signs.

(g) *Eye* : A small loop or curve formed inside the oval of the letter. This may occur inside the ovals of the letters *a, d, g, o*.

(h) *Foot* : The lower part of a letter which rests on the base-line. The small letter *m* has three feet, and the small letters *h* and *n* have two feet.

(i) *Hiatus* : A gap occurring between a continual stroke without lifting the pen. Such an occurrence usually happens due to speed. The hiatus may also be styled as pen-jumps.

(j) *Hook* : It is a minute curve or an angle which often occurs at the end of a terminal stroke. It also sometimes occurs at the beginning of an initial stroke. The terminal small curve of the letters *a, d, h, m, n, u* is a hook. In the small letter *w* the initial curve is a hook.

* For terminology, see, M.K. Mehta, *Indetification of Handwriting and Cross-examination of Experts*, N.M. Tripathi, Bombay, 1970.

(k) *Loop* : An oblong curve such as is found in the small letters *f, g, h, l*. The letters *h*, and *i* have one loop at the top while *g* has one lower loop and *f* has two loops. A loop may be blind or open. A blind loop is usually the result of the ink having filled the open space.

(l) *Oval* : The portion of a letter which is oval in shape. The small letters *a, d, g*, and *q* contain ovals.

(m) *Retrace* : Any part of a stroke which is superimposed upon the orginal stroke, e.g., the vertical stroke of the letters *d, t* which coming downwards from top to bottom may have a retracing stroke.

(n) *Shoulder* : The outside portion of the top curve. Small letter *m* has three shoulders, *n*, two and *h*, one.

(o) *Spur* : A short initial or terminal stroke.

(p) *Staff* : Any major long downward stroke of the letters *b, g* are called the staff.

(q) *Tick* : Any short stroke, which usually occurs at the top of the letters.

When the banker appreciates the individual or personal characteristics of signatories/writers, he should have a thorough understanding of the terminologies explained above. He should realize that variations do take place in the characteristics of an individual signatory. Nevertheless, if the variations in a signature are really *projected ones* and are not natural or reasonable, he has to doubt the genuineness of the signature. Forged signatures, if there are many, will have suspicious similarity whereas genuine signatures will not. The variations in genuine signatures occur in the superficial parts within a reasonable degree. Minor variations, as said earlier, take place in all genuine handwritings and signatures. Hence, no two signatures will ever be identical. The variations in the writing characteristics are shown in Fig. 2.6.

Comparison of Signatures

Whenever the banker doubts the genuineness of the signature on a

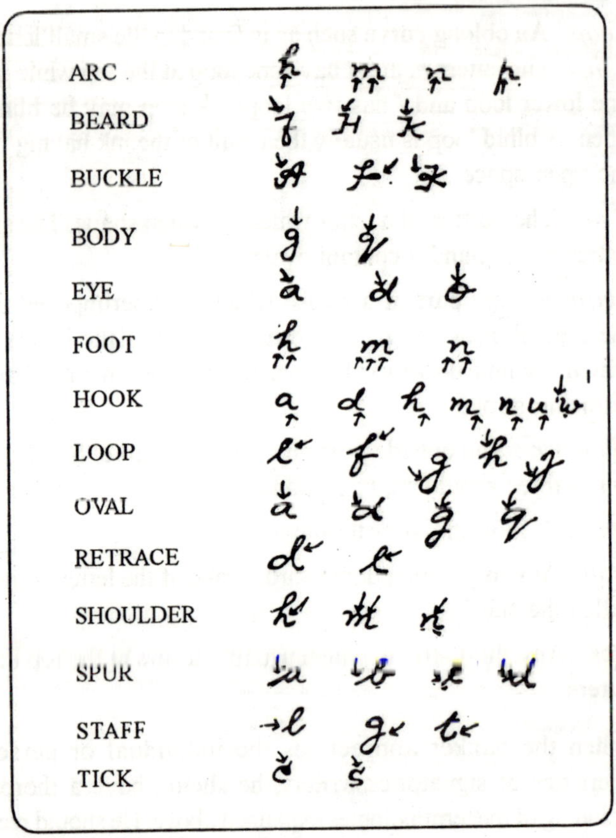

Fig 2.6 : Variations in Writing Characteristics

Note : See, M.K. Metha, *Identification of Handwriting and Cross Examinations*, N.M. Tripati, Bombay, 1970.

cheque; he usually compares it with the signature of the customer kept in the specimen signature card tray. Remember that the handwriting of one and the same person may undergo a gradual change in course of time and in the case of some other persons the change may be rapid. Hence, it is not wise to reject cheques on the basis of a casual or careful examination of the signature on the cheques and the same in the specimen card. Whenever suspicion arises, fresh signature of the customer should be obtained without offending his tender feelings and sentiments. In such instances, the specimen signature should be taken thrice on three different sheets of paper, each sheet being taken away from the sight of the customer as soon as a signature is put. It may still be advisable to give him a short interval between the completion of the first signature and the beginning of the second. He should be entertained in between so that he does not understand that the delay is purposeful. The delay will help the signatory to forget the shapes and designs of letters in the signature. If possible, provide different pens for the second and third specimen signatures. If the banker is now satisfied with the genuiness of the signature on comparison, he should ask the customer to substitute his specimen signature card. The forms of letters, the size, slope, slant or angle of letters, the arrangement etc. should be specially examined to arrive at a conclusion.

When specimen signatures on request are taken in a bank, if the person who puts the signature is a forger, he will attempt to have only free-hand forgery. Even for a 'free-hand' forgery, the forger will like to have the model in front of him. In a bank, this is not possible and therefore he will try to reproduce the signature from his memory. Inevitably, therefore, he will introduce some of his normal handwriting characteristics in such signatures. No doubt, his signature put on request in the bank and the same seen in the specimen card or on the cheque will show marked differences which can be appreciated by the banker. Whenever the forger, in such circumstances, does not get a mental picture of the letter designs or formation of letters, he is likely to pause or hesitate or to lift the pen or even to introduce retouchings. Therefore, whenever the banker asks a customer to put his signature in the bank, he should carefully watch the pen-movement, speed, pen-pauses, lifts or hesitations.

Forgery over Genuine Signatures

The banker should also know that there can be forgery over genuine signatures seen on a cheque. A case may originate when someone gets a signed blank cheque from another and presents the same to a bank with raised amounts which the person who has put the signature does not intend to give him. Likewise, certain people have a tendency to put their signatures on blank cheques and keep them. If such cheque-leaves are stolen, the thief may write an amount on the cheque and may present it to a bank for encashment. Money-lenders have a habit of accepting signed blank cheques from their customers. In such instances, it is to the interest of the bank and also to the interest of the customers that adequate caution is taken while encashing such cheques. The barker here can examine the following points :

The difference in the ink between the one seen on the signature and the one seen above it. It s quite possible that such a cheque may be stolen or criminally misappropriated, or obtained in the some way which is suspicious. If the difference in the ink is not clear for the naked eye, then a powerful magnifying glass can be used and the reasons for the difference in inks should be ascertained. The pen-track should be examined to see whether or not the writing has been done using the same pen. For this purpose, the condition of the stroke, depth of the nib furrows, width of the thick and thin strokes should be examined. If defect is seen, it can be concluded that the same pen was not used to put the signature and to write what is written above. If the writing is done after the cheque was folded, then strokes of the letters which are written across the fold will have the running of the ink into the fold of the cheque. If the fold is seen at the place where the signature comes, the running of the ink will not be seen at that particular part of the fold. Of course, if the pen-pressure is light, then running of the ink may not become conspicuous at the fold. In any case, a magnifying glass should be used here for examination.

The condition of the paper also should be studied, i.e., to see how old is the cheque?

More about the genuine and forged signatures are discussed in chapters that follow.

Questionnaire for Bankers for Examination of Genuine and Forged Writings/Signatures

The following questions should be asked by the banker when he compares two signatures/writings and he should try to get an answer to each question with respect to the admitted signature (specimen signature in the bank) and the suspected signature (signature seen on the cheque-leaf).

What do you think about the style characteristics in the signature of the cheque?

What do you see as the personal characteristics in the signature of the cheque?

What variations do you notice in the length, width, breadth and size of the signature seen on the cheque and those kept in the specimen signature card tray? Do you think that such variations are natural ones? If so, why?

QUALITATIVE TESTS

That is to say, those writing characteristics, such as *speed, movement, pen-pressure, shading, style, position of letters in relation to each other etc.*, which can be judged.

Speed

From observing the quality of strokes, style or the design of the writing, curves etc., what do you think about the speed of the writer? i.e., slow, medium or fast?

What is your observation about :
Quality of the strokes?
Quality of the curves of letters?
Style of letters?
Degree of slant in strokes?

Degree of pressure applied on the pen?

Pen-pauses and pen-lifts?

Tremors or shakiness in the quality of strokes and curves?

Terminals of strokes – i.e., coming to a point?

Movement

What type of movement do you see in the writing? slow? speedy? Are you able to say that the signature is put by a novice in writing/one who is unaccustomed to frequent writings? or one who is used to write and sign?

Are the alignments irregular? What about the connections? Do you have smooth or clear cut strokes? Are the curves round or broad? Do you notice any inconsistency in sizing and spacing of letters?

Is there any angular movement? Does the alignment assume arch type appearance?

What do you think about the outward and inward strokes and curves which are elongated?

What do you judge about the type of pen, ink and paper? And how might have they affected the signature?

What type of *Impulse Action* does the writer has?

What is your judgement about the movement of writing?

Pen-Pressure

What type of pen-pressure–light, heavy, regular/uniform, uneven, lateral, initial or graduated, do you observe in the signature? How do you judge them?

How are the strokes? What can you judge from the width of the strokes? What deductions do you make about the speed of writing from this?

Can you say from the pen-pressure that it is a normal signature? If so, how?

Is the pen-pressure even? or heavy? Do you see irregularity in pen-pressure? From the irregularity in pen-pressure, if seen, can you say that the signature is a forged one? How?

Is the signature put by a ballpoint pen? If irregularity in the pen-pressure is seen, is it due to the cheap quality ballpoint pen being used?

Is the heavy pen-pressure, if there is, owing to the fact that the writer is an illiterate/semi-literate person?

Is the inequality in pen pressure due to the poor type of the nib of the pen? –cheap quality pen? cheap quality paper?

Shading

Where do you see the shading in a conspicious manner?

From the shading, are you able to appreciate the pen-pressure?

From the shading, can you say that the signature is a forged one?

From the shading can you say that the shading is consciously done? Why do you say so?

Pen-Position

Do you see that the two parts of the nib were separated while writing the strokes? Do you see uniform strokes? Do you see smooth and deeper shade or colour of the ink in the right side of the stroke? In such cases, what do you see on the left side of the nib (rough strokes)?

Line Quality

How do you see the line quality of strokes/curves etc.?

Do you suspect any traced forgeries? If so, how does the line quality help you to arrive at this conclusion?

If the signature has poor line quality, is it because it was put by an illiterate person?

Style

Do you think that the signature is put by a person having a mental urge superior to his physical action? Why?

Do you think that the signature is put by a person having physical action superior to his mental urge? Why?

Has the signatory put his signature in one pen-operation? In other words, has the signatory lifted his pen only after the completion of the signature once he has started signing?

Does the signature possess cursive writing/running style?

Do you think that the quality of the paper, strangeness in using a particular pen, the nature of the ink and the space available to put the signature etc. have affected the style of writing? Why?

Has the signatory made any attempts to disguise the signature? How?

Is the forger successful in giving a pictorial effect to the signature forged?

QUANTITATIVE TESTS

That is to say, the alignment, slope, direction of strokes, size of letters, spacing etc.

Alignment

How is the alignment?–straight? irregular? arc–like? ascending? decending?

Are the letters in the signature resting on the base-line?

How do you see the alignment of letters in the signature to the base-line? How is the mal-alignment?

Slope or Slant

What are the angles formed by the letters to a base-line? Is the slope irregular?

Do you suspect simulated forgery in the signature? If so, how does the slope help you to arrive at this conclusion?

Spacing

How do you appreciate the spacing between letters of the signature?

Has the space available to put the signature affected the spacing?

Is the spacing narrow? irregular?

Do you suspect a simulated forgery? If so how does the spacing help you to arrive at this conclusion?

Size and Proportion of Letters

Has the space provided affected the size and proportion of letters? How?

Can you say that the signature is put in a hasty or slow manner from the size and proportion of letters?

How do you see the height of short letters in relation to long letters?

Do you suspect a free-hand forgery? If so how does the size and proportion of letters help you to arrive at this conclusion?

Form and Formation of Letters

What do you say about the form of letters? i.e., the shape of letters?

What do you think of the formation of letters?

How has the signatory developed special interest to have special formation of individual letters? If so what are they?

Dots

Do you notice dots/full stops in the signature? If so, are they below the underlining of the signature?

What is the distance between the dot and the beginning of the last letter in the signature?

Are the dots above the letter 'i' or 'j' seen almost at a constant distance from the letter?

What about the 'cutting' in the letter 't'? Is it before, after or on the vertical line in the 't'? Does it keep a constant distance from the vertical line of 't' if the 'cutting' is behind or after?

Arrangement

Has the person put his signature at a particular place on the cheque? If measured from the edges, do you see that he keeps his *own special position* while he puts the signature?

If you keep a cancelled cheque-leaf duly signed by the customer, does the *special position* of his signature on the cancelled cheque is retained in the cheque leaf surrended by him?

Size of Handwriting

What do you think about :

Size of letters?

Height of letters?

Width of letters?

Position of letters?

Space between letters?

Finally, what is your impression about the general execution of the signature? Does an overall visual impression of the signature at the first sight give you the feeling that it is a genuine one?

References

Fischhof, Julius, *New Method of Comparing Handwriting*, Szeged, Hungary, City Printing Office, 1927.

Hilton, O., Proper Evalution of Dissimilarities in Handwriting, *International Criminal Police Review*, No. 105, February 1957.

Malley, R., 'Identification and Handwriting', *International Criminal Police Review*, No. 94, January, 1956.

Nerves, N., 'Similarities in Handwriting of Relations', *International Criminal Police Review*, No. 77, April, 1954.

Osborn, Albert, *Questioned Documents*, Albany, N. Y. Boyd Printing Co., 1910.

Sulner-Fischhof, Hanna, *New Methods of Examination of Questioned Documents*, Budapest, Hungary, 1948.

Sulner, H. F., *Examination of the Document in Question*, New York, Law and Order, 1955.

3

GENIUNE SIGNATURE

'Signature generally means the name of a person written by himself' —defines *Chambers Twentieth Century Dictionary*. This definition need not always be true as there are a number of people who do not write their names when putting their signatures. They may put some symbols to represent their identity. There are many characteristics which can be seen in genuine signatures. And there can be of three kinds of signatures : (1) formal, (2) informal, and (3) deliberately disguised.

Formal signature means the one put with care and deliberation. Such signatures will be legible and firm. The signatory does not intend to produce anything unnatural in genuine signatures. And formal signatures are seen generally in wills, deeds, contracts, specimens in banks, etc. where the signatory considers that his signature is important. On the contrary, if the signatory puts his signature in a careless manner, then it becomes an *informal signature*. Such signatures are seen in office files, personal letters or other correspondences which have no special importance to the signatory. He may even put only his initials in such papers instead of his full signature. A disguised signature is a genuine one but has been written under surreptitious circumstances or in the presence of other persons. In such circumstances, the signatory consciously makes an attempt to conceal his writing habits or identity and he does this by consciously effecting changes in the style of his normal or usual manner of writing. A disguised writing is usually done in a slow manner and therefore it is quite likely to see broken letters, many pen-lifts, pen-stops, etc. in such attempts. The strokes and curves will be shaky or tremulous and the terminals of letters blunted. The spacing between words may be irregular and there will be heavy pressure applied to strokes and curves.

Genuine Signature : Things to remember

The banker should remember the following points about genuine signatures :

The signature of one and the same person put under same or different conditions may vary and differ within certain limits. These variations may take place in the size, proportion or spacing of the letters in the signature. The size of the paper and as said earlier the space provided for putting the signature may affect the pattern of the signature.

The mood, i.e., the physical and mental conditions of the signatory may affect the signature. Whether the signature is put when he is tired, when he is hurry, or as in a natural course, etc. will decide upon the execution of the signature. In such circumstances or conditions, it will not affect the cardinal features or characteristics of the signature, rather it will affect the appearance of the signature.

The difference in the writing instrument will affect the pattern of signature. Fountain pens, ballpoint pens, pencils, crayons or dried oily ballpoint pens, etc. create differences in signature in some ways.

The surface of the paper, say, smooth or hard surface, decides the pattern of signature. For instance, it is quite likely to see pen skips on a rough surface to cause interruptions and uneven writings.

The position in which the signature is put affect variations. Bending over a table, standing up and putting the signature on a paper kept in a pad, signing while lying on a bed in any moving vehicle, etc. can cause differences.

Intelligence and education of the signatories may result in natural variations in signatures.

Similarity in handwriting or signatures should not be confused to mean identity. No two signatures are identical and if that is so not two signatures of two specific individuals will ever be identical. Every individual has unique subconscious writing characteristics and features and distinct individual writing habits.

Complete identity between two signatures means a definite forgery. Hence, if a true signature appears on first impression different from another genuine or authentic signature, that fact indicates genuineness.

When forging a signature, the forger devotes most of his attention generally to the capital letters of the signature he intends to forge. Capital letters usually lack more individual writing eccentricities or characteristics than the lower-case letters. At the same time capital letters are very prominent and often contain more flourishes, particularly in signatures. The forger thinks that similarity in capital letters gives an aura of genuineness to the signature. His attention to the capital letters takes away his concentration from the controlling characteristics of the copied signature.

When a bank asks the customer to put his signature, he knows that he is being observed by the banker. This can affect his thinking process—say the mental urge—and it can cause some variations in his signature. The manner in which the signature should be obtained in suspicious circumstances by the bank authorities has been dealt with extensively elsewhere in this book. While a person puts his signature on request by the bank, the speed, execution, pen-lifts, pen-pauses etc. should be meticulously observed. When a signature is obtained on request, he should be provided with the same type of pen—fountain pen or ballpoint pen as the case may be— which has been used by him to put the signature suspected to be the forged one. The signature on request thus obtained should be compared with the signature kept in the specimen card-tray. This is the reason why it has been said earlier that six signatures should be obtained by the bank when specimen signatures are taken. This should be done by providing him both ballpoint and fountain pens.

If a person is intoxicated or is under the influence of alcohol he should never be asked to give his signature on request.

Deteriorated Signatures

There may be cases in which the signature is genuine, but the handwriting has seriously deteriorated to such an extent that it becomes practically difficult to show that the signature is authentic. This happens in the case of old people who have been sick for some time or for those who put their signature under the influence of intoxication in which case deteriorated appearance may be visible.

Guided Hand Signatures

Somctimes it so happens that a person puts his signature with his own hands but guided by another person. Such signatures can be written with one continuous line or in a series of short strokes. Usually it may not have any fine retouchings. And it can have good or bad line quality.

Illegible Signatures

If a person has lost all his control of the pen, the signature he puts will be almost illegible. This happens in the case of persons who are signing under the influence of drinks or drugs.

Ornate Signatures

A florid and ornate signature displays a super abundance of unnecessary strokes and flourishes. It is not very difficult to forge such signatures.

Forgery-proof Signatures

Ornate signatures are easy to be forged. Unlike them, a signature which is written accurately and carefully with shaded strokes is difficult to be forged. Every letter in such a signature is easily distinguished. Every forger has to study every stroke carefully if he wants to forge such a signature and to master and to be able to copy every such stroke is indeed a difficult task. Again to shade the letters as they are in the original is not an easy work.

Allonymic Signatures

When a person puts the signature of a fictitious individual or when he assumes the name of another person to put the signature, it is called *allonymic signature*. The signatory does not make any attempt to make a copy of the signature of any other person while he does so. Nevertheless, he may try to disguise his own style of writing when he puts an allonymic signature.

Allographic Signatures

When a person puts the signature of another with the latter's consent, that signature is called *allographic signature*. For instance, in the absence of a customer, his brother may submit a cheque putting the customer's signature knowing fully well that what he does in the absence of his brother will be ratified by him when he knows about it. The customer may accept the authorship of such a signature.

Characteristics of Genuine Signatures

Alignment of Signatures : Since many bank cheques do not provide a dotted line above, on or below which the signature may be put by the signatory, majority of people when they sign on cheques give a slight upward slope to their signature; many will sign in fairly horizontal and few may give a slop downward. The upward, horizontal or downward slope should be compared with their signature kept in the signature specimen cards to study the general alignment of signatures. This in fact is a fairly fixed habit of signatories.

Pen-lifts : Signatures, if they have only few letters; are often written with a continuous line. The signatory usually does not lift his pen when he puts his signature. This is particularly so in the case of people who are accustomed to sign.

Pen-halts : In genuine signatures, pen-halts are not generally seen as the signatory does not halt his pen in the process of signing from start to finish. Nevertheless, well-defined breaks (pen-lifts) may be seen in a small number of signatures.

Hiatus : Hiatus in genuine signatures does not occur although a hiatus between the initial capital letter and the remainder of the signature may be seen in some of the signatures. This means a hiatus seen elsewhere in the signature is suspicious and if at all hiatus is seen, it may be only one and generally not more.

Pen Movement : Pen moves in the case of a fluent writer even before it touches on the paper. The pen is lifted only when the signature is completely put. Nevertheless, the illeterates, semi-literates or novices may permit their pen to rest on the paper before they put their signature.

Ballpoint Pen Movement : A good number of ballpoint pens available in India refuse to write neatly until the ball of the pen rotates to a considerable extent. Hence, when signatures are put with ballpoint pens on cheques, it may be noticed that there are a number of preliminary scratches. They may have to be understood as nothing but the abortive starts to the signing.

Line Quality : The line quality indicates whether or not a line or stroke is written freely, i.e., uninterruptedly. A signature that is executed in a free and careless manner will have a smooth line quality and it indicates that the signature is really genuine.

Retouching : The retouching, if any, in a genuine signature is boldly done and the reasons for the retouching are quite obvious. Hence whenever retouching is done in an unnatural way it indicates that the signature is likely to be a forged one.

Variations : The signature of a person will vary as to its details as time advances or as he becomes old or more learned. This, however, does not mean that its general habitual characteristics very. The variations mostly occur with respect to the size and proportion of letters, modification in the formation of the slant of the letter curvature, spacing, etc. The banks are therefore advised to take the signatures of their customers once in every three years to substitute their signatures already taken and kept in the signature specimen tray.

Spelling : In genuine signature, no one bothers about the

accuracy or correctness of the spelling. Once an individual puts his signature, he seldom varifies the spelling.

Suspicious Signatures

If the bank becomes suspicious of somebody's signature, it has to obtain fresh signatures from the customer to make comparison. Normal or genuine signing is an automatic or spontaneous act requiring no conscious thought on the part of the signatory. But when he is asked to give his fresh signature in the bank, he may become nervous, particularly, if he has submitted a signature that is a forged one. Therefore, when the bank wants to have a request signature for making comparisons it is better to ask him to put his signature on plain sheets of paper as explained in the previous chapter. While doing so, he should be given the facility to put his signature in the normal physical and mental conditions.

Identification of Signatures

The following method of indentifying handwritings of different persons is meant to help the banker to examine and identify the signatures and their characteristics. Since, different persons cannot put one and the same signature in a natural way, they are asked to write a word "they" five times for comparison purposes.

The banker is advised to look at Fig. 3.1 and to appreciate the variations in the writing characteristics. He may use the following directions while he studies the many and complex writing characteristics. He can very well employ this knowledge when he compares characteristics in signature seen on the cheques to the one kept in the bank.

1. Personal characteristics :

(a) Take 3 and 5 and see the letter 'y'.
(b) Take 3 and 4 and see the distance between 't' and 'h'.
(c) Take 1 and 5 and see how 'ey' is written.

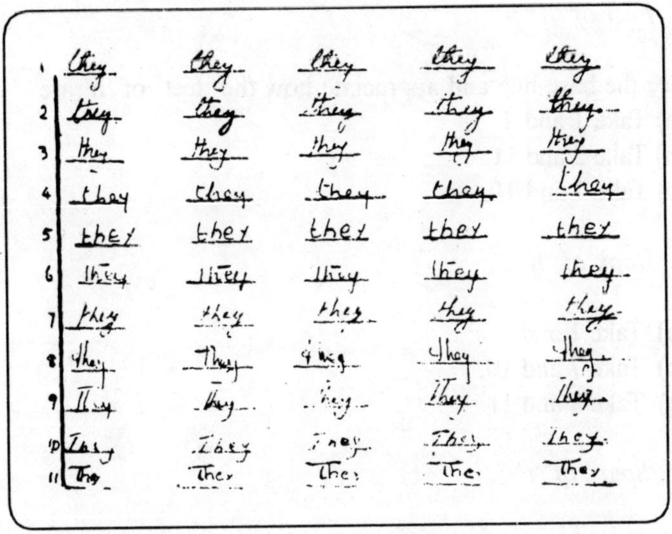

Fig. 3.1 : Writing characteristics of eleven persons

2. Size of the loops :

(a) Take 1 and 3 and see the difference in the loop.
(b) Take 2 and 4 or 5 and see the loop in 2 and no loop in 4 and 5 for the letter 'y'.

3. Eye-lets of 'e':

(a) Take 3 and 5 and appreciate the eye-lets.
(b) Take 9 and 10.
(c) Take 6 and 11.

4. Arc of 'h':

(a) Take 1 and 3 and appreciate the 'Arc'
(b) Take 5 and 10.
(c) Take 8 and 9.

5. Feet of 'h' :

See the base-line and appreciate how the 'feet' of 'h' are:
(a) Take 1 and 4.
(b) Take 2 and 11.
(c) Take 7 and 10.

6. Hook of 'h' :

(a) Take 1 and 5.
(b) Take 7 and 10.
(c) Take 8 and 11.

7. 'Spur' of 't' :

(a) Take 2 and 3.
(b) Take 1 and 10.

8. Diacritic in 't' :

(a) Take 2 and 6.
(b) Take 7 and 8.
(c) Take 5 and 9.

9. Relative height of 't' and 'h' :

(a) Take 1 and 10.
(b) Take 8 and 11.
(c) Take 9 and 10.

10. Length of the 't' crossings :

(a) Take 1 and 7.
(b) Take 5 and 9.
(c) Take 2 and 4.

11. Design of 't' :

(a) Take 1 and 8.
(b) Take 7 and 11.
(c) Take 2 and 9.

12. Length of the final stroke of 'y' :

(a) Take 1 and 4.
(b) Take 2 and 5.
(c) Take 3 and 6.

13. Slant of individual letter like 't', 'h' etc. and the degree to a base-line :

(a) Take 1 and 5.
(b) Take 6 and 10.
(c) Take 2 and 9.

14. Spacing of individual letters, say-'th', 'he' 'ey' etc.:

(a) Take 1 and 10.
(b) Take 3 and 4.
(c) Take 10 and 11.

15. Alignment of writing as a whole to a base-line :

(a) Take 1 and 2.
(b) Take 5 and 6.
(c) Take 10 and 11.

16. Alignment of individual letters to a base-line :

(a) take 't' in 2.
(b) take 'y' in 4.
(c) take 'h' in 7.

17. Shading in letters :

(a) Take 1.
(b) Take 7.
(c) Take 11.

18. Judge the following and say whether or not the following are natural ones :

(a) Size and proportion of letters.
(b) Pen-position.
(c) Pen-pressure.
(d) Line-quality.
(e) Speed.
(f) Movement.
(g) General execution.
(h) Arrangement etc. Thus, all the characteristics in the writing habits of the signatory should quantitatively and qualitatively be judged. For the purpose of comparison, the banker should take the recent signature of the customer kept in the bank and the one presented before him.

Appreciation of Genuine Signatures

When documents, cheques, drafts etc. containing signatures are obtained, the banker should try to ask the following questions to himself so as to appreciate the characteristics of the signature. To appreciate whether or not the signature in front of the banker is a genuine one, it is good to think that the signature seen on the document is a forged one. He can surely rebut his suspicion in case the signature is a genuine one if he can answer the following questions:

Questions

Is this signature legible? Is so, what is it? Can you read the signature to be the *name* of the person who is said to have signed the document? If so, what is the name?

If you cannot read the name of the signatory, then, is it a symbol to represent the signatory?

Does the signature appear to be a formal one? Why do you think so?

If the signature appears to be an informal one, why do you think so?

Do you notice broken letters? – pen-lifts? – pen-stops? – shaky or tremulous strokes and curves? – blunted terminals of letters? – irregular spacing? – heavy pen-pressure? If so what do they indicate?

How much space is provided to put the signature? Are the size, proportion or spacing of letters in the signature affected by the space provided?

Do you think that the type of the pen or the paper has affected the pattern of the signature?

Does the signature suggest anything as to the educational background of the signatory?

As people put their signature with a high degree of confidence, they are not concerned with the beauty of the letters, spelling etc. They have sufficient practice in signing and also they are usually very fluent when they sign. Does the signature suggest anything as to show that the signatory is lacking confidence while signing or is he very much concerned with the beauty of letters etc.?

Do you think that the signatory has lowered his pen on the paper and allowed the point to rest momentarily before starting to put the signature? If the signatory is a person accustomed to put the signature, the resting momentarily before begining to sign is suspicious.

The pen of the fluent writer is already in motion before it touches down on the paper and the forward motion of the pen continues till the signing is over and the pen is lifted naturally. Does the signature suggest that the pen was not in motion before touching it on the paper? Does the signature indicate that the onward motion of the pen was not continuous? Does the signature show that the pen was not automatically and naturally lifted from the paper as soon as the signing was over? [use magnifying glass if that needs be].

When the signature is examined by using a magnifying glass or otherwise, do you observe a *pointed end* at the instant of making contact with the paper by the pen? At the point when the pen is lifted from the paper at the end of signing? If so, most probably, the signature is a genuine one.

When a person puts his signature on a document, he is more concerned with the contents of the document and not on the mechanics of the production of the signature. Hence, does the signature indicate that the signatory was more concerned with the mechanics of the production of signature? In other words, is the signature written automatically and without conscious thought about the mechanics of the production of the signature?

Do you think that the signature is put by a pen which is well charged with ink? – i.e., ink which flows very freely? Hence, if you do not find *pointed ends* at the *beginning* and at the *end* of the signature, is it due to the free flow of the ink?

Do you think that the pen used to put the signature was running short of ink? Do you see the inkless traces of the pen on the signature? Or do you see some scratches indicative of the use of dry pen? Is it natural?

Is the signature put by a ballpoint pen? There cannot be any direct flow of ink from ballpoint pens to the paper (because the ballpoint pens have capillary action and rotating balls) as the thick viscous ink is transferred to the paper as the ball resolves. This being so, if at all the pen is kept stationary, there will not be any flow of ink (here the ball is not revolving) and as such one cannot see the thickening of the ends of ink lines in case a ballpoint pen is kept stationary before signing the document. The duration of the time of contact of the pen on the paper has nothing to do with the thickening of the line-endings to appreciate whether or not the pen was momentarily stopped to initate the signing.

[If ballpoint pens are used, there may be some preliminary scratches at the beginning of the signature. These scratches may be indicative of the fact that the pen refused to write until the ball has been rotated to a considerable extent].

Usually pen-lifts are not seen while a person puts his signature. Hence, Do you see unnatural pen-lifts or pen-halts in the signature? Do you see *Hiatus* in the signature? If so, is it between the initial capital letter and the remainder of the signature? If not, why does *Hiatus* occur in an unnatural way? If more than one *Hiatus* is seen, why is it so?

On examining of the signature by using a magnifying glass, do you see that signatory has lifted his pen several times and put the pen-point back to the paper on the ink-line itself so that no gap can be seen when examined by naked eye?

How is the alignment of the signature? Remember that a good many give a slight upward slope to their signature and many give fairly horizontal slope. Hence, if the alignment is doubtful, clarification to it should be obtained.

Now, the Banker should take the specimen signature kept in signature card tray of the bank and examine the signature presented to the same kept with the bank. The following points should be examined :

1. Personal characteristics, 2. Size of the loops, 3 Eye lets, 4. Arc, 5. Foot of the letters, 6. Hooks, 7. Spur, 8. Cuttings in 't', 9. Relative heights of letter, 10. Length of the 't' crossings, 11. Letter designs, 12. Length of final strokes, 13. Slants of individual letters and the degree to a base-line, 14. Spacing of individual letters, 15. Alignment of individual letters and the same of the signature as a whole to the base-line, 16. Shading, 17. Size and proportion, 18. Pen-position, 19. Pen-pressure, 20. Line quality 21. Speed, 22. Movements, 23. Arrangement, 24. General execution etc. As the banker gets more and more experience in the job these things will become very easy for him.

Law Relating to Forgeries

Chapter 4 deals with forgery of signature. The banker therefore should know what is meant by forgery in Indian law. Section 463 Indian Penal Code (I.P.C.) 1860 defines forgery as :

> "Whoever makes any false document or part of a document with intent to cause damage or injury to the public or to any person, or to support any claim or title, or to cause any person to part with property, or to enter into any express or implied contract, or with intent to commit fraud or that fraud may be committed, commits forgery".

The definition of forgery makes it clear that the forger should have an intention to commit fraud, no matter someone was in fact deceived by his act or the forger made any financial gain by his act.

The term 'document' includes everything done by the pen, by engraving, by printing or otherwise, whereby it is made on paper parchment, wood or other substance a representation of words or other equivalents addressed to the eye. Section 29 I.P.C. defines what a document is. Accordingly, 'document' denotes any matter expressed or described upon any substance by means of letters, figures, or marks or by more than one of those means, intended to be used, or which may be used, as evidence of that matter.

Explanation 1 : It is immaterial by what means or upon what substance the letters, figures or marks are formed or whether the evidence is intended for, or may be used in a Court of Justice or not.

Illustration to the above clause says that a cheque upon a banker is a document for the purposes of law.

Explanation 2 : Wherever it is expressed by letters, figures or marks as explained by mercantile or other usage, shall be deemed to be expressed by such letters, figures or marks within the meaning of this section, although the same may not be actually expressed.

Illustration : A writes his name on the back of a bill of exchange payable to his order. The meaning of the endorsement, as explained by mercantile usage, is that the bill is to be paid to the holder. The endorsement is a document and must be construed in the same manner as if the words 'pay to the holder or words to that effect had been written over the signature'.

Valuable Security

Section 30 I.P.C. reads : 'The words valuable security denote a document which is or purports to be a document whereby any legal right is created, extended, transferred, restricted, extinguished or released or whereby any person acknowledges that he lies under legal liability, or has got a certain legal right'.

Illustration : A writes his name on the back of a bill of exchange. As the effect of this endorsement is to transfer the right to the bill to any person who may become the lawful holder of it, the endorsement is a valuable security.

Section 464 I.P.C. is about making of false document. It reads :

A person is said to make a false document –

Firstly – Who dishonestly or fraudulently makes, signs, seals or executes a document or part of a document or makes any mark denoting the execution of a document with the intention of causing it to be believed that such document or part of a document was made, signed, sealed or executed by or by the authority of a person by whom or by whose authority he knows that it was not made, signed, sealed or executed, or at a time at which he knows that it was not made, signed, sealed or executed; or

Secondly – Who, without lawful authority, dishonestly or fraudulently, by cancellation or otherwise, alters a document in any material part thereof, after it has been made or executed either by himself or by any other person whether such person be living at the time of such alteration; or

Thirdly – Who dishonestly or fraudulently causes any person to sign, seal, execute or alter a document, knowing that such person by reason of unsoundness of mind or intoxication cannot, or that by reason of deception practised upon him he does not know the contents of the document or the nature of the alteration.

Illustrations

(a) **A** has a letter of credit upon **B** for Rs. 10,000, written by **Z**. **A**, in order to defraud **B**, adds a cipher to the 10,000, and makes the sum 1,00,000 intending that it may be believed by **B** that **Z** so wrote the letter. **A** has committed forgery.

(b) ....

(c) **A** picks up a cheque on a banker signed by **B**, payable to bearer, but without any sum having been inserted in the cheque. **A** fraudulently fills up the cheque by inserting the sum of ten thousand rupees. **A** commits forgery.

(d) **A** leaves with **B**, his agent, a cheque on a banker, signed by **A**, without inserting the sum payable and authorizes **B** to fill up the cheque by inserting a sum not exceeding ten thousand rupees for the purpose of making certain payments. **B**, fraudulently fills up the cheque by inserting the sum of twenty thousand rupees. **B** commits forgery.

(e) **A** draws a bill of exchange on himself in the name of **B** without **B**'s authority, intending to discount it as a genuine bill with a banker and intending to take up the bill on its maturity. Here, as **A** draws the bill with intent to deceive the banker by leading him to suppose that he had the security of **B**, and thereby to discount the bill, **A** is guilty of forgery.

(f) **Z**'s will contain these words : 'I direct that all my remaining property be equally divided between **A**, **B** and **C**. **A** dishonestly scratches out **B**'s name intending that it may be believed that the whole was left to himself and **C**. **A** has committed forgery.

Explanation 1 : A man's signature of his own name may amount to forgery.

Illustrations : (a) **A** signs his own name to a bill of exchange, intending that it may be believed that the bill was drawn by another person of the same name. **A** has committed forgery.

(b) **A** writes the word *accepted* on a piece of paper and signs it with **Z**'s name in order that **B** may afterwards write on the paper a bill of exchange drawn by **B** upon **Z** and negotiate the bill as though it had been accepted by **Z**. **A** is guilty of forgery; and if **B**, knowing the fact, draws the bill upon the paper pursuant to **A**'s intention, **B** is also guilty of forgery.

(c) **A** picks up a bill of exchange payable to the order of a different person of the same name. **A** endorses the bill in his own name, intending to cause it to be believed that it was endorsed by the person to whose order it was payable. Here **A** has committed forgery.

Explanation 2 : The making of a false document in the name of a fictitious person, intending it to be believed that the document was made by a real person, or in the name of a deceased person, intending to it be believed that the document was made by the person in his lifetime, may amount to forgery.

Illustration : A draws a bill of exchange upon a fictitious person and fraudulently accepts the bill in the name of such fictitious person with intent to negotiate it. **A** commits forgery.

The I.P.C. prescribes jail sentence for a term which may extend to two years or fine or both for a person who commits forgery by virtue of Section 465.

Section 467 I.P.C lays down :

"Whoever forges a document which purports to be a valuable security, or a will, or an authority to adopt a son, or which purports to give authority to any person to make or transfer any valuable security, or to receive the principal, interest, or dividends thereon, or to receive or deliver any money, movable property, or valuable security, or any document purporting to be an acquittance or receipt acknowledging the payment of money, or an acquittance or receipt for the delivery of any movable property, or valuable security, shall be punished with imprisonment for life or with imprisonment of either description for a term which may extend to ten years, and shall also be liable to fine."

Section 468 I.P.C. lays down punishment – imprisonment for a term which may extend to seven years, and also fine – for a person who commits forgery for the purpose of cheating. Section 471 I.P.C. prescribes punishment for using a forged document as a genuine one.

Forgery : Case-Laws

1. The expression defraud involves two elements, namely, deceit and injury to the person deceived. A benefit or advantage to the deceiver will almost always cause loss to the deceived.... Certainly, Dr. Vimala was guilty of deceit. For though her name was Vimala, she signed in all the relevant papers as Nalini and made the Insurance Company believe that her name was Nalini, but the said deceit did not either secure to her advantage or caused any non-economic loss or injury to the Insurance Company.

On evidence as disclosed, neither was she benefited nor the Insurance Company incurred loss in any sense of the term. No offence under Section 467 I.P.C. (Dr. Vimala *vs.* Delhi Administration, A.I.R. 1963 S.C. 1572, 1972 : 1963 (2) Cr. L. J. 434.)

2. If the mention with which a false document is made is to conceal a fraudulent or dishonest act which had been previously committed, we fail to appreciate how that intention could be other than an intention to commit fraud. The concealment of an already committed fraud is a fraud. (R.K. Dalmia *vs.* Delhi Administration, A.I.R. 1962. S.C. 1821 : 1962 (2) Cr. L. J. 805).

3. Ordinarily counterfeiting implies the idea of an exact imitation; but for the purpose of the I.P.C. there can be counterfeiting even though the imitation is not exact and there are differences in detail between the original and the imitation so long as the resembalance is so close that deception may thereby be practised. Explanation 2 to S. 38 lays down a rebuttable presumption where the resemblance is such that a person might be deceived thereby. In such a case, the intention or knowledge is presumed unless the contrary is proved. (The State of Uttar Pradesh *vs.* Hafiz Mohd. Ismail, A.I.R. 1960 S.C. 669 : 1960 Cr. L. J. 1017)

References

Guven, E., 'The Signature', *International Criminal Police Review*, No. 58, May, 1952.

Hardless, C.E., *The Identification of Handwriting and the Detection of Forgery*, The Hardless Press, Calcutta, 1912.

Malley, R., 'Identification and Handwriting'; *International Criminal Policy Review*, No. 94, January 1956.

Mitchell, C. A., *Documents and Their Scientific Examination*, Griffin London, 1922.

Smith, Stanley S., 'A Method of Comparing Written Documents', *International Criminal Police Review*, No. 80, August-September, 1954.

4

FORGERY OF SIGNATURE

During the busy hours of business transactions or even otherwise banks can be approached with forged or erased documents which, if not subjected to minute examination, can be beneficially used for monetary gains by the one who presents the documents and can consequently cause monetary loss to the banks. It is estimated that nearly one hundred crore of rupees is annually lost to banks by way of various frauds practised upon them[1]. It is argued that forgery of documents is, perhaps, as old as writing itself. In spite of it, the banks in India, it is found, are not very much concerned with the problem in the manner in which it should receive attention. Unfortunately, only a few training institutions of banks in India impart instructions about forgery to their employees with the result that the employees, with little or no academic training in the science of detecting forgeries, carry on their business.

What Is Forgery?

As stated in the previous chapter, every banker should have a clear idea of what forgery means in banking transactions and also in law. The word *forgery* as seen under the Indian law has been defined in chapter 3. Forgery becomes a crime only when the act can be legally perceived to be something against which legal action can be initiated. In simple terms, forgery means nothing but the making of a false document so that it may be used as genuine.

Forgery of Signature

The banks are generally concerned with signatures and therefore signatures suspected to be forged ones can be in any of the following seven classes :[2]

1. forged signature in which the forger has not made any attempt to make a *copy of the genuine* signature of the person purported to have signed;
2. forged signature of persons who are fictitions or dead;
3. forged signature, resembling the genuine signature, produced by any one of the tracing processes;
4. forged signature made free-hand which is otherwise called 'simulated forgery';
5. genuine signature which has been obtained by force, fraud, coercion or trickery;
6. genuine signature which the person who has actually signed refuses to accept it as genuine later; and
7. genuine signature, but written in an unusual way or in an illegible manner so that the signatory can disclaim it, if that needs be.

The forgery can be committed in many ways: by pencil, pen, typewriter, printing or engraving. The banker should know that the law is very clear in this matter. The following illustrations from decided cases by courts of law will show how the courts view forgery in India :[3]

1. Signing the name of any person with intent to defraud is a forgery.
2. The attempt to imitate the signature of another's name is a forgery, although the name be either of a friend or a near relation about whom the offender believes that he will not object to his action.
3. It is also forgery to induce an innocent person to write the

name of a third person, upon the false representation by the offender that the third person has authorized him to sign the name for him.

4. A person may commit forgery even though he signs his own name when his name is the same as that of another person and he signs his name with the intent that the writing should be received as written by the other person or when he impersonates the other person signing an instrument, which was to be signed or endorsed by the other person.
5. Forgery is committed by using an assumed or fictitious name in signing an instrument, when it is done with the intent to defraud.
6. It is also forgery to sign the name of non-existent person or corporation when the purpose is to defraud.

Methods of Forgery

There are only two methods by which forgery can be committed. (i) *Traced Forgery* and (ii) *Free-hand* or *Simulated Forgery*. If the signature has been forged by resorting to any one of the tracing processes, it is called traced forgery. Generally, this method is adopted by a poor pen-man or by those who lack confidence in the ability to commit a free-hand forgery in a convincing manner. Simulated forgery means the signature put by the offender without resorting to tracing processes. In other words, the offender, here, carefully studies the genuine signature intended to be forged with respect to its letter designs, letter-spacing, shading and other prominent features. He studies these characteristics taking meticulous care and in such a way that he acquires a good mental picture of the characteristics as well as the skill to reproduce the signature with its general pictorial effect. Prior to forging the signature, he makes many attempts–firstly by observing—to reproduce the signature. His practice-attempts here are aimed at the reproduction from memory the portions of the signature and then characteristics of the letters. As soon as he becomes confident of reproducing the whole signature, he puts it as a whole. After every practice-attempt, he compares the simulated signature with the genuine one and corrects the shortcomings, if any, in his subsequent attempts. His study and practice-attempts continue till he feels fully confident of forging the signature in a free-hand manner, convincingly, on the required document.

Traced Forgery

There are many methods by which one can commit traced forgery on a document. They are explained below[4] :

1. Direct Tracing Method: This method is said to be the simplest among all tracing processes. Hold the paper having the genuine signature against a window as a source of light. Then adjust the position of the paper which should bear the forged signature in such a way that the outline of the genuine signature can be clearly seen through the paper in the required place. Ink-in the outlines of the genuine signature. Instead of keeping the document against a window for getting the source of light, a photographer's retouching desk can also be used for this purpose. Since, the cheque-leaf of banks are generally made of thick papers, this method may not be successfully employed by the forger. If this method is resorted to, the forger often prefers to hold the signature to be forged upside down. This is to facilitate him to trace only a meaningless outline in which case his attention may not be directed to the accurate tracing of the signature intended to be forged. The offender generally finds it difficult in such situations as he cannot get a recognizable name. Nevertheless, if the signature intended to be forged is not kept upside down, the forger's own hand-writing characteristics or tendencies are likely to influence the final result.

As stated earlier, direct tracing of bank cheques may not be always practicable. First of all, the cheque-leaves are thicker than ordinary tracing papers and therefore only insuffcient light will be transmitted to enable the forger to see a clear outline of the genuine signature. If only both sheets are fairly translucent, the direct method of tracing can be employed.

2. Projection Tracing : In cases where direct tracing is found to be impracticable, the forger may go for projection tracing methods. In this method, the offender attempts to make a projection of the outline of the genuine signature on the document intended to be forged. For this, he places the genuine signature over the spot where the forgery is to appear and then mark with pencil along the outline of the genuine signature so heavily that grooves appear on the document that is to be forged. These grooves are then inked-in. No commerial apparatus or instrument is available in the market for projection tracing. Hence, the forger resorts to some pointed instrument or nicely sharpened pencil. Remember that some offenders employ this method to forge bank-cheques.

3. Carbon Paper Tracing : In projection-tracing, grooves appear on the cheques as a result of the application of heavy pressure during the tracing process. On the contrary, if a carbon paper is used, one can make a more detailed and clear outline of the genuine signature with the application of considerably less pressure. A smooth and pointed instrument like a needle will be all that is required for gently tracing out the outlines of the genuine signature. Like in projection-tracing process, the forger may use even sharply cut pencils for this purpose. This process makes a pencil-line or smooth and pointed line in carbon on the forged document. Along the carbon outlines of the genuine signature seen on the forged document the forger inks-in. The carbon-lines on the forged documents are called 'guidelines' about which more details are given elsewhere in this chapter. As the offender does not want to damage the paper surface of the forged cheques, he may not erase the carbon-line seen under the forged signature. Carbon paper is not found to be entirely satisfactory for a good forgery. For, apart from the general smudges wherever it has made contact with the forged document, it leaves a greasy line which is not easily erased when the inking is completed. Yet some people resort to this process to forge bank-cheques.

4. Tracing Paper Process : A tracing paper, i.e., paper which is highly translucent, e.g., grease-proof paper, can be used for forging signatures on cheques. The tracing paper is placed over the genuine signature and then pressed into close contact with the genuine signature. This helps the forger to see quite clearly the genuine signature by observing the tracing paper kept over it. Copy the signature on to the tracing paper with a soft and sharply cut pencil. Apply only gentle pressure. Then, there will be no indication to show that the genuine signature has been used to trace out the outlines of the forged signature. Some clever forgers do not use a pencil at all to trace the outlines of the genuine signature. Looking through the upper surface of the tracing paper, they directly ink-in the outlines.

After transferring the genuine signature to the tracing paper, the back of the tracing paper is generally given a coat of graphite by being rubbed over with a soft pencil. This is done to get a 'guideline' on the document to be forged. After this, the graphite-coated tracing paper is lowered on the required place of the document where the forged signature should appear and then he outlines the signature once more by tracing out with a pencil or other pointed instrument. This will give a good guideline on the document to be forged. The guideline can then be inked-in. One defect seen in this type of forged signature is that the signature is twice removed from the original and therefore considerable care has to be taken at every stage from the beginning till the completion of the forgery.

Some forgers take a copy of the signature by using copier machines. The method helps them to avoid the tracing of signature from the original document. Afterwards, fine graphite power is spread over a glass plate and the forger keeps the copy of the signature taken by copier machines over it. Using a sharp edged instrument, he writes over the outlines of the signature by employing heavy pressure. The graphite powder sticks to the outlines of the signature underneath the paper. Afterwards, it is placed over the document where the signature should appear. Once again, the outlines are marked by using a sharp-edged instrument. The guidelines made by the graphite powder is later inked-in.

The advantage of these methods is that the guideline will not be greasy as it is in the case with carbon paper tracing. A gentle erasure with an India Rubber can surely remove any graphite left on the forged signature.

Simulated Forgery

As seen before, a person who is familiar with another's signature can simulate a free-hand forgery. Here the offender has practice-attempts and therefore he does not usually give any conscious attempt to the letter designs as he is familiar with the signature intended to be forged. This type of forgery represents a *careful* and *painstaking* 'drawing' of the signature of another person. The banker may accept a simulated forgery believing it to be a genuine one because he may be judging the handwriting by its general appearance or what is otherwise called the 'pictorial effect'.

More about Forgeries

There can be good and bad forgeries. In any case there will be, in both types, some resemblance with the genuine signature. Knowledge of the language of a signature is not a *sine qua non* for committing forgeries. For, the forger is here more concerned with the letter designs and forms of the letters regardless of what he forges. If the forger is familiar with the language of the signature, he is likely to forge the signature in a more legible manner than the genuine signature intended to be forged. It is agreed upon by document examiners that a signature which is written plainly and having well-formed letters are more difficult to be forged than a signature which is put in a complex way. Many people have a false notion that the more complex they make the signature, the more difficult it is to be forged.

A good pen-man finds it difficult to forge the signature of a poor pen-man and vice-versa. It is seen that even illiterate or semi-literate people sign with considerable degree of confidence. For, signature is something which people put several times. They have sufficient practices in signing and are generally very speedy when they sign. As stated earlier, after signing on a paper, people seldom bother about the spelling and letter designs. At the time of putting the signature, most people are more concerned with and conscious of the contents of the document than on the beauty of the signature. As the signature is put automatically by many, they do not bother about the mechanics of its production. The signing is done almost in an unconscious way.

The banker may remember that people often commit forgeries for making personal gains. Therefore, the act of forgery is usually a premeditated one. The forger, therefore, often requires a model of a genuine signature to commit forgery.

A forgery will be a bad imitation if :

1. the forger is a bad pen-man;
2. the forger does not produce his imitation with increased action, i.e., with spontaneity and speed. The slightest hesitation or pause of the pen results in bad imitation;
3. the forger cannot concentrate on the work he is performing. For, he consciously attempts to conceal his own handwriting habits while he executes the imitation; and
4. the forger is forced to write in a particular way owing to the defects of the hand and fingers or because of the defective development of the muscles of the hand and fingers.

Determining Traced Forgery

Earlier in this chapter mention has been made about *guidelines*. The various methods of committing forgery of signature by tracing processes have been already discussed at length above. Except for those forgeries which are directly traced from the genuine signature, every traced forgery has a guideline through which the forger inks-in. In direct tracing, the letters of the genuine signature are clearly seen when the forger places the document over it. Here the letters of the genuine signature themselves act as the guidelines and that is the reason why in such forgeries guidelines are not required. When a forger inks-in the guidelines to commit the traced

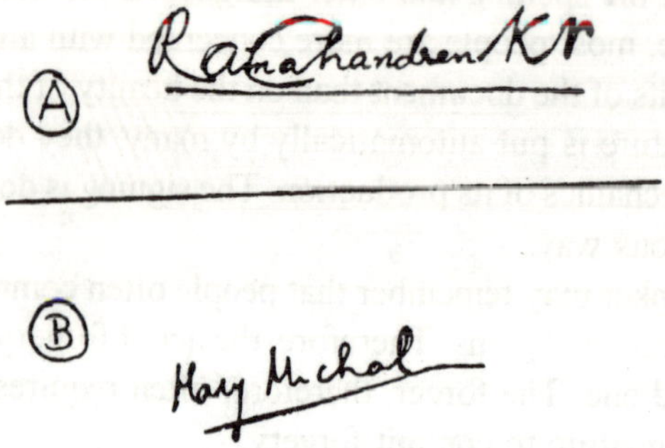

Fig. 4.1 : Note the *guidelines* through which the forger has attempted to ink-in.

forgery, he usually does not make any attempt to erase the guidelines. There are many reasons why the forgers omit to erase the guidelines. They are :

1. Few forgers know that there will be guidelines in traced forgeries. They do not know that it is by no means easy to ink-in a guideline, however meticulously they take care to ink-in the guidelines.
2. When one views the forged signature–particularly at the ends of the strokes or at the centre of the curves, it is certain that he can clearly see part of the guidelines unconvered by the ink (see Fig 4.1 A).
3. Usually the uncovered part of the guidelines can be seen by naked eye. But, there may be instances in which special care has been taken to ink the guidelines. In such cases, it will be difficult to distinguish traces of the guidelines mingled with ink (see Fig. 4.1 B). Nevertheless, a high-power microscope can reveal the traces of guidelines even in such cases. A banker is fortunate enough that he is able to see the guidelines partly covered by the ink-lines in a vast majority of forgeries even without the help of a high-power microscope.
4. Forgers often are reluctant to erase the guidelines in traced forgeries, because they are afraid that their attempt to erase guidelines will disturb the surface of the cheque where the forgery is made. Erasure is likely to cause disturbance in the

neighbourhood of the forged signature. More about erasures and their detection has been discussed in the next chapter.

5. Even when erasure on traced forgeries is being attempted, the forger does not often erase the signature at its ends. In other words, he makes the most thorough erasure in the middle of the forged signature and leaves the ends without being thoroughly cleaned up. One reason for this is that he uses the mechanical eraser to go over the signature to and fro in such a way that he does not extend the rubbed area sufficiently beyond the ends of the forged signature. This may be an unconscious act in some and in others a calculated attempt for suppressing the signs of distrurbance caused by erasure becoming visible on the blank areas of the paper adjacent to the ends of the forged signature. The banker may remember here that the speed of the eraser and its cleaning power naturally get reduced to the minimum when they reach the extreme ends of the signature. In other words, the speed and the cleaning powers of the eraser are maximum only at the centre of the forged signature.

While making an attempt to detect forgery, the banker may consider the following three points :

1. Any forgery will necessarily exhibit some good degree of similarity to the general run of the genuine signature, particularly in the more obvious features of letter designs. The forger genuinely desires that his attempt should never be detected and for this reason alone, he consciously creates similarity to the more obvious features or parts of the letter designs.
2. In traced forgeries, one can see that there will be a close resemblance with the genuine signature. For, the forger, here, accomplishes the forgery by running his pen accurately along the guidelines.
3. No two genuine signatures are ever exactly indentical in all respects.

Hence, where the banker doubts of traced forgeries, he may certainly search for the presence therein of a guideline or traces of a guideline which has been perhaps wholly or partly erased by the forger. For this purpose, the banker may examine both the ends of the strokes and also the centres of the curves of letters. It is here that the guidelines are least likely to be disturbed if at all an eraser has been applied. Also there, the guideline cannot be completely covered by the *inking* of the forger. The extremities or the signature should also be examined in case the banker suspects erasure of the forged signature.

Other aspects which should be looked on traced forgeries by the banker are :

1. As the traced forgery is done in a slow manner, it is definitely accomplished in slow speed. When the speed is slow, naturally there will be unnatural, but, generally, regular pressure in the strokes and also in curves of letters. This necessarily results in the terminals of letters, especially in final letters, blunting.
2. The forger in tracing the signature stops or even lifts his pen as and when necessary. When he stops and lifts his pen irregularly, he brings about pen-pauses and pen-lifts in irregular places, particularly in strokes and curves. He finds it difficult to trace the strokes and curves and therefore his unsteady hand results in those parts being tremulous or shaky.
3. Compared to the slant of strokes in genuine signature, the slant of strokes in traced forgeries may differ persistently, however slightly it may be. After tracing is completed or when the tracing is in progress, the forger may conclude that the tracing is faint or not satisfactory in some parts. Then he may, in a careful manner, retouch those parts. If retouching is done, there will be difference of shading in the corresponding parts of the tracing and the specimens, and it will be conspicuous.
4. If the cheque is examined on its reverse side, signs of indentation caused by the heavy pressure exerted by the

forger during the process of tracing may be seen. In case carbon paper is used to make guidelines, and the pressure is not exerted, signs of indentation may not be seen. But there will be guidelines in such cases.

5. When carbon paper is used for making guidelines, an excessively heavy looking signature is likely to be produced. As explained earlier, particles of carbon will be seen in light or heavy density, near the pen/ink strokes and curves of letters.
6. The process of inking-in an indented guideline or going over a carbon guideline necessarily impedes speed of writing. As a result, pen-pauses and pen-lifts are seen. The strokes and curves, especially the elongated ones will have tremors. Likewise, the terminals of letters, particularly the final letters, will be alienated. While inking-in the guidelines, the forger is more concerned with the filling in the guidelines with the ink than to reproduce the signature as it is. For this reason, it is believed that some forgers commit traced forgeries by holding the signature upside down.

The Fischhof Method

Professor Julius Fischhof found out a method for detecting forgeries. He took a photo-chart representing the disputed signature alongside the admitted genuine signature. They showed a great deal of similarity and very little difference. Fischhof, then, turned the same chart upside down and showed that there were perceptible differences. He said that when we are "not influenced by reading letters or words we have a more objective view". Some banks in India resort to a modified Fischhof method to detect forgeries and the banks are instructed to examine the suspected signature with specimen signature kept upside down.

Photographic Method

Banks cannot resort to photographic method easily, and particularly during business hours. Nevertheless, they may know the technique.

Here the suspected [traced] forgery (signature) and its genuine signature (model) are photo-graphed on the same photographic film. Thus the two signatures have the same dimensions. From the photographic negative, one can make prints. If the suspected signature is a traced forgery of the model, it will superimpose with the model signature. However, a traced forgery cannot coincide exactly with the model when superimposed. For instance, elongated strokes and curves in the genuine signature may be slightly more exaggerated in the traced forgery. Experts on document examination are of view that an agreement to the extent of 97 per cent will be seen between the forgery and its model with respect to the size of letters, slant of strokes, spacing between letters, etc. To get the specimen signature from which the traced forgery is made is not within the reach of the banker. Hence, in serious cases, where the bank wants to have sophisticated examination, they should register a case and get the crime investigated by the police.

Detection of Free-hand Forgery

As explained before, a free-hand forgery means an imitation made by copying the style and formation of the letters in the genuine signature with care and concentration and without resorting to any one of the tracing processes. In fact, these types of forgeries are difficult to be detected by a banker unless he examines the signature in a very scientific way. For this reason, the banker should know the following details :

1. A practised writer can make the simulated forgery in a fluent manner. Since the forger is familiar with the genuine signature, he does not require any conscious thought applied to the precise form of letters.
2. If one commits simulated forgery from a model signature that is kept just in front of him, there cannot be a swift and carefree movement of the pen. Likewise is the case when the forger commits free-hand forgery if he imitates the forgery from a form that he keeps in his memory. Here the

forger has to concentrate more on the task than anything else and in so doing he has to ensure that his pen-point reproduces the letter designs which he has in his memory. As a result, a part of his attention is always given to the execution.

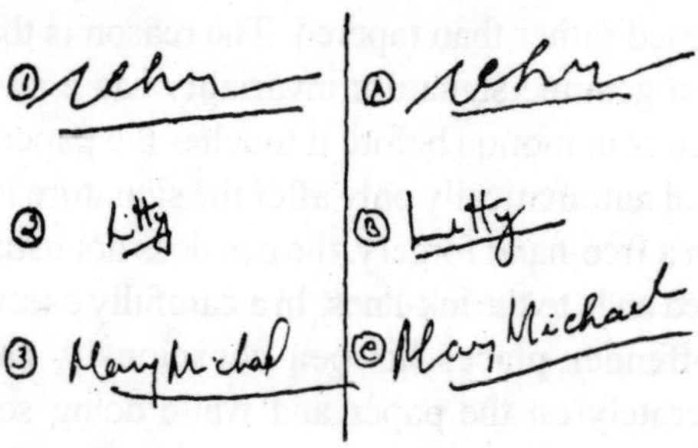

Fig. 4.2 : On the L.H.S., genuine signatures and on the R.H.S., simulated forgeries are given. Both are written using the same pen, but by different people. Try to appreciate the differences.

3. Apart from purely traced or simulated forgeries, there are composite forgeries. A composite forgery is one in which the forged signature is partly traced and partly made by free-hand. Here, the original intention of the forger has been to commit a traced forgery; but when the work is executed, the forger finds out that some part has been left out. So, he puts ink into the missing parts by free-hand forgery. Here too, there cannot be any good swift or carefree movement of the pen.

4. In free-hand forgeries, the offender has a double care, i.e., (a) he has to reproduce the signature of another as far as possible in the same way as the genuine signature is seen; and (b) he has to see that his own handwriting characteristics are consciously suppressed. Therefore, there can be only a slow and careful motion of the pen, This is the reason why it is said that the final product (i.e. the forged signature) is not 'handwriting' but is only a 'drawing'

of the genuine signature. Remember that the eye has a tendency to accept any signature as genuine by its general appearance, i.e., the 'pictorial appearance' and the banker should not be misled by the pictorial effect of the forged signatures on his eyes.

5. The ends of the ink-lines in a forgery are likely to be thickened rather than tapered. The reason is that a fluently written genuine signature invariably has a swift pen, i.e., the pen is in motion before it touches the paper and the pen is lifted automatically only after the signature is completed. But in a free-hand forgery, the pen does not usually produce tapered ends to the ink-lines. In a carefully executed forgery, the offender places his pen consciously, carefully and deliberately on the paper and while doing so, the pen is surely not in motion. When each pen-movement is complete, the offender permits his pen to rest momentarily on the paper and this causes the ends of ink-lines to be thickened. Nevertheless, if the forger knows the machanics of production of free-hand forgery, and also the methods of detection, he may simulate the signature without pen-stops and thickening of the ink-lines. Seldom do the forgers know these things.
6. In a genuine signature, no halts or pen-lifts are usually seen. This does not mean that genuine signatures do not have any pen-lifts or halts at all. If they have pen-lifts or halts, then they occur where pen-lifts or halts are expected to occur and the reason for them may be quite obvious.
7. If the forgery has been committed with ballpoint pen (otherwise this may be called an ink pencil), it is not possible to detect pen-pauses and hesitations. The ballpoint pen is lifted and placed back without leaving any interruption in the writing. The banks should therefore advise their customers not to use ballpoint pens, as far as possible, as a precaution against forgeries. Nevertheless, even in ballpoint pen forgeries, it is quite possible to detect poor line quality of a deliberately slow writing.

8. Forgers, after committing the forgery, are still doubtful of the perfection of the forged signature. They may therefore try to improve their drawing and for this purpose, they may introduce delicate retouching to improve the shading, letter outline, curves, etc. If the banker notices the presence of retouching or modified letter designs, it is almost certain that the signature is a fraudulent one. Retouching may be seen in some of the genuine signatures as well. For, in such cases, the signatory may be a careless writer. But, such retouchings are deliberately done and therefore should be different with respect to the features of retouchings seen in a forged signature.
9. Retouching in a genuine signature is generally done to improve the legibility. Such retouchings are called *genuine retouchings* and they are done by one or two bold sweeping strokes which do not usually arise suspicion. Such retouchings can be detected by naked eye. On the contrary retouchings on forged signature are unobtrusive. The purpose behind retouchings in forged signature will never be to improve legibility or things like that but purely and solely for the correction of details of letter designs and for the improvement of the appearance of curves.
10. If retouching is done with care, skill and deliberation by an expert forger, it will be no doubt difficult to detect it. At the same time, one can observe the evidence of fine retouchings even in such carefully executed signatures and if evidence of fine retouching is detected, no doubt, the signature will be a forged one. If naked eye cannot detect such retouchings, then microscopic examination will have to be conducted.
11. The positioning of the signature on a cheque is of importance to detect simulated forgeries. Almost every one has a tendency to put his signature almost exactly on the same place on all cheque-leaves that he signs. If a signature is seen in a place (on the cheque) which is not normally the place where he puts his signature, it can be an indication

that he has signed the cheque having put himself in an unnatural position or some body else has signed. This need not be always true. Therefore, it is good if the banks can get the signature of the customers on a cancelled cheque-leaf as well when they take specimen signatures on the specimen signature card.

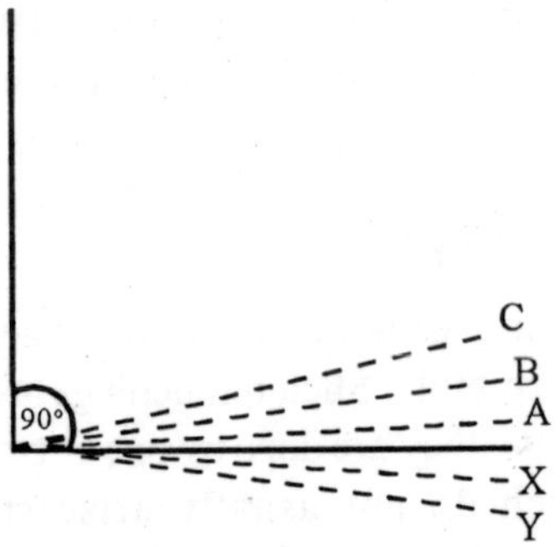

Fig 4.3 See how people may put their signatures.

A, **B**, and **C** are three lines slanted upward to a base-line. This shows how people put their signatures. This is an unconscious act and will be fairly constant unless there is obvious reasons for changing the alignment of the total signature to a base-line. If abnormality is seen in the slant of the genuine signature and the forged one, reasons for such a difference should be identified.

13. In genuine signatures, particularly of a fluent writer, the signatory, as indicated above, lifts his pen suddenly at the completion of signing. But in a forged signature, the pen rests at the end of the signature at least for a moment. The reason for this is that the forger on completion of his forgery takes stock of the imitation and mentally appreciates the beauty of the imitation. The resting of the pen at the end of the signature is perhaps done unconsciously and consequently, the end of the simulated forgery may have a thickened ink-line as discussed before.

14. If the forger, immediately or afterwards, realizes that his simulated forgery is not an imitation at all, he may try to modify the signature by additions of strokes, curves, etc. in which case the defects of additions explained in the next chapter can be detected.
15. The variations in width caused by the control of the pen position with regard to the direction of motion of pen and of the pressure exerted is called shading. In other words, shading denotes the forceful and rather an obvious increase in pen-pressure. In a genuine signature, it will be mostly unconscious as it happens owing to the personal habits of the signatory. Shading in a genuine signature should not be confused with the thick lines formed thanks to the broad concavity of the pen. To give shading as it seen in genuine signature to an imitation signature is indeed not possible. For simulating the signature of a person, the forger has to hold his pen in the manner in which the original signatory had held it, if the former wants to have the shading exactly in the manner it is seen in the genuine signature. This is not often possible.
16. Relative positioning of letters in genuine and simulated signatures is of considerable importance in identifying forgeries. Relative position of letters denotes the comparative relation of the letters or parts of the letters in respect of one another. Take for instance the word *the*–here it would be of interest to see whether or not letter *h* is higher, lower or approximately of the same height as that of the letter *t*. Similarly, the letter *e* may be examined. It is seen that the relative positioning of letters by people generally remains fairly constant. Hence, in simulated forgeries, it will be difficult for the forger to imitate the positioning exactly in the same way as seen in the genuine signature. The forger's handwriting habits will come unconsciously where he attempts for a free-hand forgery.

17. In chapters 2 and 3, a number of questions are given to enable the banker to examine handwriting and signatures. They can be used when free-hand forgery is suspected. During the induction and inservice courses for bank employees, they should be taught about comparing of forged and genuine signatures. A few practicals in the bank's training colleges with regard to this will be enough to make them self confident in this exercise.

Forgery and Cheating

The law on forgery has been explained in the previous chapter. A banker may also know the law on cheating. Cheating includes all types of acts committed in a deceitful way calculated to defraud others. Cheating therefore is a 'deceiful practice in defrauding or endeavouring to defraud another by means of some artful device contrary to plain rules of common honesty', –says Hawkins. Section 415, I.P.C. defines cheating in law. The section reads : 'Whoever, by deceiving any person, fraudulently or dishonestly induces the person so deceived to deliver any property to any person, or to consent that any person shall retain any property or intentionally induces the person so deceived to do or omit to do anything which he would not do or omit to do if he were not so deceived, and which act or omission causes or is likely to cause damage or harm to that person in body, mind, reputation or property, is said to 'cheat'.

Explanation : A dishonest concealment of facts is a deception within the meaning of this section.

Illustration : A, by pledging as diamonds, articles which he knows are not diamonds, intentionally deceives **Z**, and thereby dishonestly induces **Z**, to lend money. **A** cheats.

A intentionally deceives **Z** into a belief that **A** means to repay any money that **Z** may lend to him and thereby dishonestly induces **Z** to lend him money, **A** not intending to repay it. **A** cheats.

Section 416, I.P.C. relates to cheating by *personation*. It reads. 'A person is said to "cheat by personation" if he cheats by pretending to be some other person or by knowingly substituting one person for another, or representing that he or any other person is a person other than he or such other person really is'. Section 417, I.P.C. lays down punishments for cheating and section 419, I.P.C. for cheating by personation, and section 420, I.P.C. for cheating and dishonestly inducing delivery of property.

Cheating : Case-Laws

1. Guilty intention is one of the essential ingredients of the offence of cheating under Section 420 I.P.C. (A.K. Bose *vs.* State of Bihar, A.I.R. 1974 S.C. 1560 : 1974 Cr. L.J. 1026).
2. The accused presented a cheque, when he had only Rs. 5/- to his credit in the bank. Under rules the cheque was not accepted by the department. Hence, accused would not have been given a railway receipt for coal unless the amount was deposited in cash. The accused as a businessman knew that the cheque would not be accepted by the department, but he presented the same to gain time. No offence under Section 420 I.P.C. (Luxmi Narayan *vs.* State of Uttar Pradesh, A.I.R. 1956 S.C. 544; 1956 Cr. L.J. 948).
3. A person can be said to have done a thing dishonestly if he does so with the intention of causing wrongful gain to one person or wrongful loss to another person. Where a consignor of goods draws a hundi for the price of the consignment on some firm and supports that hundi with the railway receipt obtained by him in respect of the consignment, the party in fact pledges the consignement to the bank discounting the hundi and, therefore, in such a transaction the railway receipt cannot be regarded as anything else than a security for that transaction. If that security turns out to be worthless or practically worthless because the value of the consignement is only a fraction of what it was represented to be, the discounting of the hundi by the party drawing it must necessarily be regarded as unlawful would thus follow that the firm in question made again by obtaining credits and that these credits were obtained by them by resorting to unlawful means. Where no pecuniary question arises, the

element of dishonesty needs not be established and it would be sufficient to establish that the act was fraudulent and, therefore it may be that where an act is fraudulent, the intention to cause injury to the person defrauded must be established (Tulsi Ram *vs.* State of Uttar Pradesh, A.I.R. 1963 S.C. 666)

4. The accused took delivery of the ignots but did not pay and the complainant realised that he was cheated. If the accused had, at the time promised to pay cash against delivery, an intention to do so, the fact that he did not pay would not convert the transaction into one of cheating. But, if on the other hand, he had no intention whatsoever to pay but merely said that he would do so in order to induce the complainant to part with the goods, then a case of cheating would be established (Mahadeo Prasad *vs.* State of West Bengal, A.I.R. 1954 S.C. 724 : 1954 Cr. L.J. 1806).

Notes

1. See, V. N. Sehgal, 'Bank frauds and their detection by the application of scientific methods,' *C.B.I. Bulletin*, Vol. XVII, No. 6, M.H.A, Government of India, New Delhi, June, 1983.
2. See Wilson R. Harrison, *Suspect Documents : Their Scientific Examination*, Sweet & Maxwell Ltd., London, 1966.
3. R.L. Gupta, *Law of Forgeries, Counterfeiting and Cheating*, Law Book Company, Allahabad, 1971.
4. See Wilson R. Harrion, *op. cit.*

References

Burning, A., 'A Genuine Counterfeit', *International Criminal Police Review*, No. 58. May, 1952.

Guven, E., 'The Signature', *International Criminal Police Review*, No. 58, May, 1952.

Hardless, C. E., 'The Identification of Handwriting and the Detection of Forgery', The Hardless Press, Calcutta, 1912.

Harrison, Wilson R., *Suspect Document : Their Scientific Examination*, Sweet and Maxwell, London, 1966.

Hilton O. and Stein, E. W., 'Ballpoint Pens–Use for Signing Documents Considered', *American Bar Association Journal*, May, 1948.

Hilton, O., 'Can the Forger be identified from his Handwriting?,' *Journal of Criminal Law, Criminology and Police Science*, Vol. 43, No. 413 November-December, 1952.

Le Clere M., 'The Protection of Banking Documents against Forgery', *International Criminal Police Review*, No. 58, May, 1952.

Osborn, Albert S, 'Difficulties in Proving Forgery', reprinted from *Virginia Law Review*, Vol. XVI, No. 5.

5

ERASURES AND ALTERATIONS

Erasures are understood to mean the removal of writing from paper. This can be effected through mechanical erasers such as India Rubber, pencil erasers, ink erasers, scratch-knife, etc., and through chemical erasers like oxydizing agents which decolorize or bleach the dye of the ink. The reaction of these chemical erasers on paper results in decolorizing the colouring matter of the ink-line into colourless lines which can easily escape notice by people.

Banks use safety papers for making cheques. 'Safety paper is the term applied to paper which has been treated in such a way as to minimize the chances of a successful forgery by erasure, whether machanical or chemical, being carried out on any document of which it forms the basis'.[1]

The cheques usually have a neatly printed design which covers the entire surface of the cheque-leaf. Some banks in India use 'Cheque-Writing Machines' to type on bank-drafts, etc. This machine– a very simple form of typewriter–is intented to prevent any erasure or attempt at erasure or alteration of entries on bank drafts. This machine 'drives ink-covered type-faces into the very paper of the cheque. To produce this shredding action as it is termed, the faces of the types are scored with parallel cuts into the paper and carry with them the colouring matter of the ink. So thorough is the penetrating of the paper that the colour can usually be seen quite clearly on the opposite side. Erasure of such a heavily imprinted character is practically impossible'[2] Banks in India permit both fountain pens and ballpoint pens write on cheques. Formerly, the banks never permitted ballpoint pens to write on cheques.

Today ink in various colours and qualities are available in the market, which are made from lamp-black, log-wood, iron-gal, nigrosine, vanadium, etc. *Gum arabic* is a common igredient in all sorts of inks. If fountain pen is used to write and if it contains good ink, it necessarily penetrates slighty and smoothly into the inner layers of the cheque-paper. Cheques are made of fine quality paper and therefore when a fountain pen is used to write on it, the ink does not generally spread out in an uneven way causing rough strokes or curves. Hence if spreading of the ink is noticed, the banker can suspect of erasure of the writing on the cheques. For, when writing is done over an erased surface by a fountain pen, there will be a feather-like appearance of the writing. When an erasure by mechancial process is made on the cheque, the rubbing process invariably removes the glazing effect on the surface of the paper and thereby causing disturbance over the area. This infact is responsible for the feathering of writing over the erased surface. When the paper is of a fine quality, and the fluidity of the ink from the pen is really good, the ink penetrates into the inner layers of the paper. Likewise when writing is done on a cheap and thin sheet of paper of an inferior quality, the ink penetrates so deeply into the paper that the writer cannot write anything on the reverse side. This problem however does not arise with cheque-leaves.

Though there are a number of inks in various colours available in the market, it is good if the customers of a bank are advised to write on the cheques using carbon ink. The advantages of using carbon ink are : (i) It takes longer time for the carbon ink to fade on paper. In other words, the carbon ink fades only after several years by oxidation of the ink. (ii) It does not react with any chemical reagents just like other inks. The carbon ink writing cannot be bleached and this is a good precaution against erasures by chemical reagents known as ink-eradicators. This may be difficult for the customers; nevertheless, if they can be made aware of it, the banks can be in a safer position to transact business without being cheated. Since, the ink from the ballpoint pens do not penetrate into the deeper layers of the paper, the customers should invariably be asked to use ballpoint pens with black inks as a precaution against chemical eradicators being applied.

The banks may not permit their customers to blot their writings on the cheques. The blotting, as every one knows, removes a large proportion of the coloured matter (ink pigment) and makes the ink-writing to become dull and faint. Information leaf-lets from the bank should contain instructions as to the type of ink and also prohibition of blotting of cheques after writing down. This will help the customers take adequate precautions while they write on cheques.

Ballpoint Pen Inks

Ballpoint pen ink was first introduced around 1920. The ink then used was oily in nature and it dried very quickly on the paper because it transferred extremely small amount of ink to the paper. The early inks used in ballpoint pens were found to be unsatisfactory in many respects. The improved inks based on *polyethylene glycols of sinatable viscosity* and the ink made of it has helped to overcome many of the disadvantages of the oily inks. Some of the cheaper ballpoint pen-inks available in India are based on olein and such inks are found to "strike" very badly on certain papers. "Striking is the term given to the continued spreading of the colour over the surface of and into the paper so that the line of writing tends to lose its character and degenerate into a broad structureless streak of colour."[3] The customers therefore should be discouraged to use cheap ballpoint pen inks when they write on cheques. If possible, ask them to use only fountain pens.

Detection of Mechanical Erasures

When a cheque is presented to the bank, it should certainly be examined for the detection of erasures. For this, the cheque should be held close to the edge of a shaded lamp in such a way that the light should graze the surface of the cheque-leaf. This can be helpful to detect the disturbance of the paper fibres if mechanical erasures are made. Then the entire surface of the cheque-leaf should be thoroughly examined and the reflection of light incident upon the paper at low angles should be studied. If mechanical erasers are used, the surface reflectivity at the erased area will be quite different from the rest of the cheque-leaf. However, this is not a sure test for detection of mechanical erasures as gentle aberration on the paper has little, if any, effect upon the surface reflectivity. Therefore, if suspicion as to erasure still exists, the cheque-leaf should be held in front of a strong light which will permit detection of thin places eaten up by the mechanical eraser. Any officer of the bank exposed to some training in this aspect can easily identify such mechanically caused erasures without any difficulty.

The most reliable test for the presence of mechanical erasure on a cheque-leaf can be carried out by causing fine graphite powder to fall gently on the erased surface of the cheque-leaf. The fine graphite powder used for powdering finger-prints can be successfully employed here. After the gentle fall of the graphite powder, the cheque-leaf should be shaken so well as to distribute the powder on its surface. The excess powder is tipped off sideways. The fine graphite powder will stick to the surface where mechanical erasure has been made. This test cannot be done on all cheque-leaves particularly during business hours. Therefore, the banker should resort to this technique, in case he has suspicion about erasures on cheques presented to him. As stated earlier, one way by which erasure can be detected is through visual inspection of the cheque-leaf to find out any translucent area when the cheque-leaf is placed against a powerful source of light. The *fugitive inks* used to print the safety designs on cheque/draft leaves can help the banker to detect mechanical erasures.

At the Document Examination Laboratory, a *greenough binocular microscope* is used for detecting a skilfully made erasure. Hence, if the Staff Training College of the bank or the head office is having a Document Examination Laboratory, it is safe to send all documents submitted for getting a heavy bank loan sanctioned to detect erasures by using such sophisticated microscopes.

The banks can also resort to chemical inspection of the cheque-leaf without much difficulty. When *petroleum ether* (*benzine, carbon tetrachloride* or other organic compounds) is dropped into a cheque leaf suspected to contain a mechanical erasure, the chemical compound spreads and moistens the cheque-leaf until it reaches the erasure. On reaching the erased area, the chemical compound, instead of moistening the area of erasure, proceeds to travel along the boundary and later penetrates to the erased area. This can easily be noticed by an officer having some training in this sphere.

If the erased area is written by ink, as stated earlier, a rough feathered line is seen instead of the usual smooth line on the cheque-leaf. Now that many banks are provided with ultraviolet (UV) lamps, the erasure can be disclosed by the difference in fluorescence on appearance caused by the disturbance of the surface fibres of the cheque-leaf when made mechanically.

Detection of Chemical Erasure

If erasure has been effected by the use of chemical compounds, a careful examination under good or strong illumination will reveal discolouration from chemical erasers. As seen before, all ink writings except lamp-black (which is carbon) can be erased or bleached by using any ink eradicator now available in the market. But these ink eradicators remove not only the ink from the paper but also damage the shining and the glazing of the cheque-leaf. The damage caused to the cheque-leaf may not be very much conspicuous to the naked eye unless it is examined carefully by an experienced banker who has training and expertise in the subject. Therefore, the cheque-leaf should necessarily be examined with the help of a good magnifying glass or a low power microscope.

If chemical erasures are made, sometimes a yellow stain on the cheque-leaf can be seen. The finishing of the cheque-leaf may be disturbed then and the fibres of the cheque-leaf is loosened. This is also not easy to find out unless the banker has the required expertise. The cheque-leaf, therefore, should be examined under UV light to study the reflectivity of the surface of the paper. If chemical ink eradicators are used, the decolouration of the stained area will be shown by difference in fluorescence. However, if the eradication is not made recently or if the area is carefully washed with distilled water after the chemical eradicator has been used, it is quite possible that UV light does not reveal the presence of eradicated area. If the cheque-leaf is having a yellow tint, the UV light may not reveal a chemical eradicator. This is so because when the normal flourescence of the paper is yellowish, the chemical eradication of the ink writing cannot be easily detected as the area where the eradicator is used gives yellowish flourescence. Many banks entertain a false belief that UV light invariably exposes a chemical erasure. Because of this wrong belief some banks view the cheque-leaf under UV light in a causal manner and declare that the cheque is free from chemical erasure. The banks should never print their cheque-leaves in yellow-tinted papers. If only the cheque leaf is printed with an ink having a colour other than yellow, the erased ink will be revealed by UV lamp examinaton. The author has seen some banks getting their cheque and draft leaves printed with yellow tint and examining them under UV lamp radiation. It is futile to do so.

Documents and Deeds

In case of documents submitted for getting heavy loans sanctioned, invariably such documents or deeds should be examined for finding out chemical erasures. For this, if the bank has a document laboratory, the document can be subjected to further tests. The simplest test the document examination laboratory can do here is to place the emulsion side of an unexposed photographic plate against the site of the erasure and keep them in contact for several days in darkness. Almost all chemical eradicators, then, give off the chemically volatile products and any traces that are available in the paper will diffuse out and affect the emulsion which in turn show stains when developed. Another test is that the document may be fumed with iodine vapour and then the erased site of the paper will absorb selectively the iodine vapour. After fuming iodine vapour, the document should be kept in a warm place so that the iodine can evaporate well.

Erasures Made by Ballpoint Pen Writing

There is an erroneous belief among some of the bank officers that ballpoint pen inks cannot be erased by ink eradicators. If the ballpoint pen contains inks based on oil-soluble dye-stuffs, the writing with it can be erased by ink eradicators like hypochlorite or permanganate solutions. If better inks are used in ballpoint pens (the inks here will have lasting qualities of the writing), a good proportion of the ink can be eradicated by solvents like acetone and water mixed in equal parts. They remove the residual writings on the cheque-leaf and the last traces of the colour are further removed by treatment with a solution of any oxidizing agent.

Guidelines and Erasures

What we mean by guidelines has been explained in the chapter on forgery of signature. If traced forgery has been erased by using machanical erasers in an attempt to erase the guidelines, the most thorough erasure is seen in the middle of the signature. Here the forger rubs the forged signature by a rubber/ink eraser mechanically. He does not extend the eraser appreciably beyond the ends of the signature. As a result, the speed of the eraser and its cleaning power get considerably reduced at the two extreme ends of the signature and the maximum speed and cleaning power are seen at the centre of the signature. Therefore, the guidelines at the ends of the signature will still be noticed even when a traced forgery is erased by mechanical erasers.

Deciphering of Erasures

Banks generally do not get any documents signed by pencils. Yet, for academic interest it may be stated that if pencil lines are nicely erased, little or no trace will be left on the paper except the impressions made by the passage of the pencil over the paper. Therefore, if one examines the back of the sheet, he will be able to locate sufficient dirt sticking to the paper in the form of a faint mirror image of the writing provided the writing has been made on the paper keeping it on anything but a clean surface.

The ink writing, if erased, can be deciphered by photography, examination by UV light and infra-red (IR) light (with the image converter). When the document is put under UV radiation, a change in the fluorescence with the presence of traces of ferric compounds (in case iron gallotannate ink writing has been erased) can be observed. IR radiation in such instances affect the reflectivity and therefore, a photography or photoscopy with the help of an image converter may prove to be effective. If physical methods do not yield results, chemical methods will have to be resorted to. Banks cannot do these chemical tests except, perhaps, in their Document Examination Laboratory, and many a time the decipherment and restoration of writings are not expected to be done by the banks.

Overwriting

Some people, because of their carelessness or quickness, commit mistakes when they write on cheques. They may resort to overwriting and mostly it will be done either to correct a wrong spelling or to alter an entire word thus written wrongly. Sometimes, they may overwrite just to make an illegible writing more legible. They do so because they do not want to erase what has already been written. But in every case, where the overwriting is not done fraudulently, it is done boldly and therefore the reasons for such a bold overwriting can be understood easily since such overwriting carries no sinister implications. The banks usually do not accept cheques which contain overwriting, no matter the overwriting is fraudulent or otherwise. The customers are advised to avoid overwriting on cheqaes and whenever they are forced to resort to it for genuine reasons, they must be asked to cancel what they have already written and write afresh what they intend to write above the cancelled writing. They must put their full signature to show that the cance llation as well as the fresh writing are owned by them. Many a customer does not know this and therefore the bank should provide this advice in their information leaf-let attached to the cheque book.

Overwriting on cheques is fraudulently resorted to in the following cases :

In case of traced forgeries, overwriting may be seen, i.e. if the inking has been done on 'guidelines' (where tracing has been done by using carbon or pencil etc.), the forger invariably overwrites and in such instances, the banker should examine the cheque for locating traces of carbon, graphite, etc. near the strokes and curves of letters. If necessary, a magnifying glass can be used for this purpose. When inking-in has been done to the pencil or carbon 'guidelines', the strokes and curves of the signature would become unduly heavy. This is so because the writer makes every effort to see that his overwriting is not detected and for this he wants to cover the pencil or carbon 'guidelines' as completely as possible. Necessarily, the forger can accomplish the inking of the 'guidelines' slowly and cautiously and therefore invariably he is compelled to pause and even lift the pen whenever he has difficulty in covering a stroke or curve. If there is a gap between the pen-pause and pen-lift, the traces of graphite/carbon can be located there. If the overwriting is viewed under magnification, the 'guidelines' become distinctly clear. The examination of the cheque in IR radiation can sometimes reveal overwriting on cheques.

Sometimes, the forger may add or alter the value of figures on cheques. For example, Rs. 100 written first may be altered to Rs. 700 and Rs. 6 to Rs. 60. This he can do by alteration of strokes or addition of letters. In such instances, the forger who does it with a guilty consciousness (*mens rea*) will see that the colour of the ink which was used to write the original and the colour of the ink which is used to make the alterations show differences in their appearance. In order to conceal this difference while joining the two inks, the whole writing is overwritten again. For this, he uses the original ink-writings as 'guidelines'. Therefore, the strokes and curves must be examined to see the traces of the original ink and in such cases the writing will be having thick lines. A magnifying glass can be successfully used here.

Examination of the cheque under UV radiation can also help to identify the overwriting. Different inks give different fluorescence under the UV radiation. The examination under UV light should be carried out in darkness.

Some forgers may resort to erasing of the guidelines after the overwriting in which case the extreme ends of the writing should be examined to see traces of the 'guidelines'. As said earlier, the speed and pressure of the eraser will be minimum at the two extreme ends of the writings.

Additions

Some people, in filling out their cheques, carelessly leave space beside the 'numerical or word' amounts. This carelessness paves way for fraudulent additions into the cheque by words, letters or numbers. Forgers are very quick to recognize and appreciate the laxness and oversight of the original cheque-writer and may resort to writing on a cheque for an amount much higher than what the original cheque-writer intended. For instance, the numbers six, seven, eight, nine, etc. can be easily converted to sixty, seventy, eighty, ninety, etc. by just adding one or two letters at the end, i.e. suffixing the original writing. Six can also be changed into six hundred and the numbers 7, 8, 9, etc. can be converted to 70, 800, 9000 respectively by just adding zeros to the right hand side. Similarly, a cheque made payable to 'Jos' can be converted to 'Joson' or 'Joseph' and to 'Mr. Rajiv' to 'Mrs. Rajiv' by making small additions of letters if there is space after the writing. As a precaution to fraudulent alterations by cheque-swindlers, the banks should instruct their customers to leave no space blank when they write on cheques. The writing should be made from the extreme left. This means a line should be drawn immediately after the name is written. Likewise a line should be drawn after the amount is written. Even if it is expensive for the bank, it will be a good thing to provide carbon papers in every cheque-book so that the customer can write on the cheque by keeping the carbon surface of the paper in touch with reverse side of the cheque-leaf. If it is resorted to, many crimes on cheques, namely, alterations, additions, overwritings, etc. can be partly stopped. Providing a sheet of carbon along with every cheque-book should not be considered a waste of money, rather it is a check against forgery on cheques.

As explained under overwriting, when additions are made on cheques, the forger may write again on all the letters in his attempt to suppress the difference in colour of the ink used for original writing and the same of the ink used for making additions. The addition of an extra line to all the entries is intended to smooth out and suppress the difference between the new ink and the original ink used for writing. This can be detected if examination just like the one carried out for detecting overwriting is done.

Alterations

All additions can be alterations but all alterations need not necessarily be additions. It is possible that some people may delete letters, words, or figures on a cheque. One of the most common ways of alteration on a cheque is to try to erase. Part of it is done by any of the erasing methods. For instance, 'Mr. Gopalan' written on the cheque can be altered to read 'Mr. Gopal' by rubbing off the 'an' at the end of 'Gopalan' when Gopal and Gopalan do not mean one and the same person. It should be remembered that any alteration or addition, when the ink is still wet, is difficult to be decided about the order of writing although the alteration or addition may be very visible.

Sometimes, it so happens that the forger is able to manage a cheque belonging to somebody else. Here, he may try to write the cheque consciously altering his letter designs to simulate the handwriting to look like the one in whose name the cheque had been originally issued by the bank. In such instances of disguised handwriting, an attempt should be made by the banker to appreciate the alterations in the forged letter designs. In case of doubts, the customer may be questioned to know the alterations in letter designs. In a notorious case of banking fraud, once it so happened that the customer received a cheque book from the bank. The bank, after writing down the serial numbers in the book kept for the purpose, in fact issued the cheque book to the customer. The customer wrote on the cheque with his hand in disguised writing and surrendered seven cheque-leaves one after the other. He took nearly 2 lakhs of rupees and later made a complaint to the bank that he had not encashed any one of the cheque-leaves. His argument had been that his cheque book contained 7 cheque-leaves less than what the bank claimed to have issued to him. Ultimately, a case was registered against the bank. Hence, as a safeguard against such false allegations, it is advisable to get the signature of the customer under a statement to the effect that he received cheque-leaves bearing serial numbers from such and such to such and such whenever cheque books are issued to customers.

Obliterations

The obscuring of writing by superimposing ink, pencil or other marking materials over what is written first is called obliterations. This can be done either immediately after the first writing or afterwards. If it is immediate, the writing pigments and covering pigments are generally the same and therefore it is just not easy to decipher the contents. The intentional obliteration of writing on a cheque for fraudulent purposes is seldom resorted to by people.

Erasure of Typescript

Some people have a tendency to type the name and figures on cheques. Typescript is difficult to erase, for, erasing may, in good number of cases, remove the surface of the paper. This happens because the dyestuff in the ink of the typewriter ribbon has affinity for the cellulose fibre of the cheque-leaf. A rubber loaded with abrasive (say, carborundum) may be required for a complete erasure of typescripts on a cheque. The site of the erasure is very apparent and visible in typescripts. At the same time, deciphering what has been erased is just impossible.

Additions are quite possible in typescripts if there is gap to do so. Here, if the forger is not able to use the same typewriter with which the original had been typed, he should go for a typewriter which has similar types as the original. The forger inserts the cheque in his machine in such a way that the additions are correctly aligned with the original typescript. Some skilled forgers successfully accomplish this with enviable accuracy. When suspicion arises, the banker should compare the letter designs that are seen in the cheque so that he will be able to find out the difference with respect to one and the same letter in the entire document. He can also examine the impression, alignments and the quality of the impression which depends on the condition of the ribbon and the cleanliness of the typefaces. In India, people do not frequently use typewriters to type on a cheque.

Transplantation of Numbers

A cheque book usually contains fifteen, twenty or twenty-five cheque-leaves which bear serial numbers. The kind of forgery in serial numbers of cheque-leaves adopted by forgers are :

(i) by applying a fine mechanical erasure to a cheque-leaf and printing a number in its place of a wealthy customer of the bank. A forger, if he wants, can easily get the serial numbers of the cheque-leaves issued to wealthy customers.

(ii) by the skilful alteration of a digit to a desired one by additional strokes.

(iii) by a careful transplantation of a serial number in place of original serial number which has been skilfully erased.

It should be noted here that some banks do not have the safety printing designs on the background of the serial numbers of the cheque and draft-leaves. Though the banks are aware that the safety printing should be done using *fugitive inks*, some of them seldom do it. In a way, these two factors help the forgers to erase or skilfully transplant the numbers on the cheque-leaves. In a notorious case of forgery in which the serial number was transplanted, the forger's attempt was detected only by very careful microscopic examination. This shows how skilfully the numbers are transplanted and how difficult it is for someone to detect such forgeries. In such instances, the forger makes fine mechanical erasing of the numbers on the cheque-leaf and cuts the digits from other cheque-leaves available with him. He transplants these degits in such a way in the erased area and applies some invisible waxy material there to set the disturbed paper-fibres on the erased spots.

As the serial numbers of cheque-leaves are of considerable importance in banking transactions, it is necessary that :

(i) The serial numbers on cheques, drafts and mail transfers are printed by using carbon inks which contain some fluoresecent dye. It has been observed by the author that some banks use inks having red or blue colours to print the serial numbers.

(ii) The numbers should be printed only on a symmetrical safety printing dcsigns and *fugitive ink* must invariably be used for printing the designs. The safety printing should be done by using inks having deep colours.

(iii) As far as possible, try to give special designs to the digits in the serial numbers. Some banks in the west have developed their own special designs to the digits.

(iv) Every cheque-leaf should contain the rubber stamp of the bank in such a manner that it should cover both the cheque-leaf and its counter-foil. In chapter 6, how the counter-foils should be retained in the branch of a bank has been discussed in detail. This rubber seal should be stamped by using carbon ink and only on the back side of the cheque-leaf and the counter-foils.

Notes

1. Wilson R. Harrison, *Suspect Documents: Their Scientific Examination*, Sweet & Maxwell Ltd., London, 1966.
2. Wilson R. Harrison, *op. cit.*
3. Wilson R. Harrison, *op. cit.*

References

Bruning. A., 'A Genuine Counterfeit', *International Criminal Police Review*, No. 72, November, 1953.

Clerk, W., *Photography by Infra-red*, Chapman and Hall, London, 1946.

Downey, J.E., 'Disguised Handwriting', *Journal of Applied Psychology*, Vol. 1, December, 1917.

Edlin, C. H., 'A Case of an Altered Document', *Police Journal*. No. 11, 1938.

Harris, J., 'Disguised Handwriting', *Journal of Criminal Law and Criminology*, Vol. 43, No, 5, January-February, 1953.

Hilton, O., 'Restoring Erased Ink Writing', *Police Journal*, October-December, 1956.

Hilton, O., 'Influence of Serious Illness on Handwriting Identification', *Postgraduate Medicine*, 19 (2) A-36-A-48, February, 1956.

Longhelti, A., and Kirk, P.L., 'Restoration and Deciphement of Erasures and Obliterated or Indented Writing', *Journal of Criminal Law and Criminology*, Vol. 41, No. 4, November-December, 1950.

Mitchell, C.A., 'Erasures and Ultraviolet Light', *Analyst*, No. 58, 1933.

Mitchell, C. A., *Documents and Their Scientific Examination*, Griffin, London, 1923.

Mitchell, C.A., 'Ink and Ultraviolet Light', *Analyst*, No. 55, 1930.

O'Neill, M.E., 'The Restoration of Obliterated Ink Writing, *Journal of Criminal Law and Criminology*, Vol. 127, No. 4, November-December, 1936.

Osborn, A.S., *Questioned Documents*, 2nd ed., Boyd Printing Co., Albany, N.Y., 1929.

Rawlings, *Infra-red Photography,* Blakie, London, 1939.

Smith, S.S., 'A method of Comparing Written Documents', *International Criminal Police Review,* No. 80, August-September, 1954.

Waters, C.E., 'Blue Dye as Evidence of the Age of Writing,' *Industria Engineering Chemist and Chemistry,* No. 25, P. 1024, 1933.

6

NEW SAFETY METHODS

Banks, as shown in earlier chapters, are yet to be educated about various measures that can ensure better safety. At the time of opening a fresh account in a bank, the banks insist personal identification. For this purpose, unless the new customer is known to the bank, he needs to be introduced to the bank and this introduction is done by anyone who is already an account holder of the bank. This implies :

If 'A' is a customer, i.e., an account holder of the Bank, he can introduce 'B' who can then open a fresh account in the bank. The 'B' in turn can introduce 'C' who becomes another account holder. 'C' also can introduce 'D' to the bank and thus 'D' can become an account holder. 'A' may be a decent and honest customer. This does not mean that D also should be equally honest and decent. Here 'A' who introduces B to the Bank does not know anything about 'D' who is the last account holder from the source 'A'. A pertinent question here is: what is the criminal liability of A, B, and C to the acts of 'D' if 'D' tries to cheat the bank? In fact, there is no criminal liability in law for them. Here, just because 'C' happens to be an account holder in the bank he gets the right to introduce 'D' without any criminal liability attached to the acts of 'D'. And the bank does not expect the introducer to be responsible for the acts of the introduced. While introducing 'D' to the bank 'C' does not even attest that the signature put by 'D' is that of 'D' himself. Suppose 'D' puts signature which is not his and furnishes an address which is false, 'C' has no responsibility over the false signature put by 'D' and the false address given by 'D' and the bank does not usually verify the signature of 'D'. The following cases will indicate how the system helps people commit crimes :

Case 1 : In this case, an account holder 'A' introduced one Ragesh K.P. as Ragesh K.P. to a bank. Ragesh was having criminal intention to evade the income-tax. Therefore, he gave a false address and a false signature to the bank with intention to defraud the income-tax authorities. Ragesh thus started four accounts in four different banks with different addresses and with different types of signatures. He could evade income-tax and could suppress his black money. And he misused the existing system of 'introduction' in banks to commit crimes.

Case 2 : 'A' introduced 'B' to the bank. And 'B' started his account with a false address and signature. One day he brought a cheque worth Rs. 80,000/-. The cheque was honoured by the bank. On further enquiry it was found out that his cheque was originally written for Rs. 8,000/- (Eight thousand only). But he added one zero after Rs. 8,000/- to read it as Rs. 80,000/- and 'ty' after 'Eight to make it Eighty'. On further enquiry it was found that there was no person with such a signature and address kept in the bank.

Case 3 : A had stolen a draft worth Rs. 10,000/- from a letter addressed to one Revi Varma P.S. He got an account holder to introduce himself as Revi Varma to the bank to open an account just to encash the draft in his favour.

Case 4 : X was the Manager in a bank. X knew Y who was a customer to the bank. X was transferred and Z was posted as the new Manager to that branch. He did not know Y. Y and P were friends. P knew how Y signed and the account number of Y in the bank. When Z became the Manager, P took one B who wanted to get a stolen Demand Draft encashed. The DD was written in favour of one C. P and B went to the new Manager Z and P presented himself that he was Y, the account holder in the bank. P put the signature of Y, and got B introduced as C to the bank. B, thus successfully managed to get the DD (written in favour of C) encashed. When the cheating was detected Y said that he had never introduced any C to thc bank. The new Manager was confused and could not identify the introducer of C to the bank. It was infact P who was the villan in the fraud.

If the method of introduction is not made full-proof, one can not stop frauds and forgeries. The frauds and cheatings in banks take place because anybody can open an account with little/no identification that is worth its name or full-proof. The identification of every new account holder should be perfected if the banks desire to prevent frauds and forgery. It is here the forger plants his seeds to commit frauds. The following precautions are good safeguards against frauds and forgery :

The account holder who introduces the new customer should be known well to the bank. The procedure that any person who has an account in a bank can introduce another to open a fresh account in the bank can be encouraged; but subject to certain conditions enlisted below.

At the time of opening a new account, one photograph of the new account holder should be affixed in the application form, another behind the specimen signature card. The photograph should be duly attested by the signature of the introducer to be the photograph of so and so whom he was introduced. Taking photographs may result in having some expense to the customer. Hence a decision should be taken as to who—the bank or the customer—should bear the cost of taking the photographs. In current accounts, however, the customer can be asked to bear the expenses without much difficulty. If at all the bank has to bear the cost of taking photographs, it should not be considered as a loss or waste.

The introducer should make a statement to the effect that he personally knows the new account holder and the address and signature of the new account holder are true to his knowledge and belief. He should also state that he takes the liability for any damage to the bank in case it is subsequently proved, during the whole period when the new account holder has transactions with the bank, that the address and signature given by the new account holder now is false. This procedure will make the introducer to be more cautious when he introduces the new comer. If the new account holder, later changes his address, the matter should be informed to the bank and the new address should invariably be varified by the bank.

The new comer should be asked to give six specimen signatures on the specimen signature card in varying lengths as shown in Chapter 2. To be more on the safer side, the bank should get the left thumb impression of the new account holder on the signature specimen card. This will surely enable the bank to categorically state that so and so gave the thumb impression, along with his signature when he opened the account. The fingerprints are, as stated in Chapter 1, conclusive evidence to prove the identity of persons who put their impressions.

It may be difficult to compare the finger-prints always and everytime when the bank has some doubts regarding the specimen signature of the customer. They will be useful when serious doubts or litigations arise. Therefore, two visibly distinguishing marks on the body of the new customer should be noted down in the specimen signature card.

The new customer also should make a statement that he has given his correct name, address and signature. The signature specimen card should have the following details :

Name..Date.......................Sex.......................

Address..

Introduced by..

Two visibly distinguishing (1) ....

body marks (2) ....

Qualifications..

Specimen Signatures

Left Thumb (rolled) print of the customer	Specimen Signatures
	1. (Fountain pen), 2. (Dot pen)
	1. (Fountain pen) 2. (Dot pen)
	1. (Fountain pen) 2. (Dot pen)

On the back of this card should be pasted the photograph of the new customer and a paper pocket to keep the counter-foils of the cheque-leaves issued to the said customer. If the customer so demands, he may be issued with an identity card from the bank at the customer's expense. Every new account holder should be asked to give the names and addresses of two respectable referees of the locality. This is to enable the bank to make a reference to them about the account holder, if that is found to be necessary.

Check List

The following check list will be of use in commercial banks to ensure maximum safety when a new account holder is enlisted :

Check List for the New Accout Holder at The Time of Opening a New Account

1. Who has introduced the new account holder?
2. Is the introducer a well known person to the bank? Has he attested the photograph, address and signature of the new account holder with his own signature? Has he made the statements (duly signed) as to the identity of the photograph, address and signature of the new account holder along with the liability for giving a false address and signature in case damage is caused to the bank by the act of the new account holder?
3. Are six signatures of the new account holder by providing varying spaces and by giving ballpoint (for three signatures) as well as fountain pen (for three signatures) taken?
4. Have you marked two visibly seen distinguishing body marks of the new account holder?
5. Are the date and sex written?
6. Have the qualifications on the new account holder written?
7. Has the new account holder given two respectable referees of the locality to make some references about the new account holder if that is necessary.
8. Have you taken the fingerprint of the left thumb of the new account holder?
9. Have you issued an identity card to the account holder?

Some bank officers advance the argument that the elaborate procedure for enlisting a new customer is indeed time consuming, expensive and laborious. No doubt they are. Nevertheless the bank is supposed to take these precautionary measures only once during the entire transactions between a particular customer and the bank. A little inconvenience here should be taken as a desirable hazard to ensure safety in banking and money transactions. If the identity of the customer is not made perfect, security risk is maximum-*even ab initio*.

Another argument advanced by some bank officers seems to suggest that people are likely to be repelled from opening new accounts, if elaborate procedure at this stage is insisted. The argument seems to be quite rediculous in so far as it is against facts. Banking has become so important and widely prevelent today that a man cannot live without adequate banking facilities. Most of the money transactions are done through the banks and therefore one cannot even imagine that people will be forced to withdraw from opening new accounts. On the contrary, honest people will welcome these procedures if they are made to understand that all these are meant to ensure maximum security for their money. On the other hand, cheats and forgers will think twice once they come to know that they cannot open fresh accounts unless their identity is well established. If all banks adopt uniform procedures while personal identification of customers is made, the people in due course will reconcile with the new formalities and procedures.

Security in Money Transactions through Cheques

When an individual becomes a customer, he becomes entitled to have money transactions through cheque-leaves. The bank has to take safer measures to protect the interest of the customer and that of the bank. The present system seems to be to issue a cheque book to the customer after noting down the serial numbers of the cheque-leaves under the name of the customer in the book kept for the purpose. When a cheque-leaf is received, the bank verifies whether or not the said cheque-leaf bearing the particular serial number had been issued to the customer who surrenders the cheque for encashment. Cases have been reported that some cheque-forgers get cheque-leaves printed for the purpose of forgery. And with the connivance of some unfaithful bank employees or by some other means they note down the serial numbers of other account holders and then surrender the cheques to encash money. A number of cheque-leaves bearing the same serial number can be surrendered to the bank without the bank noting that the cheque-leaf having the same serial number had already been encashed. This happens so because the banks verify whether or not a particular leaf bearing the number, e.g. A/109: 761615, has been issued to a particular person. This they do just by looking whether or not that particular leaf bearing the number.

$$\frac{\mathbf{A}}{\mathbf{109}} : \mathbf{761615} \text{ is one in the series } \frac{\mathbf{A}}{\mathbf{109}} : \mathbf{761615} - \frac{\mathbf{A}}{\mathbf{109}} : \mathbf{761624}$$

In other words, suppose the cheque book issued to the customer contains 25 cheque-leaves starting with A/109 : 761605 and ending with A/109 : 761624. Here, any number of cheque-leaves bearing the number A/109 : 761615 can be surrendered without the bank taking note of the foul-play. Of course, the particular serial number of the cheque-leaf when surrendered and encashed is noted at the time of encashment both in the pass-book and also in the special page for the customer in the Ledger. More often than not, the banks do not verify the serial numbers of the earlier cheques already encashed. To verify this is not easy as it is time consuming and laborious. Again to know the number of a cheque-leaf is not difficult. For instance, when a person issues a cheque to a party, the party who gets the cheque can easily know the serial number of the cheque-leaves issued to a particular person. And if somebody wants to forge, he can print the number in the cheque-leaves already available with him. A country where university certificates, diplomas, degrees, currency notes are printed, it is not difficult to print cheque leaves, if one wants to do so. The banks have to take note of this fact in future days.

There are methods by which the serial number in cheque leaf can be altered or the numbers are transplanted (see Chapter 5). Cases have been detected wherein cheques are stolen and encashed.

Such methods are left deliberately obscure in this book as it is advisable not to publish such things. Nevertheless, it can be said that the serial numbers of the cheque-leaves should be printed in carbon ink having some flourescent dye which can be detected under UV lamp radiation. The numbers should have designs and should be printed over the security printing on the cheque-leaf. Hence, from the security point of view, the banks have to take meticulous care to see :

1. that the cheque-leaf that the bank receives is the same that has been issued to a particular customer;
2. that the cheque has been written with the full awareness and consent of the account holder who keeps with him the cheque book and the pass book;
3. that the money goes to the person intended by the account holder; and
4. that there are no alterations or additions in the cheque that has been surrendered to the bank for encashment etc.

How can the bank ensure these things? The author has devised a security system by which the banks can ensure maximum security. This is known as Bank-Cheque Security System.

B.C.S. System Explained

Some banks print cheque leaves on security papers having water marks. Usually the water marks are found in many places on the cheque-leaves and in some banks on the counter-foils as well. The customer detaches the cheque-leaf from the counter-foil and the perforations made as the left extreme of the cheque-leaves make this possible. The suggestion here is that one watermark on the cheque-leaf should invariably be at the portion where the cheque-leaf is detached from the counter-foil. In other words half of the watermark should be on the cheque-leaf and the other half on the counter-foil. In the new method, i.e., in the B.C.S. System, the cheque book needs a slight alteration in its making.

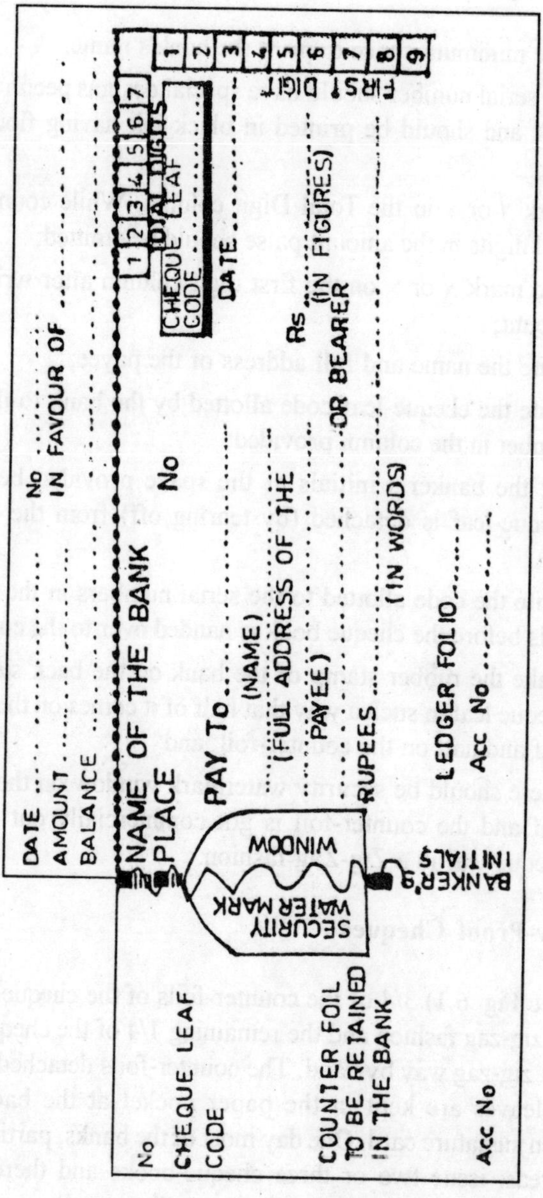

Fig. 6.1 : Design of a forgery proof cheque-leaf.

Instructions

1. Take minimum space to print the bank's name;
2. The serial number should have special designs peculiar to the bank and should be printed in black ink having flourescent dye;
3. Mark √ or × in the Total Digit column. While counting the total digits in the amount paise should be omitted;
4. Also mark √ or × on the first digit column after writing the amount;
5. Write the name and full address of the payee;
6. Write the cheque-leaf code allotted by the bank to the serial number in the column provided;
7. Put the banker's initials at the space provided before the cheque-leaf is detached (by tearing off) from the counter-foil;
8. Write the code allotted to the serial numbers in the counter-foils before the cheque book is handed over to the customers;
9. Make the rubber stamp of the bank on the back side of the cheque leaf in such a way that half of it comes on the cheque-leaf and half on the counter-foil; and
10. There should be security watermark window on the cheque-leaf and the counter-foil is got commercially out from the cheque-leaf in a Zig-Zag fashion.

Forgery-Proof Cheques

Here (see Fig. 6.1) 3/4 of the counter-foils of the cheque-leaves is cut in a zig-zag fashion and the remaining 1/4 of the cheque-leaf is torn in a zig-zag way by hand. The counter-foils detached from the cheque-leaves are kept in the paper pocket at the back of the specimen signature card. One day most of the banks, particularly in rural areas, issue two or three cheque-books and therefore this process of tearing the cheque-leaves will not take much of the bank's time. The cheque clearence officer should be provided with a small photographer's retouching desk and as soon as a cheque is surrendered for encashment, he takes the card from the signature specimen tray. Behind the card, in the paper pocket, the counter-foil of the cheque-leaf with the same serial number of the surrendered leaf is easily located. He compares the edges of the counter-foil to the edges of the cheque-leaf surrendered and satisfies himself that the edges exactly coincide. While he does so, meticulous care should be taken to ensure that the edges of the part of the watermark in the counter-foil when kept with the edges of the other part of the watermark in the cheque-leaf do exactly coincide with. The photographer's retouching desk will ensure this process in an easy way. The bank thus can be sure that the cheque-leaf surrendered to the bank is the same that was issued to a particular customer. A watermark should invariably be provided inside a window just like what is seen in rupee notes. In other words, the security printing on cheque-leaves should not be there on this watermark. The rubber stamp at the back of the cheque-leaf and the banker's initials are meant to help the banks to make comparisons.

Although the rule is that the signature on every cheque-leaf should be compared with the signature of the customer kept in the signature card tray, the practice in many banks seems to be that in a good many cases, the comparison is not seriously made. The reason for the avoidance of comparing signatures is that most of the customers are known to the bank and the bank believes their customers. As the vast majority of the customers are not criminals, the banker is very often on the safer side, even when the comparison of signatures is not seriously made. Comparison of signatures is difficult, as good many persons employed in banks are not properly given academic training in this branch of knowledge.

The counter-foil of the encashed cheque should be cancelled once the examination of the edges is made. The signature of the customer should be compared with the signature kept with the bank. Also watermark examination should be made to ensure maximum security.

The next question—Is the cheque written with the full awareness and consent of the account holder? For this, every bank should devise a code-system for each of the cheque-leaf. This can be done as follows :

Suppose a cheque-book contains 15 cheque-leaves. Then the bank should find out 15 words to be used as their permanent codes. For instance it can be as shown in the table provided below. If more cheque-leaves are there in a book, column 2 in the table can also be used. Imagine that the words given in the table are the code (words) used by a particular bank all throughout India. On the last three pages of the pass-book issued to a particular customer 18 times these codes can be printed. In other words a pass book can be used for transacting business for 36 cheque books each containing 15 leaves, i.e., 18×36 –540 times.

Table 6.1 : Code For Forgery Proof Cheques

Sl.No.	Code (Word)	Serial Numbers of Cheque-Leaves	
		Cheque Book- 1	Cheque Book- 2
1.	Pluto		
2.	Robin		
3.	Zeebra		
4.	Planet		
5.	Neethi		
6.	Maryland		
7.	Osborn		
8.	Neethu		
9.	Leopard		
10.	Cameleon		
11.	Indigo		
12.	Peacock		
13.	Moon Light		
14.	Bullock		
15.	Nickil		

When issuing a cheque book to a particular customer, the issuing officer may write the serial numbers of the cheque-leaves at his discretion in the space provided in the above table. For instance, the serial numbers in the cheque book starts with 8316 and ends with 8330, then he should write 8316 against any code (word) in the table-say, (OSBORN-8316) at his discretion and 8330 can be written against ROBIN or any other word. In other words, allotting the serial number of the cheque-leaf against the code (word) depends entirely at the discretion of the cheque-book issuing officer. After allotting the serial numbers against the code (word) in the pass book and also marking the code (word) in the counter-foils of the cheque-leaves kept with the bank, the pass book may be entrusted back to the customer. In other words, the bank should have the serial numbers and the code (words) against each serial number for its reference. The serial numbers are available on the counter-foils of the cheque-leaves kept in the bank. When cheque books are issued and before keeping the counter-foils in the paper pocket behind the specimen signature card, the code (word) allotted to each serial number is written on the counter-foils as well.

Every cheque-leaf should have a column like CHEQUE-LEAF CODE............. and when a cheque is presented, the banker can see whether or not the account holder has written the correct code allotted to the particular serial number in his cheque-leaf. This the customer can do only if he has seen the pass book and the table given at the end. This procedure will ensure that the account holder had the awareness when he issued the cheque or the forger had the accessibility to the pass book when he forged the cheque. The bank here is in an advantageous position.

Thirdly, the bank should ensure that the money goes to the person intended by the account holder. In cases where the cheque is a crossed one, the bank pays the money to an account holder in which case, there is no problem to identify the person (to whom or the account to which the money is paid). The problem comes when cheques which are not crossed ones are presented. This can be remedied if the full address of the payee is written in the cheque. Sufficient space on the cheque should be provided to enable the cheque writer to write the full address of the payee. Presently 1/3 of the cheques-leaf is occupied by the name of the bank. In the new system, a slight change in the cheque-leaf is suggested to accomodate the full address of the payee. Statutorily or otherwise, writing the full name and address of the payee may not be necessary.

To give the money to a person whose address is not known to the bank is dangerous. More about the need for writing the name and address of the payee is discussed elsewhere in this chapter.

Fourthly, the bank should ensure that there is no subsequent alterations or additions in the cheque that has been surrendered to the bank. This can easily be done by providing a sheet of carbon along with every cheque book. (A spare sheet of carbon may also be attached with every cheque book). The customer should be advised to write on the cheque by keeping the carbon paper underneath the cheque-leaf in such a way that the side having the carbon of the paper touches the back of the cheque-leaf. Chemical erasures do not react with carbon particles and mechanical erasures can not be applied if carbon paper is kept beneath the cheque-leaf. If the party issuing cheque so desires, he should be encouraged to paste cello-tape over the writings and pressed against the cheque-leaf strongly. The customer should be asked to write on the cheque as under.

Pay to Smt./Mary/James/.............or bearer
Rupees/One/thousand/ only. /1/0/0/0/-

With regard to the signature at the right extreme corner of the cheque-leaf; it is seen in the cheque-leaves given by some banks that a line is provided where one should sign. Such lines should never be provided in cheque-leaves as they affect the signing of the signatory. How should the bank compare the signature on the cheque-leaf and the specimen signature cards is given in Chapter 3 and how the forgeries in signature are detected is given in Chapter 5 of this book. Again as a precaution again alterations, every cheque-leaf should contain | 1/ 2/ 3/ 4/ 5/ 6/ 7/ 8/ 9 | at the upper right hand corner of the leaf vertically and another | 1/ 2/ 3/ 4/ 5/ 6/ 7/ | at the upper right hand corner horizontally. If the customer, suppose, writes Rs. 2841 in the cheque-leaf, then he should put '×' or √ on 2 on the vertical column to indicate the first digit of the amount written on the cheque and another '×' or √ in the horizontal column on 4 to indicate that the amount contain a total of four digits. The *paise*, if there is, in the amount needs not be taken into account when total digits are counted. Since, the '×' or √ markings are made on the extreme edges of the cheque mechanical erasures, if applied, will damage the cheque-leaf. Since, carbon paper under the cheque-leaf is kept, the '×' or √ markings can not be erased chemically and inevitably the column should be printed over security designs of the cheque-leaf. The security printing should be made, as indicated many times earlier, by using fugitive inks.

Precautions against Stolen Cheques

Sometimes it so happens that the cheques are stolen either during transit (mail) or otherwise and presented for payment. As a precaution against this, the following measures may be taken by the banks. One reason for the cheques being stolen from the post is that the banks expect that the name of the payee only to be written on a cheque-leaf. Instances are not rare that more than one person bearing the same name are available and therefore, the banks should insist that the name and full address of the payee should be written on a cheque-leaf. As pointed out earlier, presently it is seen that the name of the bank occupies more than 1/3 of the space provided in a cheque-leaf. The suggestion is that it must be limited to the minimum and more space should be given to write the name and full address of the payee by the cheque-writer. From safety point of view, this is very important. The advantages of writing the full address of the payee are :

1. More writings on the cheque-leaf makes it more difficult to make corrections, alterations, additions etc.

2. If the cheque is a crossed one, then an account holder only can get it encashed. The name and address of the payee can be easily verified by the bank. In case the address of the payee has been changed, the burden of proving that he has a new address rests with the payee.

3. If an individual opens a new account just to encash the stolen cheque, even then the precautionary measures taken at the time of opening a new account will save the bank. If the bank so desires, the bank can mail a letter in the name and address of the

payee under *Certificate of Posting* to ensure that the payee receives the letter in the address furnished. Once the cheque has been received by the bank for collection, it takes some time to get the amount transferred to the bank. And the bank can mail the letter to the payee in the mean-time. The payee can be advised in the letter sent to bring the letter/receipt as the case may be for identification purposes.

4. Suppose a cheque-leaf has been stolen along with the code allotted to the particular serial number of the cheque-leaf, the bank can ensure the safety in payment if the cheque leaf contains the name and full address of the payee. Usually the banks in such cases do not accept a cheque unless the payee has an account and if not, he can be asked to open an account in the bank with proper introduction and taking other precautionary measures at the time of opening an account. The chances of stealing the cheque-leaf along with the code alloted to each serial number from the safe custody of the account holder is remote and the frequency of occurrence is thus very rare. Whenever cheque leaves are printed with security printing on the leaf, the colour of the security printing should be contrasting to the colour of the cheque leaf. The purpose of making security printing is to provide a safeguard against erasures. And if the colour is not contrasting, white patches caused as a result of erasure cannot be easily detected. If the cheque has been sent to the payee by post it is advisable for the cheque-writer to write *by post* on the cheque-leaf so that the banks will be more cautious when they make payments. This should be made clear in the information leaf let given to customers.

Drafts Issued by Banks

Issuing of drafts creates problems for the bank. Drafts issued by the banks are as good as money and a lot of fake drafts appear in these days, more in number now than what they were before. Fake drafts are printed and the safety measures taken by the bank are found to be not up to the mark. Some banks use cheque writing type writers (machines) as a safeguard against alterations in the drafts. Writing on drafts by keeping carbon paper beneath the draft is another safeguard taken by banks against forgery. All said and done, forged drafts are presented and the banks are cheated. What can be done in this area? DRAFT SECURITY KEY SYSTEM suggested here can be effectively used for preventing forgery of drafts.

The author's discussions with a number of bank officers reveal that there is no full proof method for them to know that a particular draft has been issued from a particular branch of their bank. Usually, they compare the signature of the issuing officer and the signatures of the issuing officers, particularly in nationalised banks, run in thousands. There are well developed methods for forging signatures and a good many officers have little or no knowledge and equipment to compare the signatures or to detect forged signature. They feel it extremely difficult to transact business with self-confidence when drafts are received. As indicated elsewhere in this book, signatures are of two types– *Formal* and *Informal*. The signature of the draft issuing officer kept in the bank is a formal one and the signature put on a draft during the busy business hours is an informal one. The comparison of formal and informal signatures is indeed difficult.

DSK System Explained

The question sought to be resolved in the case of issue of drafts is : How can the receiving bank know that a particular draft in favour of an individual has been issued by their own branch at a distant place?

Usually the receiving bank is supposed to wait for the advice memo from the issuing branch for making payments. Of course, waiting for the advice memo makes the term 'Demand Draft' meaningless. Delay to get the advice memo may put the customer in difficulties. In such cases, the paying branch faces a lot of problems with the customers. A clever forger may present a fake draft to a bank and also will send an advice memo to the effcet that the payment can be made to the presentee. If he can present a fake draft, remember that he can also send an advice memo. Fake drafts are printed and recently a few such cases have been detected.

In the DSK system, each draft issued to a particular individual is provided with a key by the issuing branch and it is locked by the paying branch. The key is nothing but a plastic sheet having the thickness and the width of a shaving blade. The material used for making plastic tongue cleaners can be used for the purpose if they can be provided by some commercial firms with the thickness and the width of shaving blades. The key should have the length approximately equal to the width of the bank draft issued by a particular commercial bank.

Applying Quatlet's law of individuality, such key should be cut at the centre by chisels. The cutting edge of chisels can have any one of the shapes shown in Fig. 6.2.

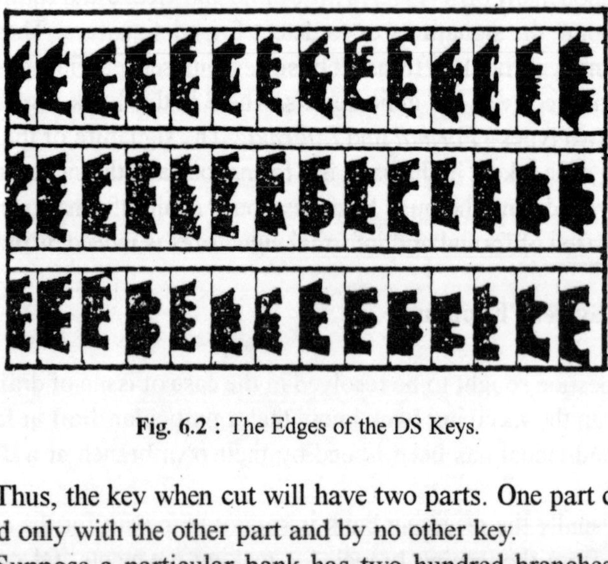

Fig. 6.2 : The Edges of the DS Keys.

Thus, the key when cut will have two parts. One part can be locked only with the other part and by no other key.

Suppose a particular bank has two hundred branches. The key should be provided by the central office (Headquarters) of the bank. It will be as under. First of all, the central office should allot 10,000/- numbers to a particular branch.

This means that TVM 1 to TVM 10000 numbers are alloted to Trivandrum branch. Likewise QLN I to QLN 10000 numbers are allotted to Quilon branch and APY 1 to APY 10000 numbers are allotted to Alleppey branch. From. TVM 1 to TVM 10000 numbers, TVM 1 to TVM 50 numbers are allotted to QLN branch and TVM

51 to TVM 100 are to APY Branch. Likewise QLN 1 to QLN 50 numbers are allotted to TVM branch and QLN 51 to QLN 100 numbers are allotted to ALPY Branch. And thus TVM 9951 to TVM 10000 will be allotted to the last branch put against TVM in Table 6.2. Likewise QLN 9951 to QLN 10000 numbers are allotted to the last branch (in the table) put against QLN. This is so because the bank is having only 200 branches and the total of 10000 numbers are equally divided among the 200 branches.

Table. 6.2 : The Numbers of the D S Keys allotted to various branches may be given in this table.

Name of the Branch	The code of the branch	T V M	Q L N	A P Y	E K M	K T M	T C R	C L T	P G T	C N R	M L P	W Y D
Trivandrum	TVM											
Quilon	QLN											
Alleppey	APY											
Ernakulam	EKM											
Kottayam	KTM											
Trichur	TCR											
Calicut	CLT											
Palghat	PGT											
Cannanore	CNR											
Malapurum	MLP											
Wynad	WYD											

DSK System and the Drafts

Some banks follow a system of making perforations in the drafts. For making the perforations they provide special columns in the draft itself. The making of perforations can be useful to prevent alterations on drafts. But making only one perforation, as done by some banks, can not offer full safety to drafts. Hence, some other banks make two or three perforations. For instance if they issue a draft worth Rs. 4850 to a party, they make a perforation at 4 in the vertical column of the draft and at 8 in the horizontal column of the draft. Since, the holes are made at 4 and 8, the banks claim that alteration in the draft is possible, only for a small amount and in this case only for at Rs. 149. For Rs. 5,000 to 5999 the perforations should be made 5 in the vertical column. With other precautionary safety measures, it is heard that the system works well in banks, The difficulty here is that the perforations made for Rs. 4850 and Rs. 48505 will be at 4 and 8. Hence, some banks make 3 perforations if the value of the amount written is having five digits. They also write the words. Below Rs... at the top of the draft. A few banks have different colours for their drafts for amounts that come within a range.

The author likes to make a change in the system of perforations. The perforation in the vertical column should indicate the FIRST DIGIT in the amount written on the draft. For example, for Rs. 2850, the perforation should be made at 2 to show that the amount begins with the digit 2. In the horizontal column, again the perforation should be made at 4 to indicate that the amount has only 4 DIGITS.

Even for them, it is difficult to say whether or not a particular draft has been issued by their own branch or is it a fake draft. Hence the author thinks that along with making perforations in a draft, the DS Key also should be provided.

How Should be the Key?

The key should be made as under. From Fig. 6.3, it can be easily known that TVM-69 is the key belonging to the Trivandrum branch and alloted to APY Branch of the bank. Hence, the part A of the key TVM 69 should be entrusted with APY branch and part B of' the key TVM 69 should be kept with the Trivandrum branch. Both part A and part B of the key have a cut-at the top of part A and at the bottom of part B. The portion above the cut of part A and below the cut of part B should be safely covered with oily paper so that neither the APY branch nor the TVM branch knows how the key is cut at the edges of part A and part B.

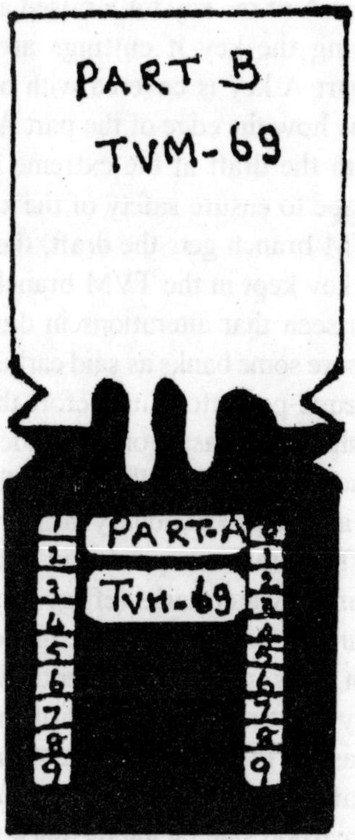

Fig. 6.3 : Part A and Part B of DS Key.

Now, that a person wants to purchase a draft from Alleppey to be sent to an individual in Trivandrum. The Alleppey branch can issue a draft in the name of the individual in Trivandrum taking the usual precautions. Then the issuing officer should take the part A of any key bearing the numbers from TVM 5I to TVM 100 kept in the branch. On the part A key one sees (Fig. 6.3) 1- 9 numbers given on the left and right hand sides. Taking the example of Rs. 2850, the issuing hank should make a *'cut'* at 4 on the L.H.S. by using a pair of scissors to indicate that the amount written on the draft has only 4 DIGITS and another cutting should be made at 2 on the R.H.S. to indicate that the amount written on the draft starts with the DIGIT 2. Suppose a person who has printed fake drafts wants to use the part A of the key for a raised amount, then he will be deprived of using the key if cuttings are made. Since, the upperedge of the part A key is covered with oily paper, the APY branch cannot know how the edge of the part A key is. The part A key is stappled with the draft at the extreme left and folded and pasted with cello-tape to ensure safety of the key while on transit, As soon as the TVM branch gets the draft, they can lock the part A key with part B key kept in the TVM branch.

Recently, it is seen that alterations in drafts occur and as a precautionary measure some banks as said earlier make perforations and also use the cheque-protector. Just before the cheque- protector is used, cello-tape should be pasted on both sides of this writings on the draft and pressed. Over this cello-tape if the cheque-protector is applied, it can be a good precautionary measure against alterations on demand drafts. The drafts are printed in security papers having watermarks. One of the watermarks (effigy of the bank) should be provided with a window so that the watermark can be easily seen by visual inspection. This is to say that over the window there should not be any security printing. The colour of the security printing, should be in contrast to the colour of draft leaf and inevitably all writings on the draft should be made after keeping carbon paper beneath it with the carbon side facing the back side of the draft and if that is not possible use the cheque writing machine and the full name and address of the payee should be written on the drafts.

The DSK system, it is argued by some bankers, is difficult to be followed in banks having many branches-say 1000 or more. This is something to be examined. If that is the case just like the cheque-books are issued by the branches, draft books should be issued by one branch to all branches of the bank. The procedure followed in the BCS system along with the special codes allotted to every leaf can be resorted to by major banks. Since, the counter-foils of the Demand Drafts are kept in the branches, the draft receiving branch can match the edges of the draft with the counter-foils along with the code allotted to the leaf. A draft book can contain 500 leaves and when they are used, fresh book can be issued. This may involve huge investment at the begining until the system is in movement and that is the reason why DSK system is recommended for banks.

The signature of the draft issuing officer should be put by carbon ink having some fluerescent dye that can be viewed under the UV lamp radiation. The banks should provide special security pens for their officers to sign on drafts.

Mail Transfers

When a party makes a requisition to the branch of a bank to transfer certain amount of money to another branch where the payee has an account, ordinarily a mail transfer is sent by the branch to which the requisition is made. Some banks have yet to know how maximum safety can be ensured when mail transfers are sent The Mail Transfer Security System (MTS System) which the author considers effective is as under :

MTS System Explained

Suppose that a bank has 3000 branches. Mail Transfer has to be sent from one branch to any branch of the bank. For ensuring security, the following code cards are to be printed. If the bank has three thousand branches, let us see how can the code card be used?

SAMPLE OF CODE CARDS

Card No. : 1

From : Trivandrum	To : Dharwar
A Q P Z Y B	X O S W Z T
Q S T U C A	X Y S T Q A
R J M P N S	M Q F A E S
D S P Q R T	J Q Y B R F
F J E P M Z	K F L S R C

(They should be alphabets and should never be words)

Card No. : 2

From	To ....
Z P T Q R I	C Z M O P T
B J N W S K	F I E S O T
R T A C Y U	G H Q N Y A
U P T O R N	H S T P L K
W J U I R D	L S Q R Y A

(Here the From and To should be written by the head quarters of the bank)

Card No. : 3

From	To ....
THUS THE CARDS SHOULD BE PREPARED BY THE BANK	

If the bank has 3000 branches, a minimum of 30 such code-cards can to be prepared. Let us take Trivandrum branch of a nationalised bank and the Trivandrum branch has to transact business with 2999 branches of the bank. Hence, 2999 cards are provided to Trivandrim branch and the cards are arranged in Alphabetical order of the receiving branches just like the author index of a library is prepared and kept in author index tray of the library.

Imagine that card No. 1 is meant to Dharwar branch in Karnataka State, then write down 'From' Trivandrum and 'To' Dharwar in the card. Keep this card in Trivandrum branch. Make a duplicate of the same card where in what is printed on the LHS of the card in Trivandrum should appear on the RHS of the card kept in Dharwar. Likewise, what is pointed on the RHS of the Trivandrum card should appear on the LHS of the card kept in Dharwar. This is to enable the Dharwar branch to arrange the cards in alphabetical order of the *mail transfer receiving branches*. Take for instance the card to be kept in Dharwar and it will be as under.

To be kept in Dharwar branch

Card No. : 4

FROM : Dharwar	TO : Trivandrum
X O S W Z T	A Q P Z Y B
X Y S T Q A	Q S T U C A
M Q F A E S	R J M P N S
J Q Y B R F	D S P Q R T
K F L S R C	F J E P M Z

After writing the usual code in the mail transfer, if that needs be, the Trivandrum branch should give the code from their card so that the Dharwar branch can make sure that the said code is written with the full knowledge and awareness of the Trivandrum branch. How should the special code be prepared? For this, the Trivandrum branch should take the card meant for Dharwar. Under Trivandrum 5 series of Alphabetical letters are given. Here the Trivandrum branch may write 62413 (B S P D E) which means that 6 represents the 6th letter in the first series, i.e., B and 2 represents the 2nd letter in the 2nd series, i.e., S. Likewise 4 represents the 4th letter in the third series, i.e., P and 1 represents the first letter in the fourth series, i.e., D and 3 represents the 3rd letter in the fifth series, i.e., E.

After writing 62413 (BSPDE), or any other, the Trivandrum branch can write 34162 (STMFF) or any other, which is meant for Dharwar branch. The decoding is done exactly like what is done in the case of Trivandrum code. In the books kept in Trivandrum as well as in Dharwar, these special code numbers are noted so that one and the same number is not duplicated when another mail transfer is sent to Dharwar by Trivandrum branch. If duplication in the number is seen in any subsequent mail transfers from Trivandrum to Dharwar, it can be safely presumed that the mail transfer is a bogus one. A bank with 3000 branches can operate this system permanently if they have sufficient number of cards. Every mail transfer contains a serial number. For example, a mail transfer sent to Dharwar branch has the serial number 21851 on January 7, 1985. This number should be written in a book meant for the purpose under the safe custody of banker. Suppose, on March 17, 1985, another mail transfer bearing the number 23478 is sent to Dharwar branch then the last two figures from the first mail transfer, i.e., 51 and the last two figures from the second mail transfer, i.e., 78 should, be taken. They should be added– i.e., 5 + 1 + 7 + 8 = 21 and this figure also should be written in the mail transfer. When an officer of a bank retires, the Head office should give secret comunication to all branches as to that changes should be made in this special number as a safety measure. They can instruct to add 2 to the total or say to substract 2 or 3 from the total so that more safety can be ensured. This should be a 'variable' in all mail transfers. Not only in mail transfers sent through ordinary posts but also, this system can be effectively used even in Telegraphic transfers. The advantage of this system is that every new transfer form one branch to another is bearing a special code which is known only to the mailing branch and to the receiving branch. This special code can also be used in Telephonic transfers and demand drafts if that needs be. The cards should be kept under the special lock and key of the Manager, so that no one else will have any accessibility to the cards. Or the key of this card tray should be under the joint custody of two officers of the bank. After the mail transfer is prepared by the clerk, the Manager can give the code meant for the particular mail transfer sent to a specific branch of the bank.

Another suggestion is to write only the letters–say BSPDE and 62413 should not be written. If the digits are added, it must make 16 to which a secret number–say 5, 7, 9 etc. can be added, substracted or multiplied as per the secret instructions from time to time. This will work as a variable in mail, telegraphic or telephonic transfers.

Travellers' Cheques

Travellers' cheques are issued by banks to protect the people from loss of money when they are on tour. The common *modus operandi* of criminals is to get travellers' cheques and with in a few days inform the bank that the cheques are lost and payment against the cheques is stopped. This creates a lot of problems for the bank issuing the cheques.

The signature seen on the cheque and put by the cheque holder is perhaps the most important means of identification of the cheque holder. As there are people who can put free-hand forged signatures, the comparison of signatures seems to be not a sure method of identification. This weakness of the banker is exploited by the Travellers' cheque holders.

After informing the banks that the cheques are lost, these same people surrender the cheque at a bank's counter at a distant place. The intimation from the bank to other branches usually takes a lot of time and this is known to the cheats. Hence, before the intimation from the 'source-bank' reaches the branches, the cheques are encashed by the cheats.

Bank officers complain that letters stopping payment against lost travellers' cheques are on increase and it is practically difficult for them to verify all the numbers of lost cheques when they are surrendered.

As a precautionary measure against this sort of cheating, the author advises the banks to clearly specify two visibly distinguishing marks on the body of the person purchasing travellers' cheques on the back of the cheque leaf. Care should be taken to note down permanent body marks. This will help the paying bank to easily identify the cheque-holder and the paying bank can make a mention of these body-marks in a book kept for the purpose. The cheque holder should be asked to sign in the book after writing the visible marks by his own hand. The cheque should be paid only after taking the finger-print of the payee and his signature. The left thumb impression of the payee should be taken when the cheque is issued so that the paying branch can compare the impression with the left thumb print taken at the paying branch.

Presuming that bogus travellers' cheques are printed, what precautions can be taken against such practices? Presently, banks use security papers for printing travellers' cheques. The water-marks, generally the emblem of the bank which is made, during the manufacture of the paper, are to be seen in every travellers cheque-leaf.' But the printing on the cheque-leaf has made it almost impossible to see the watermarks in travellers' cheques. It is therefore suggested that every travellers' cheque-leaf should have a white space (just like the rupee notes) where the watermark (emblem) of the bank should be positioned. This will surely facilitate the banker to examine visually the watermark of the bank by keeping the travellers' cheque against a source of light. Hence under no circumstances should the bank have the safety printing on the entire travellers' cheque. In other words watermark window must be provided in every travellers' cheque.

7

FORGERY OF INDIAN MONEY

Forgery of currency or bank-note is no news at all today. When the news about forged money appears in the press, some banks refuse to accept even genuine money thinking that they may be counterfeits. This happens because the banks do not have adequate knowledge in identifying genuine notes from forged ones. General defects of a forged note become apparent to the banker only when he familiarizes himself with the perfect workmanship and requisite details of genuine paper money. In India, there are two kinds of notes in circulation, viz.,

1. One- rupee note issued by the Government of India and signed by the Secretary, Ministry of Finance.
2. Rs. 2 and above issued by the Reserve Bank of India and signed by its Governor.

The former category is called currency notes and the latter, bank-notes. Thus Rs. 2, Rs. 5, Rs. 10, Rs. 20, Rs. 50, Rs. 100, Rs. 500 and Rs. 1000 are bank-notes. In bank-notes, there is a promise made by the Governor, Reserve Bank of India thus :

I promise to pay the bearer the sum of...rupees.

And this promise is not seen in the currency notes issued by the Government of India.

Obverse and Reverse Sides of Paper Money

The paper money has two sides and they are called obverse and reverse sides. The obverse side being the face of the note, it is more important than the reverse side. If the banker studies the front and back sides of Indian paper money for five or ten minutes, he will be able to know the differences in the two sides of the notes.

The obverse side of the rupee note contains :

1. the denomination;
2. the promise, if it is a bank-note;
3. the signature of the Governor, Reserve Bank of India in bank-notes and the signature of the Secretary, Ministry of Finance, Government of India in currency notes;
4. the emblem of the Government of India;
5. the issuing authority, Reserve Bank or Government of India as the case may be; and
6. the number and series of the note.

The reverse side of the note has :

1. a picture;
2. denomination of the note; and
3. the denomination of the note is printed in words in all 14 recognised languages and in English. This is printed on the reverse or obverse side of the note depending upon its denomination.

People have a tendency to look at a note consciously or unconsciously from the obverse side.

Printing of Paper Money

Forgers do not produce counterfeit money by hand; they resort to printing processes. Nevertheless, instances have been reported that paper money has been drawn by hands by people having expertise in it. It is, no doubt, time-consuming, laborious and difficult. As such the forger, now-a-days, reproduces paper money only by printing processes. Prior to the printing, one insurmountable difficulty which the forgers have is the selection of paper and inks. As the Government controls the manufacture of the paper on which all Indian money is printed, the counterfeiter has to use ordinary grades of paper to print fake notes. The Indian paper money is printed on fine quality paper which is manufactured in Hoshangabad, Madhya Predesh. Since, the paper used to print genuine notes is of fine quality, the note produces a 'cracking sound' when speedily counted or tilted and this sound may not be generally heard in fake notes owing to the poor quality of the paper. Nevertheless, this is not a sure test to detect false paper money. At the same time, it can be deemed to be a preliminary test by the banker. The forger always looks for quality paper and often he can not get the paper which can match genuine notes in texture, thickness, feel, smoothness, toughness and durability. After the selection of the paper, the forger goes for inks which are similar in colour and shade seen in genuine notes. He cannot procure the *security ink* used to print genuine notes and as a result he secures only fine inks available in the market for production of false notes. Therefore inks used in printing an imitation note lacks the body and shading seen on all Indian paper money. The forger's black ink is either too black or gray-looking and never reveals the fine lines and intricate scroll work and snake lines. The coloured inks he uses may have a dull appearance, lacking the lustre and firmness. The inks used in imitation notes have several shades, lighter or darker than the colour of the genuine notes.

Detection of forged notes depends heavily upon knowledge and appreciation of the finely and beautifully engraved print which are noticed on all genuine notes. In order to imitate the genuine notes in their beautifully engraved print, the forger should have the necessary skill to engrave the steel plates from which notes are printed. Skill is also necessary for the manufacture and mixing of inks and the printing of notes as well as the preparation of paper etc. Government of India and the Reserve Bank depend upon intricate engraving processes to protect their paper money from being counterfeited successfully. If the banker is conversant with genuine notes and critically examines them and fixes in his mind how beautiful and perfect it is in all their delicate details of genuine notes he will have no difficulty for making comparisons of genuine notes against the counterfeits which will be nothing but crude imitations. Hence, the banker should have some information about the process of manufacture of forged paper money. As shown above, formerly forgers used to make false notes by hand drawings and such notes are named *hand-made* notes and the process is called *autography*. This method is no longer used now.[1]

Lithography : This is a method in which the colour is put in by hand and the rest is produced by lithographic process. In such notes, it is found that the impressions are flat and also they lack boldness. With each impression it grows worse and therefore no forger now uses lithography to make fake notes.

Photo-lithography : In this process, the forger takes the photograph of a genuine note and it is transferred to a lithographic stone. The forger then takes an impression of this on a sheet of paper and the finishing is given by hand. This method is successful to make good imitation, but the defects and deficiencies generally inherent in lithography are seen in these notes also.

Photo-zincography : By keeping a prism in front of the lens when photographying a negative is made as for photo-lithography. The prism is kept just to make the reversal of the negative as the printing is done directly on to the metal. The plate thus made is used for printing, but the defects seen in photo lithography are noticed on the fake notes printed in this manner.

Photo-Relief Block : The forger here takes a print on a thick zinc or copper plate and it is done from the negative made for photo-zincography. Etching is done on the plate so made by using Nitric acid or Iron perchloride depending on the type of plate-zinc or copper The etching is meant to give white parts on the fake money. One can therefore feel the impression of this work if he touches the back of the forged money.

Intaglio Process : This is said to be one of the most perfect methods to make fake notes. The forger uses here copper plates. The images are etched below the surface of the plate and therefore he needs a negative print as a resist. For this, he makes first a positive from the original negatives by contact and he prints from this on copper He makes the prints from plates produced by this process in a copper plate press. The ink is rubbed into the impressions. By using coarse cloth, the ink is cleaned from the surface. He then places the plate on the press after keeping a sheet of damped paper on it. Great pressure is applied, the purpose being to force the paper into the depressed portions of the plate. The fake notes show the ink slightly in relief and therefore are easily recognised.

Numbering in Paper Money

Indian notes contain coloured serial numbers—red, black etc. depending on the type or kind of the notes. In fact, the number in a genuine note provides excellent clues to the genuineness of the notes. While printing the false notes, the forger, generally, leaves out the number and provides space to later fill in the number. The reason for this is that with the numbering machine available with him, he cannot print consecutive numbers. This being so he prints the same number on a hundred or two hundred or three hundred notes. He is sure that he is likely to be caught by the time a few notes are in circulation and the news will be flashed by the press. If the news of detecting fake notes with the number he has put appears in the press, he would like to print another number on the blank space already provided so that his fake note with the new number can be circulated until it is detected and caught.

The number and series on the face of false currency or bank notes seldom have the sharpness, firmness, beauty, and even spacing and fineness that are noticed on genuine notes. Usually, the counterfeit series and numbers are out of line, unevenly spaced, blurry and messy looking.

Security Thread in Rupee Notes

Security thread is made into the paper by the Reserve Bank during its manufacture as a precaution against forgery. Black silk thread which runs through the paper money cannot be easily imitated by the forger. The forgers therefore manufacture fake notes in any one of the following ways :

1. Taking a single sheet of paper equal in dimension of genuine notes and then they print on it the obverse and reverse sides. Since, the counterfeit note is printed on a single sheet of paper which does not have the *vein - like black thread*, the counterfeiters put it on the bill by drawing a line by carbon pencil or by black ink or printed on the reverse side of the paper. The fine silk security thread in a genuine note is barely perceptible to the naked eye unless it is viewed against a source of light. Here in the fake note, since the security thread is drawn or printed, a pencil/pen line or the printed line will be clearly seen without any powerful source of light on the reverse side when it is examined. Usually the line is drawn on the reverse side because the counterfeiter knows it well that people have a tendency to look at a genuine note for security thread from the obverse side keeping the reverse side placed against a source of light.

Genuine notes of Rs. 5 and above have security threads and the counterfeiter finds it extremely difficult to put such a delicate metal band ingrained exactly in the same place as it is seen in genuine notes. The exact distance from the edges of a genuine note to this metal thread is a security secret. In order to facilitate the drawing of the line in a false note, some forgers, during the printing process itself or afterwards, make colourless ink markings on the reverse side almost exactly at the same place where genuine security thread is seen in rupee notes. The author has seen a number of fake notes having such colourless ink-markings when imitation notes have been seized from the counterfeiter's storehouse. The banker, therefore, should examine the reverse side of the fake notes and see whether or not pencil/pen drawings or printed lines are conspicuously seen.

2. Taking two thin sheets of paper and the forger prints the obverse side of the genuine note on one sheet of paper and the reverse side of the genuine note on the other sheet of paper and the two sheets are then pasted so well that ordinary people will find it extremely difficult to detect the pasting. Here the sheets of paper used are, as indicated above, very thin ones and perhaps this method is now widely employed by counterfeiters as it enables them to put the security thread into it with little difficulty. The paper sheets are pasted taking meticulous care. But, unfortunately, air bubbles which are inside the two sheets make the pasting at certain places uneven and thereby the fake notes made by pasting lack smoothness on the surface of the paper. This is not very easy to detect unless the imitation money is carefully examined by the banker. If the banker has some suspicion, he should apply a little water on the corner of the fake money and he can be sure that the note has been made by pasting of two sheets of paper, for, when water is applied the two layers of the paper sheets can be separated by just rubbing the corner by the thumb and fingers. If the false notes are printed on two sheets of paper and then pasted together, some forgers make the pencil or pen drawing (to simulate security thread) on the back of the paper on which the obverse side of the genuine note is printed. Since it is a drawing in such cases, on examination it can be seen that the drawing is highly visible when the fake note is viewed from its obverse side and similar visibility is not seen when the note is viewed from its back side. In genuine notes the security thread is seen alike when it is viewed from the face side or back side of the note. Another method to make security thread into the fake note is to insert a fine silk or plastic thread in between the two layers of the paper sheets. This he does while pasting the paper sheets. Since, the pasting is done manually, the silk/plastic thread kept in between may not have a straight line appearance. By touching the location where silk/plastic thread is put one can feel the projection and the thread in the fake notes. Such a feeling is not there when genuine notes are examined by the fingers. It is good if the bank officers are taken to a police museum and are exposed to the section where counterfeit notes are kept so that they can see, touch and feel the difference between fake notes and genuine ones.

About some seven months ago, photographs of genuine notes which are made by pasting sheets of paper appeared in Malayala Manoramma (Kottayam Edition). The paper then gave the serial numbers of such notes as 3 GR 146939 (100 rupees, note), OFE 305889 (50 rupees note), 55Q 766863 (10 rupees note), 43B 039323 (5 rupees note), 25F 203910 (1 rupee note). The paper says further that all genuine notes are made by pasting two sheets of paper and it is possible to seperate the two sheets of paper from genuine rupee notes by taking meticulous care and caution. The photographs that appeared in the paper show the genuine notes with separated sheets. However, the observations made by the press are yet to be confirmed by the Reserve Bank. Presuming that the genuine notes are made by pasting two sheets of paper, the fact remains that the pasting is so well done that it is not possible to see any traces of pasting. In forged notes, the pasting can be detected just by visual inspection and the air bubbles that are available in between the two sheets of paper prior to pasting and the crude way in which the pasting has been done make it all the more easy for detection. The forger pastes two sheets of paper to insert a thin fibre inside the two sheets to simulate security thread (sometimes to make the water-marks) and if that is the case, one doubts why should the Government of India pastes two sheets of paper even in one rupee note wherein the security thread is not necessary. However, the points raised by Malayala Manorama needs further clarification from the Reserve Bank and the Government of India.

Shadow Printing in Indian Money

Although some of the general public and bank officers are aware of security threads in genuine notes, they have little or no knowledge about shadow printing in genuine notes. Genuine notes when viewed against a powerful source of light, one can notice printing which has a shadow-like appearance. If a one rupee note is viewed from its obverse side against a powerful source of light, the word Bharat in Hindi is seen printed vertically in shadow at the place where the Government's emblem appears If the shadow printing cannot be seen by viewing the note in this way, then keep the note straight against the eye in such a way that the upper surface (obverse side) of the genuine note comes in straight lines to the eye. View the note against sunlight/powerful source of light. Then the shadow printing can be seen without difficulty. The letters seem to have an appearance of wax printing when viewed in this manner. As stated earlier, the one rupee note is printed by the Government of India and that is why Bharat is seen printed in shadow in this note.

ONE RUPEE

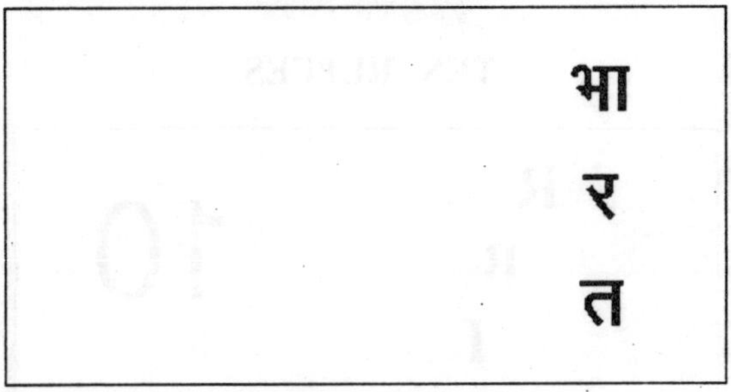

Fig. 7.1 : Viewing from the obverse side, Bharat in Hindi is seen as shadow printing in one rupee notes.

On the contrary, Rs. 2 and above have RBI and the denomination printed in shadow if viewed against a powerful source of light. In a two rupees note the denomination in shadow is printed at the centre of the note and RBI printed vertically down on the place where the Government's emblem is seen. In a five rupees note, RBI is printed at the centre and the denomination on the Government's emblem.

TWO RUPEES

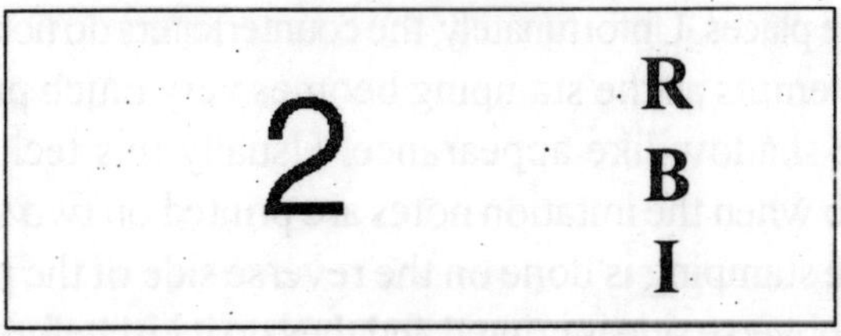

Fig. 7.2 : RBI and 2 are seen as shadow printing in two rupees notes

FIVE RUPEES

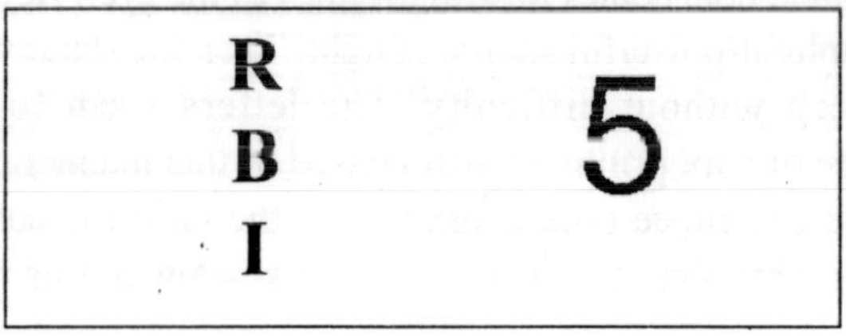

Fig. 7.3 : RBI and 5 are seen as shadow printing in five rupees notes

TEN RUPEES

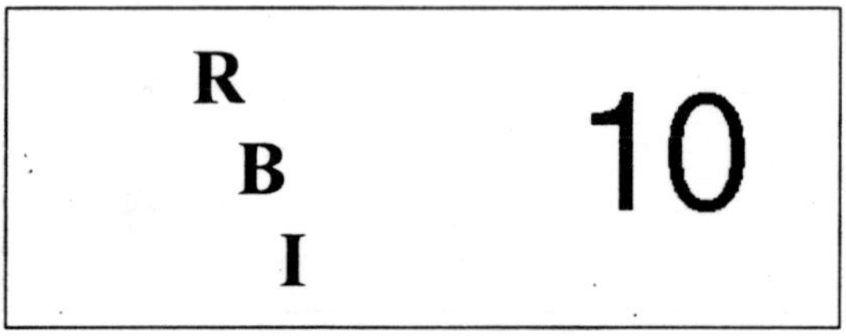

Fig. 7.4 : RBI and 10 are seen as shadow printing in ten rupees notes

In a hundred rupees note, RBI is printed at the centre in a crowded manner and the denomination just below the emblem. A banker can take genuine notes of various denominations and study how the shadow printing is seen in each of them. Fake notes usually do not contain shadow printing. Nevertheless, there are instances in which the counterfeiter has attempted to put shadow printing as well in hundred rupees note. Here he makes rubber stamps and stamp the denomination and RBI with thin black pad-ink at the appropriate places. Unfortunately, the counterfeiters do not succeed in their attempts as the stamping beomes very much projected losing the shadow-like appearance. Usually this technique is resorted to when the imtation notes are printed on two sheets of paper. The stamping is done on the reverse side of the paper on which the obverse side is printed and they do it just before pasting the two sheets on which the obverse and reverse sides are printed.

Since this method does not guarantee success, the forgers generally are reluctant to stamp the shadow printing in imitation money. Hence, this can be taken as the surest indicator to identify genuine notes from fake notes.

HUNDRED RUPEES

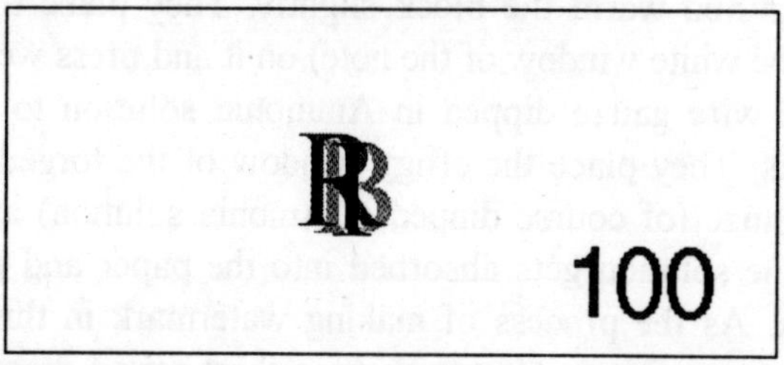

Fig. 7.5 : RBI and 100 are seen as shadow printing in one hundred rupees note.

Watermarks in Indian Paper Moeny

Every genuine note has an apparently white blank space where watermark may be seen. The national effigy, i.e. Asoka Pillar, is seen in the blank white space and this can be seen by viewing the note from its obverse side against a source of light. The watermark, just like shadow printing and security thread, is built into the paper during its manufacture. It has a light and shade effect, i.e., translucent effect. The counterfeiter finds it extremely difficult to make the translucent watermark on the white space of the note. What is available to him is only a crude method in which he makes a metal seal containing an Asoka Pillar and he smears glycerine or similar oil into the seal and stamps the seal on the white space. At times, he uses candle wax to bring about the light-and-shade effect. He uses fine sand paper to make the paper thin. Hence the imprint of the Asoka Pillar can be seen on the reverse of the note. Projection of the outlines of the Asoka Pillar is clearly visible at the backside. The paper gets torn and thin. The method that the forger uses is no superior than the crude method employed by school-children to transfer the engravings of a coin on a sheet of paper by using wax and the back of a pencil by means of rubbing the paper after keeping a coin underneath the paper. Here too, the counter feiter places the white space of the imitation note over the block on which the Asoka Pillar is engraved and rubs it with wax and a hard substance. As stated above, the forgers produce watermark on the forged note by the use of wax, glycerine or paraffin. Some forgers resort to this method of spreading the wax, glycerine etc. on the block for watermarks and warm the block slightly. They place the effigy window (the white window of the note) on it and press well. Some others use wire gauze dipped in Ammonia solution to produce watermarks. They place the effigy window of the forged note on the wire gauze (of course dipped in Amonia solution) and when doing so the solution gets absorbed into the paper and produces watermark. As the process of making watermark in this way is found to be imperfect as it lasts only for a short period, many forgers are reluctant to adopt this method. Also, it is easy to detect such watermarks. If the forged note is printed on two thin sheets of paper and pasted them together, the watermark on such a note is made by scraping the back of the front sheet where the obverse side is printed. Now a days, the picture of Mahatma Gandhi may be seen instead of Asoka Pillar.

Stiching and Stapling

The notes are released from the Reserve Bank after stiching or stapling them. The commercial banks too stitch the bundles and for this purpose, they use the white space where the watermark is seen. They are not supposed to stitch the bundle by making holes on the printed part of the note. The Reserve Bank staplings are usually found on the printed part of the notes just near the white space for the watermark. This is not always true. In some notes, the RBI staplings may be seen on the watermark as well. For, the distance of the stapling holes from the edges of the note is a security secret. The banker by observing stapling holes on genuine notes can easily make out the difference between the holes made by the RBI and other commercial banks. Holes put by the RBI are neatly done. Some bank officers have a tendency to write on the white space provided on genuine notes. This practice should be discouraged at any cost.

Designs on Notes

The designs on genuine notes–*schorles* and *rosettes*–and lettering are the effect of excellent craftmanship and skill for perfect execution. The netlike designs are called *schorles* and the snakelike designs are known as *rosettes*. They are very complicated and change from design to design. For printing these designs, blocks are nesessary. Steel engravings are really the perfection of art. The finished note-printing plate is the result of combined individual skill of many master engravers and produces master work as effective as it is humanly possible. This is done as a precaution against counterfeiting. Without the necessary skill, precision instruments and highly sophisticated printing presses, it is just impossible for any croaked craftsman, or any gang of craftsmen to produce a rupee note without it being detected. The counterfeiters use acid-etched plates. As the counterfeiter has no control over the acid, the acid while etching the design into the forger's plate eats into the metal unevenly and quite often eats away small pieces of metal that should be on the plate. The unfortunate result of this eating away is that open white spaces appear in the counterfeiter's note. He cannot print fine shading lines in his imitation notes.

In counterfeit note, the netlike and the snakelike designs are either etched too deeply or not enough. This causes white squares on the forged money. The result of this will be that there will be some designs formed and they will not be like the ones seen in the genuine notes. The designs will be dull, smudgy, unnaturally coloured and have irregular and broken lines etc.

Inks in Notes and Chemical Tests

The forger usually prints the paper money by using inks available in the market and the Reserve Bank/Government prints the paper money by using security inks. Therefore, the inks that are found on a forged note can be dissolved in one or other solvents.[2] The solvents are:

1. Concentrated muriatic acid.

2. Concentrated solution of oxalic acid.
3. Solution of caustic soda.
4. Solution of sulphurous acid.
5. Solution of chloride of lime.
6. Solution of protochloride of tin.
7. Dilute nitric acid (1 : 50 ratio of acid and water).
8. Dilute sulphuric acid (ratio is 1:10 of acid and water).

The test may be difficult to be done in a bank; yet the banker should know how the test can be done. Draw lines on the note suspected to be forged ones and the lines should be drawn crosswise by using all the eight solvents, For drawing the lines, quill pens should be used. And seperate pens should be used for each solvent. It is not advisable to use pens having nibs of steel as the steel suffers from chemical actions of the solvents. If any discolouration occurs anywhere in the notes where the solvents are applied, it is a sure indication that the notes are forged ones. Security inks can never be discoloured by the above solvents.

Instructions to Banks when Forged Notes are Detected

---

1. Do not return it.
2. Inform or telephone police at once.
3. Delay the passer under a pretext.
4. Avoid arguing with him.
5. Write down a description of the passer if he leaves the counter before the police arrives. How to describe the passer is given in chapter 9 of this book.

The bank should remember that all counterfeiters are likely to be strangers and the Government never redeems counterfeit money.

LEGAL PROVISIONS REGARDING FORGED NOTES

Section 489 A, Indian Penal Code 1860 runs as :

Whoever counterfeits, or knowingly performs any part of the process of counterfeiting, any currency note or bank note shall be punished with imprisonment for life, or with imprisonment of either description for a term which may extend to ten years and shall also be liable to fine."

The offence is cognizable but not bailable; not compoundable and triable by Courts of Sessions as a warrant case.

Section 489 B, I.P.C. reads :

"Whoever sells to or buys or receives from, any other person or otherwise traffics in or uses as genuine, any forged or counterfeit currency-note or bank-note, knowing or having reason to believe the same to be forged or counterfeit, shall be punished with imprisonment for life, or with imprisonment of either description for a term which may extend to ten years and shall also be liable to fine."

Possession of forged or counterfeit currency notes or bank notes is made punishable under the Indian Penal Code. The law is laid down under Section 489 C:

"Whoever has in his possession any forged or counterfeit currency-note or bank-note, knowing or having reason to believe the same to be forged or counterfeit and intending to use the same as genuine or that it may be used as genuine, shall be punished with imprisonment of either description for a term which may extend to seven years, or with fine or with both."

Section 489 E, I.P.C. reads :

"Whoever makes or causes to be made, or uses for any purpose whatsoever, or delivers to any person, any document purporting to be or in any way resembling, or so nearly resembling as to be calculated to deceive, any currency-note or bank-note, shall be punished with fine, which may extend to one hundred rupees."

However, while the counterfeiting of any currency note or bank-note constitutes an offence under the I.P.C, there exists no legal provision to prohibit the reproduction or the production of imitation of currency and bank-notes for such purposes as advertisement or the like where there is no intention to practise deception on anyone or even a knowledge that deception is likely to be practised with the help of imitation. The above observation has been made in the objects and reasons put forth in the I.P.C. (Amendment Act VI of 1943).

In the explanation given under section 489 A, I.P.C. it has been stated that "For the purposes of this section, and of sections 489 B, 489 C, 489 D and 489 E, the expression "Bank-note" means a promisory note or engagement for the payment of money to bearer on demand issued by any person carrying on the business of banking in any part of the world, or issued by or under the authority of any State or Soverign Power, and intended to be used as equivalent to, or as a substitute for money.

Counterfeit Coins

Counterfeiting of coins is a rare occurrence in the recent past. The reason for this has been that it is not profitable to counterfeit coins now. Hence, the subject is not elaborately dealt with in this book.

The common method of counterfeiting coins is by casting base metal in a suitable mould. They can easily be detected by examining the corrugated (reeded) edge of the coin. The edge will show file marks. The counterfeiter makes an attempt to simulate the corrugated edge where he has filed from the coin the metal which adhered to it that took the shape of the mouth of the mould. The methods of detecting counterfeit coins are :

1. by weight of the coin;
2. by the thickness of the coin;
3. by specific gravity of the coin;
4. by examining the rim of the coin;
5. by conducting chemical test to identify the metal used to counterfeit the coin;
6. by seeing the beads and pearls;

7. by observing the surface of the coin;
8. by doing magnetic tests;
9. by the ringing test (of course, this is not a conclusive test);
10. by examining the security edges; and
11. by observing the colour of the coin etc.

The surface of a counterfeit coin will generally appear to be imperfect and pitted. The lettering, figures and design will appear round. On the contrary, they, in genuine coins, will be sharp and clear cut. The counterfeit coins are usually heavy or too light and they produce a dull, thudlike sound when thrown on a hard surface. Genuine coins have a ring to them. This test may not be applicable to all types of genuine Indian coins. Most counterfeit coins have a greasy feeling. The ridges on a genuine coin are distinct, clear-cut and evenly spaced. But, they are poorly spaced and are irregular in a counterfeit coin. In many of the counterfeits, the metal is soft and can be cut by a knife, whereas genuine coins cannot be easily cut as they are hard. Genuine coins made of aluminium are not counterfeited at all.

When the banker suspects a coin to be a counterfeit, he should compare it with one or more genuine coins of the same denomination. The examination should be conducted in good light preferably with the help of a magnifying glass. Since gold weighing balances are available in all banks, the suspected coin should be weighed against a genuine coin. It has been observed that a good number of counterfeit coins are either lighter or heavier than genuine coins. Mint Masters employ specific gravity test to ensure certainty.

If the banker resorts to ringing test to hear a clear high note when rung on a stone slab or similar hard surface, he should remember that most of the modern genuine coins do not give a good ring. Hence, the test is not conclusive. Moreover, the high note, if at all there is, can be recognised only if the one who does the test is an experienced officer having no auditory defects.

The colour of the genuine and counterfeit coins should be examined. It is seen that a counterfeit coin has a brassy or dull leaden appearance. Sometimes, a peculiar glazed appearance may be noticed in counterfeit coins. A genuine coin particularly 25 ps.,

50 ps, Re. 1, Rs. 2 etc. should be silvery, dull or bright according to the treatment such coins have received. If the banker sees coins which when feel greasy to the touch, he should examine them with meticulous care and caution. Whenever colour test is employed, do the test with the help of a genuine coin with similar description.

In all genuine coins, the thickness at the rim is seen to be the same all round. On the other hand, it will be sometimes thicker at one point than at another in a fake coin. It is also observed that fake coins are sometimes bent or destorted. The result is that such fake coins do not lie evenly between two other coins of the same denomination. Likewise, rough, jagged edges in a coin are highly suspicious.

Remember that the rim of a genuine coin is regularly milled all the way round with straight angles to the faces. In a fake coin, the lines of the milling are generally seen at a slant. Likewise, in a counterfeit coin, the spaces between the teeth are found to be irregular, uneven and broken. The banker can easily verify this by placing the counterfeit coin between two genuine coins of the same denomination. When doing so, he can see that the rims of all the three coins are close together and he can see them at the same time. If he can not see them, as stated earlier, doubtlessly, it is a suspicious case. Nevertheless, he should not make false judgements by keeping much worn genuine coins. While it is true that coins which show good milling are seldom fake ones, it does not mean that all genuine coins always maintain the good milling characteristics. There can be much worn genuine coins as well.

The pearls on the inner side of the rim of the fake coins are found to be badly shaped, uneven in size and spaced at irregular intervals. On the contrary, the beading on the genuine coins are found to be even and regular all round and the pearls to be uniform in size, shape and spaced at regular intervals. In some counterfeit coins, the pearls are found to be very small and far apart.

There should be clearly cut and well defined edges particularly in the outlines of genuine coins if one examines the front and back side of the coin. Hence, if blurred lines or imperfect edges and impressions are noticed, it is a suspicious case. However, imperfect impressions or edges etc. can occur in genuine coins owing to wear and tear. In such instances, they are quite obvious.

The inscriptions—letters and figures on the genuine coins are very clear, well defined and sharp-edged. Counterfeit coins suffer from blurred, irregular or double lines. It is also quite possible to see very thick letters in fake coins. The portion where inscriptions are not made, i.e., the plain surface of the genuine coins–will have smooth appearance and will be even and free from blemish. Hence, an uneven, spotted or rough appearance on the plane surface of the coin is suspicious.

Fake coins are sometimes made by cast-method. Hence, in a cast coin, the surface may be granulated or pitted with minute pin-holes. They appear as black spots even to the naked eye. In cast-coins, the milling is quite defective and this can be felt at the point where the metal has been poured into the mould. In cast coins, there may not be square and sharp edges for the letters and figures. They will be having almost a rounded appearance.

Law on Counterfeit Coins

According to Indian law, a coin is defined as a metal used for the time being as money, and stamped and issued by the authority of some State or Sovereign Power in order to be so used (see section 230, I.P.C. 1960.) And 'Indian coin is metal stamped and issued by the authority of the Government of India in order to be used as money.'

Section 231, I.P.C. reads:

> "Whoever counterfeits or knowingly performs any part of the process of counterfeiting coin, shall be punished with imprisonment of either description for a term which may extend to seven years, and shall also be liable to fine.
>
> **Explanation :** A person commits this offence who intending to practise deception, or knowing it to be likely that deception will thereby be practised, uses a genuine coin to appear like a different coin".

Section 239, I.P.C. is about the delivery of coin, possessed with knowledge that it is counterfeit. It reads :

> "Whoever, having any counterfeit coin, which at the time when he became possessed of it he knew to be counterfeit, fraudulently or with intent that fraud may be committed, delivers the same to any person or attempts to induce any person to receive it, shall be punished with imprisonment of either description for a term which may extend to five years and shall also be liable to fine."

Also section 241, I.P.C. reads :

> "Whoever delivers to any other person as genuine, or attempts to induce any other person to receive as genuine, any counterfeit coin which he knows to be counterfeit, but which he did not know to be counterfeit at the time when he took it into his possession, shall be punished with imprisonment of either description for a term which may extend to two years, or with fine to an amount which may extend to ten times the value of the coin counterfeited, or with both."

And finally, section 242, I.P.C. lays down :

> "Whoever, fraudulently or with intent that fraud may be committed, is in possession of counterfeit coin having known at the time when he became possessed thereof that such coin was counterfeit, shall be punished with imprisonment of either description for a term which may extend to three years, and shall also be liable to fine."

The word counterfeit has been defined under section 28, I.P.C. 1860 as follows :

> "A person is said to "counterfeit" who causes one thing to resemble another thing, intending by means of that resemblance to practise deception, or knowing it to be likely that deception

will thereby be practised.

Explanation 1 : It is not essential to counterfeiting that the imitation should be exact.

Explanation 2 : When a person causes one thing to resemble another thing, and the resemblance is such that a person might be deceived thereby, it shall be presumed, until the contrary is proved, that the person so causing the one thing to resemble the other thing intended by means of that resemblance to practise deception or knew it to be likely that deception would thereby be practised."

Notes

1. See, A. C. Bose, *A Handbook of Criminology*, Ambica Charan Bose (Publisher), Calcutta, 1960.
2. A. C. Bose, *op. cit.*

Refecences

Gupta, R. L.. *Law of Forgeries, Counterfeiting and Cheating*, Law Hook Co., Allahabad, 1971.

Hardless, H. R., *Handwriting and Thumb-Print Identification and Forensic Science*, Law Book Co., Allahabad, 1970.

Wilson, Frank J., 'Detection of Counterfeit Money' in *Elements of Police Science*, The Foundation Press, Chicago, 1942.

8

MODUS OPERANDI AND CRIMINALS IN BANKS

The term, *modus operandi*, etymologically comes from Latin which means the *method of operation*. In other words, it is the specific manner in which a particular person commits crimes. Usually, he does not deviate from his method of operation. For instance, a person who breaks open the window to commit a burglary in a bank will usually resort to that method even when he has other options. Professional criminals thus mostly adhere to their established *modus operandi* and go on committing crimes in the same manner. The taste, aptitude, ability, habits, training, proficiency and confidence which the professional criminal has qualify him to commit crimes in the same fashion for which he is best suited and well trained. Having found that a particular *modus operandi* has successfully turned out results, the professional criminal often clings to that method of operation with an almost blind faith in its effectiveness and efficiency. Thus, the concept of *modus operandi* is based on the normal pattern of human conduct and habit formation flowing from psychological compulsions. In other words, if a person has started his professional career as a pick-pocket, he likes to continue as a pick-pocket and so do the burglars, cheats, forgers etc. The technique employed by them will also be the same. In other words, they follow the same techniques throughout their life with an unbelivably firm faith in its efficacy.

Though strong rooms are necessary to keep the money, valuables and documents in banks, one wonders whether or not such rooms are available in all banks. In some banks, only the doors are strong enough and are the ones recommended for strong rooms and the rooms as such cannot be considered to be strong. Some '*modus operandi* criminals' are aware of this fact although the bank administration has still to be serious about it.

In a bank, it is seen that there will be more valuables (received by way of gold loans or otherwise), than money. Therefore, *modus operandi* criminals are keen about the valuables than perhaps the money. Wherever gold loans are received, it is therefore very necessary to have a detailed description sheet of every item received. This can help the bank to identify the property stolen in case a burglary takes place in a bank. The bank can ask the lonee to fill up the details of every item and can check the veracity of the lonee's description when a gold loan is given. These description sheets must be filed separately.

Entry, means of entry, object of crime, time, style, means of transport, etc. are of importance in understanding and appreciating the *modus operandi* of criminals. As far as a banker is concerned he must know the *modus operandi* of the criminals so that he can successfully take counter-measures to foil the designs of criminals likely to commit crimes in banks.

Strangers to Banks

Many people come to bank to transact business or on the pretext of transacting business. Professional criminals may come to a bank to assess the possibility of committing a burglary. The banker and his security staff should therefore maintain really sharp observations of all people coming to the bank. The method of describing strange persons coming to the bank has been discussed at length in Chapter 9. They may come to the bank on the pretext of clearing doubts, taking loans or with queries to open an account etc. During their visits, they may take note of the situations of the premises and its interior parts to facilitate the planning out of a burglary. Hence, if strangers come to the bank, look upon them with an eye of suspicion and if possible provide them with a visitor's slip to write down their personal particulars and signatures.

Armed Customers

Some banks provide loaded rifles to their security guards. Sometimes professional criminals may come to the bank in an organized manner. They may come in cars/jeeps and may have weapons with them. If strangers come to the bank in vehicles, the security staff should immediately take note of the registration numbers of the vehicles and observe them closely. The managers and cashiers in the banks are advised to keep some handy weapon in an unexposed manner. If necessary, they can use the weapon against aggressive thieves to banks.

Quarrelling Customers

Some people come to the bank to fetch a quarrel with the bank employees. This is a calculated attempt on the part of such people to deviate the attention of other employees in the bank. Other employees in the bank may come to the help of their friends during which time the associates of the aggressive customer quarrelling in the bank may commit theft of gold ornaments or cash from the bank. Therefore, when a quarrel takes place between a customer and a bank employee, the security staff and others should make a close watch on all the customers present and their activities. The cashier should, on no account, leave his seat to settle the quarrel and so does the officer entrusted with the task of gold loan. The officer having the custody of the keys of the bank should take special care to see that the keys are not left on the table or in the drawers. Quarrels and attacks on bank employees are premeditated and are usually made by them during busy hours of work. Hence, the bank should be vigilant and alert in such situations. A few *don'ts* in banks are provided in Chapter 9.

People of Criminal Gangs

There are people belonging to professional and criminal gangs coming to the bank to commit theft of money/ornaments of customers. They have special *modus operandi*, i.e., when a customer counts money to be deposited or to be taken home, one of the gang members puts a one-rupee, two-rupees or five rupees note down on the floor near the customer. He then asks him to see whether the note fallen belongs to him or not. While answering the question, he looks down and thereby his attention is diverted. Here he forgets momentarily about the money that he is counting, perhaps a part of which may still be kept on the counter. During that split moment, another member of the gang takes away the money kept on the counter. The security, therefore, must have their attention always focused on the customers, particularly those who count money at a counter. The 'Badgis' from West Bengal, 'Banfars' from Bihar, 'Barwar' from Uttar Pradesh, 'Baurahs' from Rajasthan, 'Bediyas' of Jessore from Bengal, 'Bhadaks' from Uttar Pradesh, 'Bhagris' from Gujarat, 'Bhamptas' from Karnataka, 'Chhattisgarh Chamars' from Madhya Paradesh and many others are notorious for their criminal activities—particularly in burglary, theft, pocket-picking, cheating etc. Each one of these gangs has its own '*modus-operandi*' for committing crimes. It is not necessary for the banker to know the specific methodology of these gang operators. At the same time he must know how the strangers are described and the method of describing them. A few *don'ts* to customers, given in Chapter 9 should be published in the banks in a conspicuous way.

Security Watch During Nights

During night hours, the security guards should sit inside the bank, unapproachable by people who want to attack them. If they sleep during night hours, they should do so in such a way that the professional thieves cannot cause them to smell something to render them unconscious so that they are not able to make a cry. The security staff during night hours should not accept anything, particularly edible things, even from people known to them. They should politely refuse the offer or say that their stomach is upset, Likewise, they should not ask or receive beedi or cigarette from strangers or even from people known to them. If a burglary in a bank is premeditated, there is all likelihood of putting sedatives in the eatables, cigarettes, etc. The security staff should be educated about the serious consequences of their acceptance of edibles, or cigarettes/beedies from strangers and others during night hours.

Withdrawals of Huge Amount of Money

Huge amount of money may be withdrawn by a customer who may carry it home after counting the amount received from the bank. Counting money in public is always an invitation to the thief. Hence, if huge amount of money is withdrawn, the bank has the responsibility to provide adequate facilities for the customer to count the money in secret, i.e., not in public visibility. He should be called to a room and should be asked to count the money in the presence of an employee of the bank. It is to the interest and safety of the bank to see that their customers are not robbed off on their way back home. Therefore, it is necessary for every bank to fix an amount above which the customers are offered special facility to count their money. Letters of credit, if necessary, should be issued to the customer in case he should carry large sums of money with him. He should be advised on this, if he does not know about it. If he asks for a vehicle for his transport, the bank may arrange a suitable vehicle for him after noting down the particulars of the vehicle and the driver.

Bogus Mail Transfers

Bogus mail transfers may be presented to the bank when the bank is in busy transactions. T. Ramanujam in *Prevention and Detection of Crimes*, enumerates a number of cases in which bogus mail transfers were presented to various banks. To cite a few :

1. In May, 1969, the State Bank of India, Coimbatore, received two mail transfer orders, one for Rs. 63,000 and another for Rs. 59,000 from the Thallakulam (Madurai) branch in the names of two textile concerns in Coimbatore. The agent of the former bank contacted the Madurai branch and it was found that both the mail transfers were forged ones.

2. In August, 1969, the Indian Bank at Tirupattur received a mail transfer from Delhi for Rs.85,000 in the name of one Sethuramalingam who had earlier opened a current account in the former bank with Rs. 100 only. He withdrew gradually the entire amount noted in the mail transfer (Rs. 85,000) and disappeared. In Chapter 6, precautions while issuing mail transfers have been discussed at length.

Bogus Demand Drafts

Some people are quite capable of getting demand drafts printed and get them cashed: Many banks, it seems, have to develop better safety measures when they issue demand drafts. Such measures are discussed at length in Chapter 6. Likewise, alterations in demand drafts, cheque-leaves etc. are often reported in the press. Chapter 6 deals with precautionary measures against fraudulent alterations as well.

Armed Robbery of Cash Vans

Professional criminals may commit robbery of bank's cash vans. This can take place in public roads and in broad daylight. Broad daylight robbery is committed in a daring manner by armed criminals. Hence, if huge amount of money is transmitted in bank vans, it is necessary that they may make a requisition for police escort. If that is not found to be necessary, the van should be escorted by the security guards of the bank.

While bank vans with huge amount of money is sent, it should be sent only with security guards who are changed from time to time. The van should not be taken regularly through the same route, and the route should not be told to the escort guards until the van moves on with the money. Likewise, the time of the departure of the van should be changed whenever necessary.

Experts in banking security suggest that special type of van with security grills and metals should be used for carrying cash. Likewise, the cash chest should be chained with the van so that the culprits cannot essily remove it. The practice of carrying huge amount of money in taxi cabs should be discouraged.

Recently newspaper reports about armed robbery at the point of gun has become no news for the public. Security guards must be fully trained to face such situations. They should be trained in the use of firearms. It seems that some banks appoint old and inactive ex-service men as their guards or others with little or no training for preserving the security of banks. Young ex-army or ex-policemen are good security guards. They have training in weapons and also in unarmed combat. It is high time that banks may appraise their security system so that sufficient security can be ensured. There should be adequate armed security strength in every bank.

Bank Keys and Safety

Rules regarding the custody of the keys of the banks should be strictly adhered to. If the officer having the custody of the key carries it home, it should be kept under lock and key. For, the servants/visitors who have criminal tendencies can take a print of the key in a moulding clay or even in a cake of soap and thereafter make a key to commit crimes in banks.

Surprise night checks should be done by the managers of the bank to see whether or not the security staff is vigilant. The surprise checks should be done regularly at irregular hours.

Burglary in Banks

Banks should be aware of the fact that they can be subjected to burglary which is a crime against property. The burglars operate mostly during night hours. Therefore, there should be special night security in every bank if the crime of burglary is to be prevented. Burglars are of two categories : 1. the casual and 2. the professional. A casual burglar attacks only if the premises are easily accessible for attack and also if there is ample scope for escape after the burglary. But a professional burglar plans his action carefully and uses tools and equipments. Once the burglary takes place in a bank, a total and complete list of items and articles taken away by the burglar should be furnished to the police for investigation. Hence, it is to the interest of every bank to see that all items/articles, valuables/ornaments are properly listed out in duplicate so that one can be kept in the bank and the other sent to the regional or head office. Every new item received in the bank every day should be properly included in the list before the closure of the bank on a particular day and a duplicate list should be mailed to the regional or head office on the same day. This procedure will ensure the up-to-date list of everything kept in the bank both in the branch as well as in the regional/head office.

Safe Burglaries

Every banker should know how safe burglaries are effected by criminals. A safe is a container meant to keep valuables safe from fire or burglaly (or both) attack. Therefore safes are principally of two types : 1. fire resistive and 2. burglary resistive. Although all banks use safes, one wonders whether or not they are safe enough to resist attacks from fire as well as burglary. Remember that some of the safes used in banks in India are old and they can be attacked by burglars with ordinary burglary tools without much difficulty. It is to the bank to see that every branch is given the most modern burglary-proof safes for protecting valuables.

The banker should have a working knowledge of the various methods used by safe burglars to open safes in banks. They are elaborately described below[1] :

1. Punch : In this method, the burglars break off the dial knob and places a punch on the exposed spindle. They then drive back the spindle by exerting force and thereby break the lock-box from its mounting. After turning the handle then, they open the door. As a precaution against this method, now there are safes having relocking devices.

2. Carry Out (Haul Away) : The burglars carry way the safe to some isolated place and open it. This type of burglary is not often resorted to banks as the safes in banks are very heavy to carry away easily. Some banks have permanently fixed their safes well so much so that carrying way will be difficult. Nevertheless, there are banks which are not having permanently fixed safes. If that is the case, immediate steps should be taken to permanently fix the safes to the floor.

3. Rip or Beel : This method is not employed against burglar resistive safes. Light weight metals are used in fire-resistive safes and the burglar here peels off the door plate with a bar or he rips the sides open.

4. Hinge Attacks : Some burglars remove the hinges and remove the entire face of the door when the safe is properly peeled.

5. Chopping : Here the burglar, by using a sledgehammert chisel and hammer, hand-axe, etc. chops out the bottom metal plate and fire-proof material. He then makes a hole to insear his hand to take away the money/valuables or both.

6. Drag : Here the burglar uses a drag plate, i.e., a heavy metal plate having three or more adjancent bolts. The bolts are gradually tightened so that it pulls out the knobs and spindle by the application of the force caused by tightening the bolts.

7. Torch or Burn : The ozyacetylene cutting torch can burn a hand-size hole in the safe which in turn can open the door. As a precaution against money being burnt, the thieves use water to fill the compartment. Burglar-resistive safes can be opened by this method.

8. Drill : The safe bolt is identified and drilled with a high carbon-drill as large as the bolt. If the bolt cannot be drilled completely, then it is broken with a centre punch and hammer. The door is unscrewed and removed.

9. Explosives : The burglars use nitroglycerine for this purpose.

10. Lock Shot : A drilled hole is made and explosive is placed and discharged. Sometimes, burglars drill the hole near the lock and destroy the locking device to open the safe.

11. Door Shot : The door seams are first packed with clay, putty or brown kitchen soap. An opening is made at the top where a cuplike shape is given and also at the bottom. Nitroglycerine is then poured into the cup which seeps around the door. When nitroglycerine comes to the bottom, the hole is sealed and the cap is discharged. The door of the safe then is broken into pieces.

12. Sawing : Here a high-speed power saw having a carborundum blade (also sometimes a diamond-edge blade) is used. This makes a hole through which human hand can be inserted.

13. Force : This method is used to open fire-resistive safes. The cabinet of the safe is forced away from the door. To achieve the end, hammering is done. When hammering is forcefully done, a bulge appears between the cabinet and the door. By the help of pry bars, the cabinet is forced back and the bolts are taken out. Then the door is opened.

Counterfeiters and Forgers of Money

The counterfeiter does not come to the bank with forged currency or bank notes for the purpose of converting them into genuine ones; rather he inserts one, two or three forged notes in a bundle of genuine notes and comes to the bank on the pretext of depositing them or getting a bank draft for the amount. If the cashier counts the money carelessly, the counterfeiter wins his game. If the counterfeiter understands that the cashier is very cautiously counting the money, he may try to raise some casual questions to distract the attention of the bank employee. Once the counting is over, and a draft is issued in his favour, he gets it cashed soon and repeats the same *modus operandi* to the same bank or to other banks.

Some counterfeiters bundle the genuine notes as well as forged notes along with the bundle slips of recognised banks in such a way so that the money will be counted without taking adequate precautions. The banker thinks that after all this is issued by another bank. Hence, whether the bundle of money has a bank slip or not, every bundle has to be counted with meticulous care. Some bankers have a feeling that they can sense the genuine and forged notes by touch. This does not always turn out good results. Detection of forged currency notes is not easy; but once a banker has formed suspicion on a currency note, genuine or otherwise, he can make sure as to the genuineness of the note if he knows the methods of detecting false notes (see Chapter 7).

Time and *Modus Operandi* Criminals

Time is an important factor in the case of *modus operandi criminals*. They will approach a bank only in busy hours of transactions and they do it because they know that the banker then cannot pay adequate or meticulous attention to the false cheques presented or forged notes surrendered. They may pretend to be very busy and they will not allow the banker to do his work calmly. They may converse with the banker in pleasing manners and may smoke costly cigarettes to project their ego, social status and economic stability. They will be quite impatient until their money is accepted or the cheque is passed by the bank. They may tell a tale to impress upon the banker that the money or draft is required before a specified time or the taking off of the aeroplane, etc. It is said that the style and tale are really pointers in the *modus operandi criminals*. There may be associates with them who may come and support the *modus operandi criminals's* claim. The associates may help them in their attempts to speed up the business in the bank. Hence, when a person is unusually busy and he is a stranger to the bank, unusual care should be taken in counting the money and in passing the cheques. Time of committing crimes by professional criminals is of considerable importance from the point of view of committing burglaries in banks as well. Some criminals prefer to commit burglary in the early hours of night when people in the neighbourhood (particularly in urban areas) may think that some official transactions are going on inside the bank. Others may commit burglary late in the night while a few others may prefer small hours of the morning.

In any case, if a burglary has taken place, the banker must immediately and invariably report the matter to the police. For this purpose he must try to be sure about :

1. the property attacked;
2. point of entry;
3. method of approach;
4. the time;
5. transport, if any etc;

If the banker can give these information to the police, no doubt they are valuable clues to the police. If he does not know them clearly, he should not try to mislead the police and for ascertaining the facts, he should not enter the scene of crime and contaminate the physical clues likely to have been left by the criminals. How should the scene of crime be guarded is dealt with in detail in Chapter 10 of this book.

Foot-prints, finger-prints, implements (instruments) for committing burglary, matches, cigerette ends etc. are quite likely to be left at the scene of crime by the culprits. There may be signs of assembly and despersal. It is quite likely that burglars leave or abandon their own or the bank's property and if so they should be allowed to be there without being touched or removed.

Bank Employees and Crimes in Banks

There may be cases in which the servants of the bank work with *modus operandi criminals*. In such instances, it is not quite unusual that transactions are done without taking adequate care and caution. Superior officers and colleagues have a tendency to believe what their subordinates or associates tell them to be true. They put their signature in all places shown by the subordinate/ associate criminals. Business is business and therefore, it at all some subordinates/ associates approach with special requests, the superiors and colleagues should not take it for granted that things represented by them are always true. You are dealing with money that belongs to another and it should be done in the manner in which it is done in the formal way in the bank. Oversightedness and carelessness have landed many men in difficulties. It has been found that some employees of the bank give precise details about the bank to some *modus operandi criminals*. Beware of such persons in the banks.

Surveillance in banks means the secret or open watching of a particular bank employee who has been suspected for illicit transactions, corrupt practices, undesirable associations with known bad characters, drankards, etc. for the purpose of learning as much as possible about his activities, operations and contacts outside the working hours in the bank. It is not as simple or as easy as it appears to be. It is really delicate and laborious to have surveillance of the employees in a bank. The proper surveillance requires a variety of techniques and skills. Its success lies in the fact that the employee with criminal contacts is watched without his knowledge. The surveillance system is not available in banks and it is to the advantage of any bank that they develop a surveillance wing in their head quarters. This wing should be given adequate training in surveillance techniques, shadowing methods and watching the employees suspected to associate with underground criminals. It can surely prevent a number of crimes which are committed with the knowledge and concurrence of bank employees. In some of the western countries, banks entrust the surveillance work to known non-governmental detective agencies. In India too, such agencies are now available.

Periodical and Casual Works in Banks

Whenever the bank needs white-washing, painting or repair-works etc. entrust the work to some known people in the locality. When work men are employed on casual basis, see that strangers are not appointed. In case the bank asks someone to do some job for the bank, take note of their names and addresses and also keep an eye on them lest they steal things from the bank. They may pass information about the bank to some *modus operandi* criminals. They themselves may have criminal tendencies or may be associated with the people of bad characters. They may plan and attempt for a burglary in the bank.

Bank Managers/Accountants and Safety

The managers or those having the custody of the keys of the safe where money and valuables are kept should, as far as possible, avoid going alone at late hours of night—particularly through deserted and insecure routes. They should never carry large amounts of money when they go alone after the work. Such officers should carry weapons with them to resist an attack in case they are faced with it. They may not succeed in fully overpowering the criminals; nevertheless, they can at least keep them at a distance, for some time. Meanwhile, help may come from some persons or means.

It is a welcome idea if the bank managers are given training in judo and unarmed combat and this can be imparted by the police department or gymkhanas available everywhere in the country. This may be a strange suggestion, but it appears that matters have developed into such an extent that judo and similar self protecting techniques are essential things in the contemporary society. The managers of the bank and similar officers who keep the key of the bank should refrain themselves from accepting lifts offered by strangers. It has become no news today that people are abducted by organized criminal gangs who are notorious men of the underworld. If such officers go by taxis or autorikshaws, see to that the number of such hired vehicles are noted done and entrusted to the watchman on duty. It is always advisable for officers having the custody of the key of the bank to travel in their own vehicles and if this is not possible, they should depend upon the public transport. In many banks, the managers' quarters are attached to the bank building and if this system can be extended it will be surely a safer method. Wherever quarters are provided to bank managers, it is advisable to have sentries posted during night hours to protect them. If banks construct quarters for their employees, they should be constructed like a complex where all will be living together.

Bank Drafts for Small Amounts

Some banks issue bank drafts, particularly of small amounts, by inscribing the entries by hand. Small amounts are altered into big amounts and therefore every bank should be provided with cheque-writing machines and it should be insisted that they write on the drafts only by the machines and never by hand. Safer methods are discussed elsewhere in this book. When bank drafts are written for small amounts by bank employees having criminal tendencies, they see to it that it is written in such a way that the small amount is altered into big amounts. A few months ago, a demand draft worth Rs. 1000/- was converted to Rs. 91000/- in a nationalized bank. The investigation proved that the clerk who wrote the draft saw to it that sufficient space is provided in the draft to enable alterations. Therefore, it is to the interest of the bank to see that the officer who signs the draft may see that nothing can be inserted into the writing on a draft when it is issued.

It has been learnt that in a bank in South India, a clerk managed to secure a blank draft leaf, forged the signature of the officer and got Rs. 100,000. Further investigation proved that he had done the same thing five times in his service causing a damage of Rs. 500,000 to the bank. This indicates how things can move in commercial banks. Adequate security measures are to be taken to see that crimes by the bank employees are prevented.

Lighting the Premises of the Banks

Lighting the premises of the bank building during night hours should not be considered a waste. The entire area should be lighted with powerful electric lamps so that any suspicious characters wandering around the premises of the bank can easily be located and questioned. It has been proved that when electric lights have been put during night hours in streets and buildings; crimes against property during night hours could considerably be reduced.

If a large amount of money is kept in a particular bank for some reason or other for a particular day, the local police should be informed so that adequate patrolling near the premises of the bank can be arranged by them. If the manager who resides in the bank building is out for some days, the matter may be intimated to the police so that they will arrange special vigilance in and around the bank premises.

Finger-prints

Lack of knowledge in taking finger impressions of people has resulted in disputes between the banks and the customers. Litigations have failed in courts just because identity of the customer could not be proved. Hence whenever finger-prints are taken, it should be examined by another to see that the ridge-characteristics are sufficiently clear to make the identity of the customers. The chapter on finger-prints deal with this extensively. Some criminals purposefully exert heavy pressure when finger impressions are taken and this is done to see that crude and blurred impressions are taken by the bank so that they can dispute the case if that needs be.

Fictitious Accounts

In an over enthusiasm to maximise the deposits in banks some self-serving managers permit one and the same customer to open two or three accounts in fictitious names and addresses. It has been reported that the customer who puts the signature of the fictitious person forgets how he had put the signature. Some self-serving managers take the signature card kept in the bank to show him how the signature of the fictitious person looks like. He puts the signature accordingly and draws the money and the managers get their share. These few managers carve out a poor image of the bank in public minds.

Greedy Employees

Some employees of the bank conduct business within the business. They accept money from the customers and pay them the usual interest given by the banks. And the deposits so received are diverted to money-lenders to get more interest and thereby misuse their official positions. This is really a bad state of affairs and it should be discouraged and stopped.

Accepting illegal gratification from customers who want to take loans, coercing people to canvass deposits in case the loan is to be sanctioned, etc. are some of the evil practices that are seen operative in some banks. The employees who indulge in such unauthorized practices are to he watched closely so that they do not enter into transactions that can affect the fame of the banks. In fact, every bank should have a vigilance and surveillance unit which is empowered to investigate into cases, to shadow the suspected employee and if their investigation finds that there is truth in the case, departmental proceedings against such employees should be initiated.

In a reputed bank in South India it is learnt that an officer who was in charge of keeping the pledged ornaments in custody once pledged ornaments for an amount of Rs. 15,000. After a few months, the officer stealthily took the ornaments without effecting the repayment of the loan. The bank took no notice of her act and the entire thing came into light only when the Reserve Bank made its auditing. The payment slip for the loaned amount was missing and it resulted in the detection of this offence. This shows how some officers manage to get things done.

In another bank, one officer managed to get a draft without paying the money. Since he was an officer, his subordinates took it for granted what he said was true. The officer managed to see that all papers in connection with the said draft were in perfect conditions. After a few days, the draft was brought back with a request to cancel it and after cancellation, he received the money back from the bank. The account of the bank did not tally and further investigation brought to light how he managed to get the draft and setting all papers right in a surprisingly stealthy manner.

It so happens that there are individuals and organizations who do not periodically check their balance amount in the account of the bank. The employees of the bank in the pretext of making entries in the pass book get the pass book and keep it with them. They take a cheque-leaf and write a cheque with forged signature when they are in short of money. When their financial need is over, they deposit the money back and the customer does not take note of the alterations in the account. It has also been noticed that some employees do not deposit back the money at all in the bank. And if the amount withdrawn is considerably less, say, Rs. 25, Rs. 35, etc., the depositor may not know about it.

Cases of temporary misappropriation of money by the 'teaming and lading process' has been reported to have been committed by some of the employees of the commercial banks. The employees receive money from one customer and do not enter the same in his account. They temporarily misappropriate the money and later when another customer deposits an amount equal or more than the first customer, they credit the amount equal to the misappropriated one to the former customer's account. The first customer may not take note of this temporary misappropriation at all as the employees do not take undue delay to put the misappropriated amount. This process goes on until the employees get sufficient money to see that no more misappropriation is required. Often, this takes place by an understanding among two or three employees who are concerned with the acceptance of the cash, recording of the deposits, making entries in the book, etc. Such cases have been reported to the police and investigation into such successive and successful misappropriation by bank employees has proved that the employees have taken undue advantage of the lack of sufficient internal checks in the banks. Some banks elsewhere obtain the statements of accounts from customers selected on random basis and compare the same with their accounts kept in the bank.

Advances and Security Measures

Now, all banks give advance to people for some purpose or other. Development loans, direct credit for the purchase of fertilizers, machinery, development of irrigation facilities, construction of farm buildings, loan for securing seeds, construction of wells, advance for development of small-scale industries, financial assistance to technically qualified enterpreneurs, to importers and exporters etc. are in vogue today. The banker is supposed to use his discretion when he grants loan and advance to people. Cases have been reported that some agents and managers abuse their discretionary powers and with ulterior motives help the cheats defraud the banks and draw funds under various schemes. The misuse of discretionary authority by unscrupulous bankers shows the lack of proper supervision and periodical checks by the higher-ups in the bank. Fox ensuring adequate security, the following precautions are to be taken by every bank[2] :

(1) No credit should be granted in cases where the credit is not sufficiently covered by collateral security.

(2) Prior to sanctioning the credit, strict verification of the history and nature of the business, ownership, assets and liabilities should be conducted.

(3) The storage for keeping the goods should be examined for its adequacy and the goods to be pledged should be properly examined in quality and quantity. Expert advice should be sought for, if that needs be.

It is suggested for ensuring security of the banks that at least 15 per cent of all the advances and loans sanctioned by the branches should be rechecked by the supervisory and inspecting officers of the bank and if found unsatisfactory, strict disciplinary action should be taken against the defaulters.

Frauds Through Clearance Houses

Another method of committing crimes is to open two accounts in two different banks with fictitious names, addresses and signatures. The cheat surrenders a cheque for a huge amount in one account and requests the bank to accept the cheque for collection. Consequently, the bank which received the cheque sends it to the clearing house. If on examination, it is seen that the cheques can not be honoured in the clearing house, the cheque is sent back to the bank which surrenders it.

Prior to surrendering the cheque, the cheat gets hold of the bank employee who in turn sees that the cheque is misplaced before it comes up for clearance. As a result, the cheque is not returned and the bank to which the cheque has been surrendered persumes that it had been cleared. The cheat then withdraws the money from the bank and a share always goes to the bank employee who assists the cheat. Cases of this nature have been detected and in one notorious case, a women clerk managed to accumulate an amount worth of over Rs. 1.5 lakhs. She was employed in the clearing house and she saw to it that the false cheques sent to the cleaning house were destroyed and clearance slips promptly returned.

Fixed Deposits and Frauds

Some of the bank employees make undue money from fixed deposits. A case has been unearthed wherein a bank issued a regular receipt when a customer made a fixed deposit. Entries regarding the deposit were not made in the book kept for the purpose. The employee misappropriated the entire deposit for his benefit. It has been estimated that he pocketed almost Rs. 5 lakhs by this way. When the case was further investigated it was found that a number of customers were made the victims of his criminal act.

In another case, the manager of a reputed bank was found to indulge in criminal activities. His method of operation was as follows. The bank had a provision to issue cash certificates. It could be pledged if the certificate holder wanted to take a loan. The manager of the bank entertained the certificate holders when ever they came to the bank to pledge the cash certificate. Then he used to give them the requested money after getting their signatures in the prescribed forms for the purpose. The rule was that the certificate holder could take 75 % of the total amount deposited in the bank. After the certificate holders left the bank, the manager wrote in the prescribed from that he gave 75 % of the deposit to the certificate holders whereas the certificate holders demanded and were paid only 30 % or 40 % of their deposit as the case might be. The balance amount, i.e., 75 % minus 30 % or 40 % as the case might be, was taken by the manager who in turn utilized the amount for conducting his private money-lending business. When the certificate holders came to get back the cash certificates after paying the loan and the interest, they were issued with regular receipts and were asked to come to the bank after a week. When they came as suggested by the manager they were given the cash certificates and at the same time the manager made huge amount of money by way of interest which he collected from his private money-lending business. Thus, he could do his business well with the customers' deposits. On investigation, it was further brought out that the manager could get certificates pledged with private money-lenders and could get further loans for conducting his business.

Hypothecation and Frauds

Cases have been again reported that people hypothecate their godowns with materials to more than three or four banks and receive huge amount of money and more often than not, it is done with the understanding of the bank employees. They submit forged documents—even title deeds—for this purpose. Sometimes, it is noticed that the materials hypothecated to the bank might not be worth anything.

Bank Lockers and Crimes

Many banks have safe-deposit lockers. It so happens that the locker-holders, sometimes, complain that their locker had been opened by the bank and the contents misappropriated. Some banks entrust all the keys of the lockers to the locker-holders while some others give only one key to the locker-holders and the other key is kept in another branch of the bank. The purpose behind keeping one of the keys with the bank is to enable the bank to open the locker in case the key kept with the locker-holder is found missing. Any way, this system has created unnecessary problems between the locker-holders and the bank.

The locker can be opened only by two means—one by using a duplicate key or by using a genuine key. If duplicate keys were used, doubtlessly, the levers of the lock will surely show tool marks on it and it could prove that the locker was opened by using a duplicate key. If a genuine key is used, no such tool mark can be noticed.

Some banks give *pass-words* to the locker-holders and this *pass-word* is known only to the bank and the locker-holders.

Whenever the locker-holder wants to open the locker, he tells the *pass-word* to the manager who in turn allows him to open it in the presence of himself or an employee of the bank. The *pass-word* as a means of identification of the locker-holder has proved to be less effective as the *pass-word* can be leaked out by some way or other. Hence, the best method of making personal identification of the locker-holders coming to the bank to open the lockers, is to take their finger-prints (left thumb) whenever they are allotted the lockers. When the locker-holders come to the bank to open the locker, again the left thumb impression should be taken to make comparisons. On comparison, if the bank is satisfied with the identity of the locker-holder he can be permitted to open the locker. After opening the locker, the newly taken finger-impression should be pasted so well on the key-hole of the locker so that the locker-holder can verify whether or not the finger-impression has been disturbed by the use of a duplicate or genuine key. Hence, if the existing lockers do not have the provision to paste such finger-prints, it should be seen that such provisions are made so that there will not be any chances of disputes between the locker-holders and the bank-employees.

Inoperative Accounts and Frauds

There will be dormant or inoperative current/saving bank accounts. An employee with criminal tendencies may take note of these accounts and try to make fraudulent withdrawals of money by forging the signature of the dormant account holder. It goes without saying that the banks should make periodical verification of all account holders at least once in every five years and should see why the accounts remain dormant.

Cash and Credit Facility and Frauds

Cash and credit facility offered by the bank can result in colossal losses to the banks. Some times it so happens that some dishonest businessmen may obtain fictitious orders from distant places for their products. Such orders are backed by false bills and fictitious motor transport/railway receipts showing that the consignment had been despatched. Thus the cheat gets sizeable amount of money by way of credit from the bank. As soon as he receives the amount, he winds up the business and disappears.

Faulty Methods of Recruitment and Crimes

Allegations are levelled against some of the banks that large bribes are demanded and accepted even at the stage of selection of candidates to be employed in the banks. It should be remembered that anyone who joins the bank after having had to pay heavy bribe to someone involved either directly or indirectly in the process of recruitment can hardly be enthused to remain honest when he becomes a full-fledged officer in a bank. He will be looking forward to get an opportunity to make money by resorting to different modes of earning money and if he can be dishonest in his official transactions where he has to use his discretion, he may avail of the opportunity. Cases have been reported wherein some agents demanding bribe for sanctioning advances and loans to people. S.K. Ghosh in his book *Economic Offences* writes :

"An efficient and seemingly fool-proof system has been evolved by corrupt officials of the department and the office-bearers of the co-operative bank to get rich quick. As the loan realization period closes on 30 June every year, thousands of farmers, who are unable to pay the principal are offered fresh loans on 1 July. The amount comprises the principal and the interest on it. Many debtors willingly pay the interest because they are not asked to repay the principal and the interest is pocketed by office-bearers of co-operative banks, and supervisors of the co-operative department."

The banker should understand that if he accepts a gift in return for some special favour and the transaction is done in strict secrecy, it is nothing but bribery and corruption. After the nationalization of commercial banks in India, the bank officials also come under the purview of the operations of the Prevention of Corruption Act. Sections 161 and 165 of the Indian Penal Code 1860 and Section 5 (2) of the Prevention of Corruption Act. deal with taking of illegal gratifications in respect of official acts. The managers, agents and others employed in the bank should know the provisions of law regarding the acceptance of illegal gratifications.

Section 161, I.P.C.

Whoever, being or expecting to be a public servant, accepts or obtains or agrees to accept or attempts to obtain from any person, for himself or for any other person, any gratification whatever, other than legal remuneration, as a motive or reward for doing or forbearing to do any official act or for showing or forbearing to show, in the exercise of his official functions, favour or disfavour to any person, or for rendering or attempting to render any service or disservice to any person, with the Central or any State Government or Parliament or the Legislature of any State or with any local authority, Corporation, Government, Company referred to in section 21 or with any public servant, as such, shall be punished with imprisonment of either description for a term which may extend to three years, or with fine, or with both.

Explanations

Expecting to be a public servant : If a person not expecting to be in office obtains a gratification by deceiving others into a belief that he is about to be in office, and that he will then serve them, he may be gulity of cheating, but he is not guilty of the offence defined in this section.

Gratification : The word "gratification" is not restricted to pecuniary gratifications or to gratifications estimable in money.

Legal Remuneration : The words *legal remuneration* are not restricted to remuneration which a public servent can lawfully demand, but include all remuneration which he is permitted by the Government, which he serves to accept.

A motive or reward for doing : A person who receives a

gratification as a motive for doing what he does not intend to do, or as a reward for doing what he has not done, come within these words.

Section 165, I.P.C.

Whoever, being a public servant, accepts or obtains or agrees to accept or attempts to obtain for himself, or for any other person, any valuable thing without consideration, or for a consideration which he knows to be inadequate–

from any person whom he knows to have been, or to be, or to be likely to be concerned in any proceeding or business transacted or about to be transacted by such public servant, or having any connection with the official functions of himself or of any public servant to whom he is subordinate,

or from any person whom he knows to he interested in or related to the person so concerned,

shall be punished with imprisonment of either description for a team which may extend to three years or with fine or with both.

Section 5, Prevention of Corruption Act,[3] 1947

(1) A public servant is said to commit the offence of criminal misconduct in the discharge of his duty –

(a) If he habitually accepts or obtains or agrees to accept or attempts to obtain from any person for himself or for any other person, any gratification (other than legal remuneration) as a motive or reward such as is mentioned in section 161 of the Indian Penal Code;

(b) If he habitually accepts or obtains or agrees to accept or attempts to obtain for himself or for any other person, any valuable thing without consideration or for a consideration which he knows to have been or to be likely to be concerned in any proceeding or business transacted or about to be transacted by him, or having any connection with the official functions of himself or of any public servant to whom he is subordinate, or from any person whom he knows to be interested in or related to the person so concerned; or

(c) If he dishonestly or fraudulently misappropriates or otherwise converts for his own use any property entrusted to him or under his control as a public servant or allows any other person so to do; or.

(d) If he, by corrupt or illegal means or by otherwise abusing his position as a public servant, obtains for himself or for any other person any valuable thing or pecuniary advantage.

(2) Any public servant who commits criminal misconduct in the discharge of his duty shall be punished with imprisonment for a term which shall not be less than one year but which may extend to seven years and shall also be liable to fine.

The officers employed in banks are well paid in India and yet they become corrupt at times. When they become corrupt, they commit crimes just like a forger, a counterfeiter and a cheat. Nevertheless, they enjoy social status. Their desire for money, gift, material, gains and luxury in life makes them to indulge in the obnoxious practice of corruption. The high cost of living and the banker's fixed salary cannot be taken as an explanation or excuse for their criminal acts, if they indulge in the misuse of their official position for their personal advantage. Strict departmental as well as legal action should be initiated against officers who indulge in such practices.

Law and Crimes in Banks

The Indian laws about forgery, forgery of notes, counterfeiting of coins, cheating, etc. have been discussed earlier. The criminal laws that follow relate to offences against property given under Chapter XVII of the Indian Penal Code 1860. An understanding of these laws are important for the conduct of banking business, if safety is to be ensured.

Section 378, I.P.C. : Theft

"Whoever intending to take dishonestly any movable property out of the possession of any person without that person's consent, moves that property in order to such taking, is said commit theft.

Explanation l : A thing so long as it is attached to the earth, not being movable property, is not subject of theft, but it becomes capable of being the subject of theft as soon as it is severed from the earth.

Explanation 2 : A moving effected by the same act which effects the severance may be a theft.

Explanation 3 : A person is said to cause a thing to move by removing an obstacle which prevented it from moving or by separating it from other thing as well as by actually moving it.

Explanation 4 : A person, who by any means causes any animal to move is said to move that animal, and to move everything which, in consequence of the motion so caused, is moved by that animal.

Explanation 5 : The consent mentioned in the definition may be express or implied, and may be given either by the person in possession, or by any person having for that purpose authority either express or implied."

Illustration : If A, having pawned his watch to Z takes it out of Z's possession without Z's consent, not having paid what he borrowed on the watch, he commits theft, though the watch is his own property, in as much as he takes it dishonestly.

Section 383 I.P.C.: Extortion

"Whoever intentionally puts any person in fear of any injury to that person, or to any other and thereby dishonestly induces the person so put in fear to deliver to any person any property or valuable security, or anything signed or sealed which may be converted into a valuable security commits "extortion."

Illustration : A, by putting Z in fear of grievous hurt, dishonestly induces Z to sign or affix his seal on a blank paper and deliver it to A. Z signs and delivers the paper to A. Here, as the paper so signed may be converted into a valuable security, A has committed extortion.

Section 390 I.P.C. : Robbery

"In all robbery there is either theft or extortion. Theft is "robbery" if, in order to the committing of the theft, or in committing the theft, or in carrying way or attempting to carry away property obtained by the theft, the offender, for that end, voluntarily causes or attempts to cause to any person death or hurt, or wrongful restraint, or fear of instant death or of instant hurt, or of instant wrongful restraint.

Extortion is "robbery" if the offender, at the time of committing the extortion, is in the presence of the person put in fear, and commits the extortion by putting that person in fear of instant death, or of instant hurt, or of instant wrongful restraint to that person or to some other person, and, by so putting in fear, induces the person so put in fear then and there to deliver up the thing extorted.

Explanation : The offender is said to be present if he is sufficiently near to put the other person in fear of instant death, or of instant hurt, or of instant wrongful restraint."

Illustration

(a) A holds down, and fraudulently takes Z's money and jewels from Z's clothes, without Z's consent. Here A has committed theft, and, in order to the committing of that theft, has voluntarily caused wrongful restraint to Z. A has, therefore, committed robbery.

(b) A meets Z on the high road, shows a pistol, and demands Z's purse. Z, in consequence, surrenders his purse. Here A has extorted the purse from Z by putting him in fear of instant hurt, and being at the time of committing the extortion in his presence, A has, therefore committed robbery.

Section 391 I.P.C. : Dacoity

"When five or more persons conjointly commit or attempt to commit a robbery, or where the whole number of persons jointly committing or attempting to commit a robbery, and persons present and aiding such commission or attempt, amount to five or more, every person so committing, attempting or aiding is said to commit "dacoity."

Section 403 I.P.C. : Criminal Misappropriation of Property

"Whoever dishonestly misappropriates or converts to his own use any movable property, shall be punished with imprisonment of either description for a term which may extend to two years, or with fine, or with both.

Explanation 1 : A dishonest misappropriation for a time only is a misappropriation with in the meaning of this section.

Explanation 2 : A person who finds property not in possession of any other person, and takes such property for the purpose of protecting it for, or of restoring it to the owner, does not take or misappropriate it dishonestly, and is not guilty of an offence, but he is guilty of the offence above defined, if he appropriates it to his own use, when he knows or has the means of discovering the owner, or before he has used reasonable means to discover and give notice to the owner and has kept the property a reasonable time to enable the owner to claim it.

What are the reasonable means or what is a reasonable time in such a case, is a question of fact.

It is not necessary that the finder should know who is the owner of the property or that any particular person is the owner of it; it is sufficient if, at the time of appropriating it he does not believe it to be his own property, or in good faith believes that the real owner cannot be found."

Section 405 I.P.C. : Criminal Breach of Trust

"Whoever being in any manner entrusted with property, or with any dominion over property, dishonestly misappropriates or converts to his own use that property, or dishonestly uses or disposes of that property in violation of any direction of law prescribing the mode in which such trust is to be discharged, or of any legal contract, express or implied, which has made touching the discharge of such trust, or wilfully suffers any other person so to do, commits "criminal breach of trust."

Cheating under Section 415 I.P.C. is given in page 91 of this book.

Section 425 I.P.C. : Mischief

"Whoever, with intent to cause, or knowing that he is likely to cause, wrongful loss or damage to the public or to any person, causes the destruction of any property, or any such change in any property or in the situation thereof as destroys, diminishes its value or utility, or affects it injuriously, commits "Mischief."

Explanation 1 : It is not essential to the offence of mischief that the offender should intend to cause loss or damage to the owner of the property injured or destroyed. It is sufficient if he intends to cause, or knows that he is likely to cause, wrongful loss or damage to any person by injuring any property, whether it belongs to that person or not.

Explanation 2 : Mischief may be committed by an act affecting property belonging to the person who commits the act, or to that person and others jointly."

Illustration: A, voluntarily burns a valuable security belonging to **Z** intending to cause wrongful loss to **Z**. **A** has committed mischief.

Section 441 I.P.C. : Criminal Trespass

"Whoever enters into or upon property in the possession of another with intent to commit an offence or to intimidate, insult or annoy any person in possession of such property,

or having lawfully entered into or upon such property, unlawfully remains there with intent thereby to intimidate, insult or annoy any such person or with intent to commit an offence,

is said to commit "criminal trespass."

Section 442 I.P.C. reads :

"Whoever commits criminal trespass by entering into or remaining in any building, tent or vessel used as a human dwelling or any building used as a place for worship, or as a place for the custody of property, is said to commit "house trespass."

Explanation : The introduction of any part of the criminal trespasser's body entering is sufficient to constitute house-trespass"

Section 445 I.P.C. : House-breaking

"A person is said to commit house-breaking who commits house-trespass if he effects his entrance into the house or any part of it in any of the six ways hereinafter described; or if, being in the house or any part of it for the purpose of committing an offence, or, having committed an offence therein, he quits the house or any part of it in any of such six ways, that is to say–

First : If he enters or quits through a passage made by

himself, or by any abettor of the house-trespass, in order to the committing of the house-trespass.

Secondly : If he enters or quits through any passage not intended by any person, other than himself or an abettor of the offence, for human entrance; or through any passage to which he has obtained access by scaling or climbing over any wall or building.

Thirdly : If he enters or quits through any passage which he or any abettor of the house-trespass has opened, in order to the committing of the house-trespass by any means by which that passage was not intended by the occupier of the house to be opened.

Fourthly : If he enters or quits by opening any lock in order to the committing of the house-trespass, or in order to the quitting of the house after a house-trespass.

Fifthly : If he effects his entrance or departure by using criminal force or committing an assault or by threatening any person with assault.

Sixthly : If he enters or quits by any passage which he knows to have been fastened against such entrance or departure, and to have been unfastened by himself or by an abettor of the house-trespass.

Explanation : Any out-house or building occupied with a house, and between which and such house there is an immediate internal communication, is part of the house within the meaning of this section."

Illustration

(a) A commits house-trespass by making a hole through the wall of **Z**'s house and putting his hand through the aperture. This is house-breaking.

(b) A commits house-trespass by entering **Z**'s house through a window. This is house-breaking.

(c) Z, the door-keeper of **Y**, is standing in **Y**'s doorway. **A** commits house-trespass by entering the house having deterred **Z** from opposing him by threatening to beat him. This is house-breaking.

Notes

1. See John H. Horgans *Criminal Investigation*, New York, 2nd. ed., McGraw-Hill Book Company.
2. S.K. Ghosh, *Economic Offences*, Culcutta, Satchidanande Prakashani, 1977.
3. The 1947 Act is substituted by a new Act now.

References

Soderman, Harry, *Modern Criminal Investigation*, New York, Funk and Wagnalls, 1962.

Jones, Laland, *Scientific Investigation and Physical Evidence*, Illinois, Charles C. Thomas, 1959.

9

CUSTOMERS :
Their Psychology and Safety

Safety in banking and money transactions is becoming more and more important and complicated in the day-to-day functionings of commercial banks. While the banks are highly conscious of their security and also the security of their customers, it must not be forgotten that the ultimate objective of any bank is service to the people. An important aspect of the efficiency of a commercial bank is what is called the 'response-time'. This is the time taken by the bank to act on receipt of a cheque, a draft, a bill etc. A person who comes to bank to do a particular transaction naturally desires the banker to respond quickly to his need. He cannot tolerate any undue delay in the name of functional security. Therefore, the banker must remember that the customers, in general :

1. want immediate attention to their needs;
2. are not bothered about the difficulties and problems of the bankers;
3. are not forgers, counterfeiters, cheats, thieves and dacoits;
4. do not like to see that they are doubted or looked upon with suspicion;
5. express impatience in the delayed response-time;
6. get irritated at the slightest provocation from the bank; and expect desirable human qualities, like courtesy, decency, politeness, responsiveness, calmness, efficiency etc. from the bank.

Having borne in mind the above facts, the banker has to transact business with the customers. In his enthusiasm to guarantee functional security in banking and money transactions, the banker should never antagonize his customers. The success of any banking depends heavily on the wholehearted support and satisfaction which the bank derives from its customers. Therefore, any branch should have the following equipments to ensure speedy response-time. Such equipments include the following :

1. Hand Magnifiers

A linear magnification of about four times will be more than enough in most of the documents/cheque examination. A magnifier which has a diameter of nearly two inches is recommended for the purpose. A trained officer in a bank can use this magnifier effectively to detect forgery, guidelines, overwriting, etc. with very little time spent on it.

2. Illuminated Magnifiers

If the bank can provide a hand-magnifier with an illuminating system built into the handle, the flash-lamp bulb in the system can be directed to the object of examination. Illuminated magnifires which work on dry battery are available in the market. If the lighting is poor, these magnifiers are of considerable use while examining documents/ cheques in banks.

3. Microscopes

Stereoscopic microscope, compound microscope, comparison microscope, etc. are good devices in document/cheque examinations. They are, no doubt, very costly and as such cannot be provided to every branch. Hence, it is suggested that every bank should have a Central/Regional Document Examination Laboratory at the head quarters/regional offices. The management of the bank should bear in mind that some documents are not always what they appear to be, particularly so when documents are submitted to the banks for getting heavy loans sanctioned. Well qualified document experts are now available and the banks may not find it difficult to get the services of trustworthy document examiners. These examiners will be able to assist the banks whenever necessary or large sums of money are transacted on the basis of documents or whenever the branches of the bank have serious doubts about a cheque, draft, bill, etc. It is a sad state of affairs that most of our banks in India, in spite of their affluence, do not take adequate advantage of scientific document examinations. Document examination has now developed into such an extent that well-qualified document examiners use highly sophisticated techniques for analysis. A few training colleges in India impart instructions to their officers and clerks regarding forgery, erasure, overwriting, handwriting, etc. It is necessary that the training curriculum of banks should be revised to include topics of document examination, forgery of money and other security measures for their trainees at various levels.

4. Measuring Apparatus

For general measurements of handwriting or typescripts, a metal scale (1 foot length) should be provided to every branch. Such a scale should be made of stainless steel and should have measurements both in inches and centimetres. At the end of the scale, there should be subdivisions–thirty sections of an inch with half millimetres on the metric scale. The scale can be used for rough measurements or the document, alignment errors in typescript, etc. More precise or sophisticated measurements, if necessary, should be undertaken by the Central/Regional Document Examination Laboratories. Such a laboratory may require the measuring microscopes, micrometer, screw-gauge, special scales, etc.

5. Ultraviolet Lamps

Every branch of a commercial bank should be provided with an ultraviolet (UV) lamp which are useful for the visual examination of documents/cheques. The UV light can reveal very important facts invisible to the naked eye. The light is used for detecting corrections, erasures, additions and also to differentiate and separate as well as establish colour contrasts of ink, pencil writing, paper, etc. What may appear to be similar or identical to the naked eye, often, shows difference when viewed under UV lamps. The UV radiation does not injure, affect or change the conditions of the documents and cheques. A portable UV lamp in a branch can invariably help the bank officer to examine cheques, drafts, etc. in a very speedy manner.

Every branch can also make arrangements for oblique lighting and also for examination under transmitted light. For the examination under oblique lighting, a lamp on an opaque shade held in a fitting can be used and for the second, a single 100 watt bulb backed up by a metal reflector will be more than enough. They are not at all expensive, and therefore every branch can make use of them. But, soft x-rays which can show up watermarks and any thinner places on the cheque/document (at the site of erasures) can be provided in the Central/Regional Laboratory.

6. Infra-red Radiation

Infra-red (IR) lamps are not very costly and they should be given to every branch of commercial banks. The IR radiations can bring out a writing which has been obliterated, i.e. erased by a rubber or by chemical methods. The radiation can show the overwriting and also sometimes decipher what had been written particularly on a partly charred document. Any branch of a commercial bank provided with the equipments given above and a trained officer/clerk can transact his business in a secure manner without any undue delay or reaction-time.

Photographer's Retouching Desks

A Photographer's Retouching Desk available in the branches can aid the banker to examine the documents in a more effective manner.

PSYCHOLOGY OF THE CUSTOMERS

If a banker is conscious about functional security without irritating the customers, he should have a basic understanding about human psychology in general and that of the forger, counterfeiter, thief etc. in particular. Every person who submits a counterfeit note, a forged cheque, a false draft, an erased document, will experience anxiety and mental conflicts. He desires very much to resolve his anxiety or mental conflicts and towards this end he may resort to every or all defence mechanisms to maintain his mental equilibrium/ homeostasis. Defence mechanisms are the escape mechanisms by virtue of which a person resolves or attempts to resolve his anxiety, frustrations or mental conflicts.

Often it so happens that a forger, a counterfeiter, or a thief, makes his own forecasts about the possible evil consequences of his act. No doubt, he experiences anxiety. The knowledge of the after-effects or the consequence of being caught guilty leads certainly to fear and anxiety of the consequences in the form of humiliation, loss of prestige or personal status, embarrassment, social stigma, etc. The fear and anxiety in a nefarious customer to a bank make him employ various defence mechanisms to save himself from the embarrassing situations. Such defence mechanisms can be : (1) rationalization, (2) projection, (3) compensation, (4) regression, (5) identification, (6) withdrawal, (7) tolerance, (8) aggression, and (9) repression. The defence or escape mechanisms can be seen among the offenders when a bank transact business with them. An understanding of some of these mechanisms will surely help the banker adopt an appropriate attitude to people and situations.

1. Rationalization

Rationalization is a defence mechanism by virtue of which an individual resolves or tries to resolve his frustrations or mental conflicts by offering a good reason and not the correct reason. The story of *the fox and grapes* is an example to this. The fox, when it felt frustrated as it did not get the grapes, tried to resolve its frustration by telling 'grapes are sour'. It offered a good reason and not the correct reason. Likewise, in a bank, for instance, the banker tells the customer :

The banker : The signature on this cheque does not show similarity with the signature on the specimen card.

The customer : It was signed in a very hasty manner.

Here, the cheque may, on close examination, prove to be a simulated or free-hand forgery. But the forger tries to give a good reason–hasty execution in signing–and not the correct reason. Hence, when a forger is questioned under suspicious circumstances, one should never accept everything he tells. Think that he is likely to rationalize and convince the banker.

2. Projection

Projection is an escape mechanism by virtue of which an individual resolves or tries to resolve his conflicts by externalizing his thoughts, feelings and activity by projecting his needs, wishes or desires to some other. A forger/counterfeiter may refuse to recognize his faults and deficiencies or even disown his demerits by blaming others. For example, a bank employee may blame his colleague seated near to him for his failure to detect a counterfeit currency note. A forger may accuse of the bank clerk for slackness and lethargy to see that the bundle of notes is counted fast.

3. Compensation

A person by this defence mechanism called compensation attempts to overcome his anxiety by resorting to various methods of compensating his defects. His anxiety may be closely associated with his guilt feeling. A customer who is a cheat may compensate his weakness by pretending to be scrupulously honest. When he approaches for a loan, he may compensate his pauperism by showing himself as rich, i.e. by coming in a foreign car, by smoking foreign cigarettes or by wearing a costly watch. The banker should be fully conversant with various methods of compensation so that he is not cheated.

4. Regression

People, psychologists think, attempt to reduce their guilt feelings and anxiety through their psychological return to earlier and more primitive forms of behaviour. Every person progresses through a series of developmental stages in his personality growth and he returns to any one of such earlier stages when he experiences mental conflicts. For example, among adults, we see them weeping (particularly women) when they face acute problems. Instead of weeping, some may bite their nails. When a cheat or a forger smells the possibility of being detected, he may start smoking cigarettes or beedies to resolve his anxiety, Chain-smoking may be the expression of oral regression. Some people may show keen interest in urination when they face anxiety and conflicts.

5. Identification

This is a mental mechanism resorted to by some people when they face mental conflicts/irustrations by identifying themselves with superior persons, institutions or ideals. A person who is poor may identify himself with richer people by wearing costly garments. Some people who want to impress upon others may speak in English when vernacular can be used. Likewise, people may come to a bank with a few 100-rupees notes in their pocket in such a way that they can be seen by others. They may come with gold ornaments, the intention being that they should be seen by others.

Immediately after coming to the bank, some people may go to the manager's room, pull out the chair to sit and smoke costly cigarettes and offer them to the manager. They may speak of the VIPs in the locality and try to impress upon the manager that they are all friends to them. They may surrender their cheques to the manager in person and it may be a calculated attempt to see that their cheques are not meticulously examined by the clerk who works under the manager. They may entrust a bundle of notes to the manager with an aim in mind that the amount should be counted only on a casual way.

6. Withdrawal

Here the individual realizes that his goal is not attainable. The moment he understands that he is in trouble, he tries to escape from the scene. Offenders who come to the banks are of two types: (1) the first offenders; and (2) the repeaters. The first offender will usually exhibit more anxiety and as such he may show symptoms of neurosis. He is clever enough to quit the place. The repeater may not be showing intense anxiety just like the first offender. But realizing the danger, he too may retire from the scene. Therefore, it is to the safety and advantage of the bank to note down a vivid description of the offenders before the bank starts questioning them. The offenders should be entertained by the bank and in the meantime, the police should be contacted. This technique should be invariably be adopted when counterfiet money is detected.

7. Tolerance

In tolerance, the offender, realizing that he cannot achieve his goal, tolerates. For example, he may say, 'Well, if you cannot do it, give it back to me. I will go to another bank.' He resorts to this technique knowing fully well that be is in for danger. Tolerance is said to be a healthy approach in resolving mental conflicts, but here he resorts to it as a means of withdrawal. The fact should be intimated to the police and till that time he should be entertained.

8. Aggression

Some offenders, knowing that they are not going to realize their goals, exhibit aggressive symptoms. They may, to begin with, enter into verbal abuse and may culminate in snatching away the forged document or currency note. If they fail in their attempts, they may even make an attempt to physically assaulting the banker. This is an extreme step and is not often resorted to as the offender knows that he is not going to win the case if such extreme steps are taken.

When an individual resorts to aggression, he reacts to the situation in an emotional way and may even destroy the goal. He takes a hostile attitude. When hostility and anger come to the picture, destruction may be the outcome.

9. Repression

Some offenders, to resolve their tension, may put back their complexes, instincts and needs which are not wanted/desired or which threaten their normal adjustment with the environment. The offenders control their troublesome urges and impulses by repression.

Banks, though they deal with money and documents, do not enjoy authority and power to question suspicious characters. This indeed is a delicate state of affairs and therefore the banks have to be extremely cautious when transacting business with customers. They see to it that their behaviour does not affect their business and put their customers in difficulties. Instances have been reported that some officers employed in banks do not bother about reporting even cases of forged currency notes as they are not prepared to take up the botheration connected with the investigation of cases by the police. This attitude should never be encouraged.

Criminal Psychology

The banker will find that a thorough knowledge about psychology of criminals – particularly those who commit crimes in banks–is one of the basic requirements for the conduct of banking transactions in the contemporary times. An individual who commit a crime intentionally against banking is presumed to commit the same after exercising his freedom of will in the choice of the offence. He finds out good reasons for his commission of the crime. When caught, he may say that the cheque was forged because he wanted to purchase food for his children or to pay a bill in the hospital. If he is handed over to the police, he may make a confession of his guilt followed by rationalizing his act. Unlike the above category of criminals, there are professional criminals who know and fully realize all the implications of their criminal acts in the bank. They are very intelligent people and commit the crime in a neat and business like manner. Those who come to the banks with forged currency notes, knowing that there are forged ones in the bundle, belong to this category. They are efficient and well-trained in their commission of the crime. Such people are indeed hard nuts to crack not only by the banker but also by the police. *Modus operandi* of such criminals are of importance.

Here the banker should be aware of the questioning methods and techniques of eliciting truths from the suspects. He can very well use *direct method* of questioning. If the banker is sure or almost sure about the guilt of the culprit, he should assume an air of confidence in the customer's guilt. By his attitude and mannerisms, the banker should give the customer a feeling that his criminal intention is detected and he is not in any way innocent. He can calmly point out the implications if the guilt is proved. The banker should be sympathetic towards the offender and should say that it is to his advantage that he tells the truth. If the banker is convinced of the guilt of the offender, the *direct method* of questioning the customer pays well even with professional criminals.

On the other hand, if the banker has only a suspicion about the commission of crime by the customer, i.e., the guilt is indicated with something less than reasonable certainty, he should question the suspect by using *indirect method* of eliciting truths. Whatever may be the method of eliciting the truth, the banker should be able to appreciate the symptoms of guilt from the customer when he is being questioned. The symptoms may be physical, emotional, psychological or a combination of all.

The physical manifestations are the increased perspiration, paleness of the skin, increase in pulse rate, drying of mouth and tongue, excessive swallowing, change in respiration rate, etc. Licking the lips, tics on face, excessive smoking, stuttering, blurred speech, etc. are other physical symptoms during questioning.

Emotionally, the guilty customer will become nervous and anxious. He may exhibit fear, anger, visible efforts to reestabilish his homeostasis, delicacy to look at the banker's face, long pauses to reply questions and hesitations. There will be attempts on the part of the guilty customer to lie, to lie successively and to lie successfully. In his attempts to lie, the physical, emotional and mental symptoms are visible.

Lying is said to be the oft-resorted defence mechanism of the forgers, counterfeiters and cheats. They may plead innocence, for, they know that their integrity and credibility are otherwise doubted by the banker. They do not want to cause the least suspicion in the banker and as such they try to be innocent in the whole transactions. If more questions are asked, they may get angry and the anger is often found to be a defence mechanism. In such instances the banker may ask him why he gets angry if he is innocent in the whole affair.

The banker should always remember that he is to question the customer just to rebut the suspicion formed against him. He is not supposed to question the customer as a police officer or a detective may interrogate. Therefore, the customer should invariably be questioned in private, i.e., in secret so that he is likely to confess the guilt. No guilty person likes to make a public confession of his guilt. When a customer is questioned by the banker he should try to *induce*– meaning to influence the suspect customer by motivating him to admit the guilt. The inducement should never be in the form of accusations. When inducing the customer to accept his guilt, it is advisable to have no one else in the room. Once he accepts the guilt, he can be dealt with as per law and in spite of sincere attempts to induce him to accept the guilt, he refuses to admit his guilt, the banker may hand him over to the police or deal with him as per the standing orders of the bank.

The banker, while inducing the customer to admit his guilt should never forget that ultimately his is a business enterprise and therefore assuming a police role while questioning is not only unwarranted but also is dangerous. There may be cases in which the customer is an innocent possessor of forged notes. Hence, the banker should be calm, decent, sympathetic and considerate to the innocent victims of criminal action. While questioning the customer:

1. ask only one question at a time. Ask the next question only after he has answered the first ore;

2. raise brief, clear, simple and concise questions. He should not be confused during the inducement;
3. never try to make the customer emotional by the use of 'repulsive' words.
4. never threaten the customer. Avoid arguing with him There should not be any personality clashes. Never degrade yourself in your acts and words.

While inducing the customer in a room away from the visibility of others is recommended, it should be borne in mind that women customers should be induced only in the presence of another woman if the inducement is done in private by a male personnel. This is a percautionary measure against her later attacks on the banker with respect to his sexual decency and integrity.

Every banker should have a thorough training in the science of transactional analysis and psychology of inducement so that he can assume the ego-states which may be necessitated during his inducement to the customer to admit the guilt. If the customer seems to be an innocent one, the circumstances under which the forged currency notes, forged cheques, erased document, etc. came to his possession should be ascertained. Hence, the banker has to keep away all his prejudices against the customer. He should explain to him the problems he may face in case the forged document/currency note is honoured by the bank.

A FEW DON'TS TO BANKERS

The following don'ts are important for ensuring safety in banks :

1. Don't leave your counter or office unattended during business hours. Articles such as fountain pens, handbags, cheques, unwritten cheque-leaves and similar items are easily stolen by people who have criminal tendencies.
2. Don't defraud your employer. Remember that any effort on your part, successful or otherwise, to obtain some special benefit for yourself in a deceitful and dishonest manner is quite

unbecoming, degrading and immoral.

3. Don't keep the keys of the bank in a conspicuous place upon a table, or under the table clothes, or in the drawer of your table. Keep them in the safest way possible.
4. Don't permit a stranger to the cash counter unless he is watched closely by the security. If a stranger moves in a suspicious manner, he should be asked for the purpose of his visit.
5. Don't allow the customers to leave their handbags or wallet on the visitors' seats. There is a likelihood of these being lost when they come after their business transactions at the counter. Ask them to carry them wherever they move unless there is special security arrangements made in the bank to keep them in the custody of an employee of the bank.
6. Don't allow the customers to leave their valuable property in a conspicuous way in their cars if cars are not fitted with a steering lock. Cases are reported that cars with locked doors are stolen.
7. Don't permit one and the same person to open more than one account in fictitious names to show increase in deposit or to reach the target soon. By this, you encourage a person to forge the signature of a fictitious person.
8. Don't think that the documents submitted to the bank are always what they are represented to be. The crime of forgery is perhaps as old as the writing itself.
9. Don't think that all criminals are suspicious; looking; or all customers are criminals.
10. Don't leave the draft-book and other important ledgers accessible to all employees in the bank. There may be a person with criminal tendencies among you.
11. Don't allow a customer to carry a large sum of money with him. If he must, then ask him to carry it under proper security.
12. Don't accept the passbooks and retain them with you to make the entries. Make the entries then and there and entrust them to the customers. If you are very busy on that day, ask them to bring them on another day.

13. Don't count the money and pass the cheques under insufficient light or candlelight. It is dangerous to do so for the employees and safe for the forger to get things done.
14. Don't hesitate to entrust a counterfeiter of money to the police even when you are sure that he is an innocent possessor of fake money. The police will be able to prevent further flow of false notes into your banks.
15. Don't leave the scene of crime unguarded if the bank has been made a target of crime and never permit curious spectators to enter the scene until the police come and take charge of it.
16. Don't accept gifts, offers and other materials from the customers. They may be doing a charity with a hook.
17. Don't think that all your friends and relatives are honest people or they will not do something which is detrimental to your interest. They also should be dealt with just like any other customers. Remember that you are dealing with the money of the bank and not yours.
18. Don't try to 'interrogate' a customer suspected to have committed a crime. Try to induce him to accept his guilt. If he does not plead guilty, entertain him until the police take charge of him.
19. Don't think that yours is the only bank in the locality. There may be others too. But yours must be one where maximum caution is taken–maximum service is rendered

A little foresight saves a lot of heartbreak

Observation and Description of Customers

Observation means a purposeful looking, i.e., forming a precise and clear mental picture of the observed. One needs not *observe* all customers to the bank, nevertheless he should *observe* those who are suspicious-looking. A banker should develop the habit of minutely observing the people, their conduct and actions, and his security staff should be specially trained as good observers. They should develop their ability to observe and describe people who are suspicious-looking. When they describe people, the one who listens to them should be able to form a clear mental picture of the persons described.

How to Observe the Customers?

Observe a person—systematically or methodologically—from his head and progress to the feet. The following is the recommended listing of what to observe :

1. **Sex :** male, female.
2. **Age :** estimate the approximate age and you can say—between 20 and 25, 25 and 30, 30 and 35, and so on.
3. **Religion :** appears to be a Christian, Hindu, Muslim, Sikh, Parsi, etc. There may be indicators to show the religion.
4. **Caste :** Caste can be decided from the manner of dress. dialects, etc.
5. **State :** Keralite, Tamilian, Maharashtrian, Punjabi, Bengali, etc. This can be decided from the language spoken, manners, dress, etc.
6. **Region :** North of Kerala, south of Tamil Nadu, east of Maharashtra, west of Bengal, north of Uttar Pradesh, coastal area, mountain area, etc. This can be decided from the colour, language, dress, etc.
7. **Place of residence :** urban, semi-urban, rural, etc. This can be judged from the dress, manners, conversation, etc.
8. **Occupation :** can be decided by guessing. Can also go wrong.
9. **Height :** approximately estimate this by comparison with own height.
10. **Weight :** approximately estimate this by comparison with own weight.
11. **Build :** stout, lean, large, very large, medium, etc.

12. **Posture :** erect, stooping, hunchback, normal, head-up.
13. **Complexion :** dark, black, oily black, fair, wheat coloured, sallow, etc.
14. **Hair :** hippy-like, thick growth, bald, partly bald, thin, curly, grey, black, partly grey, cut, wavy, etc.
15. **Beard :** long, short, arranged well like Sikhs, or cut well, French beard etc.
16. **Mustache :** size, shape, pointed, well-cut, turned-up, drooping, police-mustache, etc.
17. **Hair :** hair-dyed or not, recently dyed, well-cut, not cut, well-combed, not combed, long, short, etc., and with women their style of hairdress.
18. **Forehead :** high, low, bulging, receding, narrow, wide, any religious marks, etc.
19. **Eyes :** Protruding, sunken, partly sunken, Manipuri type, squinted, cat's eye, size of the iris —small, large, medium, etc.
20. **Eyebrows :** Slanting up or down, bushy, plucked, arched, wavy, horizontal, connected, grey, partly grey, heavy, thin texture, penciled, long, short, etc.
21. **Nose :** Small or large, nose-rings, pierced, straight, flat, broken, large nostrils, small nostrils, growth of hair in the nostrils, skewed right or left, etc.
22. **Mouth :** large, small, drooping corners, upturned corners, lipsticks applied, any distortion when speaks or laughs, foul smell when speaks, etc.
23. **Lips :** thick, thin, puffy, drooping lower, upturned upper, protruding, etc.
24. **Teeth :** Arrangement, large, small, prominent, protruding, colour, pan-eater, heavy smoker, tooth missing, false tooth, dental work, etc.
25. **Ears :** hair growth, large, small, pierced, ear-rings or ornaments, close to head, wide opening, cauliflower appearance, etc.

26. **Chin** : small, large, square, triangular, double, jutting, flat, etc.
27. **Face** : round, square, long, sunken cheeks, prominent checkbones, pimples, visible identification marks, etc.
28. **Neck** : thick, thin, long, short puffed, back-folds, hair growth at the back of the neck, prominent Adam's apple, ornaments, gold chains, religious marks or symbols, etc.
29. **Shoulders** : square, narrow, one shoulder higher than the other, broad, sloping, round, etc.
30. **Stomach** : pot-belly, flat, bulging, etc.
31. **Hands** : long, short, large, small, etc.
32. **Walk** : fast, slow, bouncy, sloping, sailor's gait, lameness, etc.
33. **Identifying marks** : any visible marks of identification.
34. **Fingers and toes** : missing, abnormality like six fingers etc.
35. **Dress** : nature of cloth, nature of stitching, colour, dhoti, pants, jubba, modern, old, etc.
36. **Hair style and dress style in women** : should be noted specially.
37. **Jewellery in women** : should be clearly described.
38. **Slippers, shoes** : model, old or new, etc.
39. **Habits** : pan-eater, smoker etc.
40. **Tics and mannerisms**
41. **Disabilities**.
42. **Any other peculiarities.**

If the banker cannot say clearly about something, he needs not bother much about it. Observation means, as stated earlier, a purposeful looking to describe something or somebody precisely, accurately and completely. A little training can make oneself quite competent in observing persons and things. If necessary, he should write them down so that whenever they are needed, such description will be of great use.

References

Andra, Evans, The Investigator in Court, from *Criminal and Civil Investigation Hand Book*, by Joseph J. Grauied., New York, Mc Graw Hill Book Company, 1981.

Bingham, M.V. and B.V. Moore, *How to Interview,* New York, Prentice-Hall, 1950.

Garrelt, Annelte, *Inrerviewing : Its Principles and Methods*, New York Family Welfare Association, 1962.

Larson, John, A. *Lying and Its Detection*, Chicago, University of Chicago Press, 1932.

Mulbar, H., *Interrogation*, Springfield, C. Thomas, 1951.

10

CRIMES IN BANKS : Investigation and Prosecution

When a crime has been committed in the bank or in its vicinity, the banker has to be extremely careful in every step so that a proper investigation of the crime can be conducted by the police. A crime scene, in simple terms, is the location where the offence took place. Technically speaking, a scene of crime means the place or places where material evidence to prove the crime can be located. There may be cases in which crime scenes are not available. For, in such cases no material evidence can be found out if at all an inspection is conducted there. For example, in a case of forgery of a cheque in a bank, a scene of crime will not be there and in such instances it is called the scene of occurrence of crime, i.e., a place where the crime has taken place. The offender may have forged the cheque in the compartment of a train and therefore it is futile to conduct an inspection of the scene in the bank as there may not be any physical evidence available in the bank. On the contrary, if a burglary has taken place in a bank, there is a scene of crime and in which case the banker has to protect the scene from being contaminated until the police come and take charge of the scene.

How to Protect the Scene?

Every banker has to take the following precautions to see that the material evidence available at the scene of crime is not disturbed.

For this purpose, he should :

1. take a careful stock of the situation;
2. isolate the scene of crime and guard it;
3. prevent trespassing into the scene by all people including those employed in the bank;
4. disallow anything at the scene of crime to be moved or in any other way interferred with;
5. note down the names and addresses of the suspects in the crime and the names and addresses of the witnesses to the incident, if there are, for entrusting to the police; and
6. keep a watch over all people gathered around and listen to all passing remarks made by them; never allow anyone to introduce fresh materials like cigarette butts, cigarette ash, footprints, etc. at the scene of crime.

PRINCIPLES OF SCENE INSPECTION

Every banker should have a basic knowledge of the principles of inspection of a scene of crime in criminal investigation. This will surely aid him to take adequate precautionary measures to protect a scene of crime.

1. Locard's Principle of Exchange

The principle is that when two things come into contact there is always an exchange of materials. The more the contact, the more will be the exchanged traces. According to this principle when a burglar or his instrument comes into contact with anybody/anything/any place, there is always an exchange of traces between the criminal/his instrument and the person/thing/place. The police are interested in collecting the exchanged traces and that is why the banker is advised to see that the scene of crime is not disturbed or contaminated.

Examples

1. If a burglar enters the bank through a ventilator, he may leave his footprints on the sill.
2. A burglar who opens a safe by an explosive leaves the area around with the clothes covered with insulating material as well as some exploded and unexploded substances.

2. Quatlet's Law of Individuality

The law is that nothing created by God or made by man is ever identical. In other words : 'Every object natural or manmade has an individuality which is not duplicated in any other object'. The banker, therefore, should realize that identification is an important aspect in crime investigation. In a bank burglary, the criminal, his associates, tools used, the *modus operandi* etc. will have to be identified. It is for identifying these things that he is instructed not to damage the scene of crime by entry of unwanted people into the scene of crime.

3. Law of Progressive Change

Everything changes with the passage of time and the rate of change varies with different objects. The change can take place in people, articles and places. Hence, the banker should see to it that the crime is immediately reported to the police so that the latter can conduct an inspection of the scene of crime before any *change* takes place. For example, the finger-prints, foot-prints, etc. at the scene of crime may be contaminated or destroyed if delay takes place for the police to come and inspect the scene of crime. Police dogs may not be of much use as the smell of the culprit is not likely to last long on physical clues. The burglary-tools may acquire additional surface patterns if they have been used after committing the crime. Hence, in course of time the physical evidence may lose all their practical utility and identity if delay takes place between the commission of the crime and the inspection of the scene of crime by the police.

Types of Physical Evidence

The banker should understand that finger-prints of the criminal are likely to be seen in the doors, windows, knobs and handles, glass-panes, polished surfaces, safes and locks. They can also be located on tumblers, plates, saucers, bottles, cups, spoons, utensils, boxes, furniture, rexine, plastic goods, purses, bags, letters, currency notes, tools, weapons of offence, etc.

Documents such as account books, cheques, receipts, bills, files, letters, applications, forms, etc. may have to be required for examination. Exploded products, fuses, tins, explosives, devices etc. may have to be collected. Thus, the list is endless and that is why crime scene should under no circumstances be permitted to be disturbed or contaminated by unwanted people.

How to Report a Crime to the Police?

A report can be filed to the police under section 154 Criminal Procedure Code,1973. The section reads :

> Every information relating to the commission of a cognizable offence if given orally to an officer-in-charge of a police station, shall be reduced to writing by him or under his direction and be read over to the informant and every such information, whether given in writing or reduced to writing as aforesaid, shall be signed by the person giving it and the substance thereof shall be entered in a book to be kept by such officer in such manner as the State Government may prescribe in this behalf.
>
> A copy of the information as recorded under sub-section(1) shall be given forthwith, free of cost to the informant.

The banker should know that the facts contained in the report relate to the first information in point of time of a cognizable offence to an officer-in-charge of a police station and as such its importance lies in the fact that it is presumed to be an untutored, unplanned and unthought out version of the incident just as it reaches the police and therefore the F.I.R. is admissible in evidence to corroborate or contradict its maker.

It seems that there is a tendency among the first informants to give an exaggerated version regarding the commission of an offence. This should not be there. The banker should file a factual and honest report to the police. After getting the F.I.R. recorded by the police, the banker should request the police to read the report and then only he should put his signature.

Cognizable and Non-Cognizable Offences

The offences committed in banks are mostly cognizable offences and they mean offences in which a police officer may in accordance with the First Schedule of the Criminal Procedure Code 1973 or under any other law for the time being in force arrest the culprit without warrant and logically it follows that non-cognizable offences are those in which a police officer cannot arrest the criminal without a warrant from a magistrate. Offences committed in the banks are serious ones and the following schedule shows the offences indicating whether or not they are cognizable under the Indian law :

	Offences under the Indian Penal Code, 1860	*Whether Cognizable or Not*
1.	*Section 161* : Being or expecting to be a public servant and taking gratification, other than legal remuneration in respect of an official act.	Cognizable
2.	*Section 162* : Taking gratification in order, by corrupt or illegal means, to influence a public servant.	Cognizable
3.	*Section 165* : Public servant obtaining any valuable thing, without consideration from a person concerned in any proceeding or business transacted by such public servant.	Cognizable
4.	*Section 231* : Counterfeiting, or performing any part of the process of counterfeiting coin.	Cognizable
5.	*Section 232* : Counterfeiting or performing any part of the process of counterfeiting Indian coin.	Cognizable
6.	*Section 239* : Having any counterfeit coin known to be such when it came into possession, and delivering, etc the same to any person.	Cognizable

7.	*Section 241* : Knowingly delivering to another any counterfeit coin as genuine, which when first possessed, the deliverer did not know to be counterfeit.	Cognizable
8.	*Section 243* : Possession of Indian coin by a person who knew it to be counterfeit when he became possessed thereof.	Cognizable
9.	*Section 379* : Theft.	Cognizable
10.	*Section 380* : Theft in a building, tent or vessel.	Cognizable
11.	*Section 381* : Theft by clerk or servant of property in possession of master or employer.	Cognizable
12.	*Section 384* : Extortion.	Cognizable
13.	*Section 385* : Putting or attempting to put in fear of injury in order to commit extortion.	Cognizable
14.	*Section 386* : Extortion by putting a person in fear of death or grievous hurt.	Cognizable
15.	*Section 387* : Putting or attempting to put a person in fear of death or grievous hurt in order to commit extortion	Cognizable
16.	*Section 392* : Robbery.	Cognizable
17.	*Section 393* : Attempt to commit robbery.	Cognizable
18.	*Section 394* : Person voluntarily causing hurt in committing or attempting to commit robbery, or any other person jointly concerned in such robbery.	Cognizable
19.	*Section 395* : Dacoity.	Cognizable
20.	*Section 397* : Robbery or dacoity with attempt to cause death or grievous hurt.	Cognizable
21.	*Section 398* : Attempt to commit robbery or dacoity when armed with deadly weapon.	Cognizable
22.	*Section 406* : Criminal breach of trust.	Cognizable
23.	*Section 408* : Criminal breach of trust by a clerk or servant.	Cognizable
24.	*Section 408* : Criminal breach of trust by a public servant or by a banker, merchant or agent.	Cognizable
25.	*Section 417* : Cheating.	Non-Cognizable
26.	*Section 419* : Cheating by personation.	Cognizable
27.	*Section 420* : Cheating and thereby dishonestly inducing delivery of property, or the making alteration or destruction of a valuable security.	Cognizable
28.	*Section 447* : Criminal trespass.	Cognizable

29.	*Section 448* : House trespass.	Cognizable
30.	*Section 451* : House-trespass in order to the commission of an offence punishable with imprisonment for life.	Cognizable
31.	*Section 452* : House trespass in order to the commission of an offence punishable with imprisonment.	Cognizable
32.	*Section 453* : Lurking house-trespass or house-breaking.	Cognizable
33.	*Section 456* : Lurking house-trespass or house-breaking by night.	Cognizable
34.	*Section 461* : Dishonestly breaking open or unfastening any closed receptacle containing or supposed to contain property.	Cognizable
35.	*Section 465* : Forgery.	Non-Cognizable
36.	*Section 467* : Forgery of a valuable security, will or authority to make or transfer any valuable security, or to receive any money, etc.	Non-Cognizable
37.	*Section 468* : Forgery for the purpose of cheating.	Cognizable
38.	*Section 471* : Using as genuine a forged document which is known to be forged.	Cognizable
39.	*Section 489* : (A) Counterfeiting currency notes or bank-notes.	Cognizable
40.	*Section 489* : (B) Using as genuine forged or counterfeit currency or bank-notes.	Cognizable
41.	*Section 489* : (E) Making or using documents resembling currency notes or bank-notes.	Cognizable

Lodging the F.I.R. to the Police

The first information report (F.I.R.), as stated earlier, forms the basis of crime investigation. Hence, the banker should attempt to give an accurate, precise and concise but complete details of the occurrence of the crime to the police. The following information should be furnished, if possible, on all crimes reported to the police :

1.	Date and time of the occurrence of the crime	As far as possible the date and time of the occurrence of the crime should be accurate. If the exact time is uncertain, indicate the parameters, viz. between 9 p.m. and 10.30 a.m., etc.

2. Place of occurrence, distance and direction from the police station	The information regarding the place of occurrence should be furnished to the police by the banker in specific and precise manner. Of course the distance from the police station to the scene of occurrence can be approximate.
3. Full name, address and residence of the informant/complainant	The banker should give his temporary and permanent address to the police.
4. Name and residence of the accused/suspects	If the banker can name the accused and if he knows the addresses of the suspects/the accused, the names and addresses should be furnished.

How should the Offence be Described to the Police?

It should be borne in mind that there are certain technical aspects when the police record the F.I.R. In order to help the police record the F.I.R. in a perfect manner, the banker should cooperate with the police. They may ask a number of questions and all should be answered if one can. If you cannot, then be frank about it. There is nothing wrong to say 'I do not know'. Never mislead the police when you are questioned. If one and the same question is asked by the police officer several times, do not get irritated. It is necessary for initiating a good investigation. The questions usually asked by the police to the first informants are :

I.

1. What is the crime?
2. What is the reason for the commission of the offence?
3. What is the name of the suspect(s) in the crime?

4. What is the temporary/permanent address(es) of the suspect(s)?
5. What is the professional occupation of the suspect(s)?
6. What is the relationship with the suspect(s)?
7. What is the value of the articles stolen?
8. What is the method of committing the offence?
9. What is the reputation of the suspect(s)?

II.

1. Who else can be involved in the commission of the crime ?
2. Who has informed the crime to you? What is/are the reason(s) for the same?
3. Who has visited the scene of crime after the commission of the offence?
4. Who is the culprit?
5. Who were present at the scene of crime before, during or after the commission of the crime? If they have not seen the commission of the crime, why?
6. Who gave provocation first? What is the reason for the same?
7. Who was contacted by the informant after the crime has taken place? and why?
8. Who was behind the actual commission of the crime? Any abettors, etc.?
9. Who is the informant? Temporary and permanent addresses?

III.

1. Why did the crime take place?
2. Why did the culprit choose the particular spot, person, property, etc. as the target of his attack?
3. Why was the victim/witness(es) unable to identify the culprits?
4. Why does the informant prefer the information to police?
5. Why can't the victim prevent the commission of crime if he could at the time of committing the offence?
6. Why was the victim not taking precautions for safeguarding himself/his property?
7. Why was the information delayed to be reported to the policc?

8. Why did the perpetrator use the particular tools/weapons?
9. Why did the perpetrator use the particular means of entry?
10. Why did the perpetrator injure the victim?

IV.

1. Whose property is stolen
2. Whose brain is behind the commission of the offence?
3. Whose provocation was there for the commission of the offence?
4. Whose injury is serious – the victim's or offender's?
5. Whose name could be suggested as the possible offender?

V.

1. Where is the place of occurrence?
2. Where is/are the suspect(s) now? Where can he/they be located?
3. Where is the property? Where can it be found out?
4. Where is the victim now? Why?
5. Where did the perpetrator obtain tools and weapons from?
6. Where was the perpetrator last seen?
7. Where were the witnesses at the time of committing the offence?
8. Where were the informants at the time of committing the offence?
9. Where can the tools and weapons of offence be located?

VI.

1. When did the crime occur?
2. When did the informant come to know the incident? Why? If delay is seen, why?
3. When was the suspect seen in the vicinity of the scene of crime by witnesses?
4. When did the suspect leave the scene of crime?
5. When was the victim last seen alive and by whom?

6. When did the witnesses see the incident? When did the witnesses arrive and leave the scene?
7. When did the victim leave or was the victim removed from the scene?
8. When was the offence discovered?

VII.

1. Which are the pieces of evidence likely to be seen at the scene of crime?
2. Which are the pieces of evidence likely to have been destroyed?
3. Which are the methods likely to have been adopted by the culprit to conceal the crime?

VIII.

1. How did the crime occur?
2. How did the criminal approach the victim / the scene to commit the offence?
3. How did the criminal approach the victim /the scene to commit the offence?
4. How did the culprit escape the scene of crime after the commission of the crime?
5. How difficult or easy was it for the culprit to commit the crime?
6. How best can the crime be proved in the court of law?
7. How much is the loss? How is the loss estimated?
8. How much is the gain to the culprit? How is the gain estimated?
9. How far is the scene of crime from the police station?
10. How did the witnesses happen to be at the scene?
11. How did the perpetrator obtain the tools and weapons used?

The F.I.R. if filed before the police only in cognizable cases, and if the offence is a non-cognizable one, a complaint before a competent magistrate should be filed under section 190 of the Criminal Procedure Code 1973. While the information is preferred to the police and questions are asked by the latter, the banker should not think that he is being interrogated. No, it is not the purpose. All questions given in the above list will not be asked. Depending upon the nature of the offence and the type of the crime, the investigating officers will ask perhaps more questions other than what are given above. This is why it is advocated that the banker should personally file the report to the police.

Can the Banker Send a Telegramme or give a Telephonic Message to the Police?

Section 154 of the Criminal Procedure Code 1973 makes it mandatory for the informant to affix his signature/thumb impression on the F.I.R. Though the police officer can register a case *suo motu* on the basis of a telephone-message/telegramme-message provided he is convinced of the commission of a cognizable case, it is better that the banker goes to the police station to file an informantion regarding the commission of a cognizable offence.

More About Filing the F.I.R. by the Banker

Under no circumstances should the banker delay the filing of the first information after he has come to know of the commission of a cognizable crime in a bank. In *Thuliakall vs. State* (A.I.R. 1973 S.C. 501 Cr. L.J. 1260), it has been made clear by the Supreme Court that 'Delay in lodiging the F.I.R. quite often results in embellishment which is a creature of after-thought.' Hence, if delay in lodging the F.I.R. is there, the banker has to satisfactorily explain the reasons for the delay. Hence, 'undue or unreasonable delay in lodging the F.I.R., therefore, gives rise to suspicion which puts the court on guard to look for the possible motive and the explanation for the delay and consider its effect on the trustworthiness of the prosecution version' (*Apren Joseph vs. State of Kerala,* A.I.R. 1973 S.C.I., 1973 Cr. L.J. 185) and in *Kartar Singh vs. State of Punjab,* it has been observed by the Supreme Court that 'The F.I.R. was made very soon after the incident, and there is no justification for the argument that it discredits the statement of its maker (A.I.R. 1977, Cr. L.J. 214; A.I.R. 1977 S.C. 349).

Thus, if and when a crime takes place in a bank, the matter should be intimated to the police immediately so that speedy action can be initiated. Some bank officers seem to be quite reluctant to go to police, for, they want to avoid botheration connected with police investigation. Instances have come to notice that some employees in banks do not inform even cases wherein 'counterfeit money' has been detected by the bank. This attitude on the part of the bankers, if it exists, shows lack of civic-mindedness and citizen's responsibility. Not only so, it is a disservice done to the self, to the bank and to the society. The banker should co-operate with the police to keep the criminal out of business.

Criminal Prosecution : The Banker Before the Court

The banker should bear in mind that, once the F.I.R. is filed before police and when the investigation by the police is over, he will be summoned to the Court to give testimony. The conviction or acquittal of the case can considerably depend on the banker's ability to present facts, explain the incident etc. to the Court. Hence, when the banker is called to the Court, he must ask the following questions to himself and try to answer them one by one.

Questions

1. Who are the accused persons?
2. Who is the first accused and why?
3. Who responded to the first information?
4. Who questioned the informant when the case has been registered?
5. Who recorded the first information?
6. Who came to the scene of crime?
7. What has actually happened?
8. What damages were done to the bank?
9. What is the motive of the accused for committing the offence?

10. What is the delay between the occurrence of the incident and the report to the police? If delay is seen what is the reason for the delay?
11. When was the offence committed? – Hour? Day? Date? Month? and year?
12. When was the offence reported? – Hour? Day? Date? Month? and year?
13. When was the offence investigated? – Hour? Day? Date? Month? and year?
14. When did the culprit arrive at the scene? When did he leave the scene?
15. Why was the offence reported?
16. Why did the culprit use a particular *modus operandi* to commit the offence? Why did the culprit use a particular means of entry? Why did he use a particular tool or weapon ?
17. How did the accused arrive at the scene of crime? How did he leave the scene of crime?
18. Where was the informant at the time of committing the offence? Why?

These are a few questions which the banker should ask to himself. He can ask as many questions as possible and try to answer them so that he will prove to be successful when he is being examined or cross-examined in a court of law.

How to Give Testimony Before the Court

Giving testimony before the Court is a noble act of all civic-minded persons. Remember that the judges are also human beings and just like all other people, they too make their first impressions of others at the first sight, i.e., when the people walk into the court room and take the oath. Hence, the banker's walk and appearance— especially his actions and manners – should make the judge feel that the officer is there to perform a dignified job. Hence, the banker is advised :

1. to approach the witness-stand in a dignified manner – i.e., in a deliberate and unhurried way;
2. not to glare at the accused or the defence counsel;
3. to stand erect and to show a pleasing countenance;
4. not to be overconfident;
5. to give an impression to the judge that you are taking things with due seriousness and sincerity;
6. to take oath seriously, pronouncing each word in a clear and audible way;
7. to look at the Judge and wait patiently for the proceedings to begin;
8. not to make sounds or movements which are distracting. Clearing of throats, frequent crossing and uncrossing of arms, wiping the face always with towels and similar nervous mannerisms should be avoided;
9. to be truthful; tell the truth and nothing but the truth;
10. to answer the questions slowly and specifically using normal language. Don't try to be wiser than the Judge and never use a word or jargon that is not clearly known to the Judge.
11. to look always and everytime at the Judge. Answer all questions looking at and looking at the Judge only. The defence counsel may make attempts to confuse you; may show signs and facial expressions to fool you. Therefore, don't look at him so that his attempts will not have any impact on you. You need only your ears to hear him and need not see how he acts or performs his rituals in the court;
12. not to answer the questions without understanding the full meaning and implications. If the question is not clearly understood, ask the counsel to repeat it;
13. ask the lawyer to repeat the questions if he is consciously or purposefully asking lengthy questions. The same procedure can be resorted to if he is asking questions in an angry tone. In such instances, more often than not, the lawyer will not be able to

repeat the questions with the same vigour he had when he asked the first. This will, sometimes, put him in a confusion as to the question itself;

14. to answer the questions in a loud tone—but with due politeness and courtesy;

15. to ask the counsel to explain what he actually means by a question which he has put in a confusing manner. This is likely to confuse the lawyer himself;

16. to think well before answering. A pause before answering a question proves to be always rewarding and good. Slow answers give the impression that the answers are believable. "If you respond slowly enough to consider your thoughts before speaking, your testimony is enhanced. Speaking hurriedly can result in the misunderstanding of testimony, because words were slurred, answers were improperly phrased, or the question was misinterpreted. Before replying, wait until you are sure that the question has been completed. Answering before the question is completed may be perceived as eagerness to help your side of the case or, on cross examination, an attempt to avoid a difficult question. Adopt a deliberate pace, but avoid speaking so slowly as to cause your listeners to doubt your testimony";[1]

17. not to volunteer information unless called for. If it is very necessary and unavoidable, then it can be done. Remember that an information which is not asked for is almost certain to be objected to;

18. to remember that hearsay evidence is not made admissible in Indian Law. Hence, in replying to questions, never say things that someone else told you or you heard it from somebody else speaking to another. State only those facts and information about which you have personal knowledge. Such phrases like : *I must like to say, I am to think, I must believe* or *I am of opinion* etc. must be avoided. What you know is more important and relevant than what you think or believe to be true. You are not summoned to give an opinion in the court;

19. not to be worried very much if you commit a mistake while

giving testimony. Recognize the mistake at the earliest and acknowledge the same. In this context Andre Evans writes, "The simple statement that you have made a mistake and would like to correct it is far better than having your entire testimony discredited later. If you have not recognised your mistake, but it becomes apparent, perhaps, during cross-examination, admit it. It is better to acknowledge an error than to adamantly maintain a position that is plainly wrong and thereby discredit your entire testimony";[2]

20. to remember that no one will be able to make accurate estimate of the distance, height, weight etc. unless he has actually measured them or verified through measuring instruments. The same is the case with time, speed, depth, slope etc. Being not exact in such matters simply proves that you are honest in your testimony;
21. to know that the defence lawyer is likely to interrupt the prosecutor when you are being examined in the court. Sometimes, the objections and interruptions are purposeful and unnecessary. In such instances, wait until the matter is ruled on and you are instructed to give your testimony by the Judge;
22. to realize that cross-examination is really *torturous*. Hence politeness and calmness will be more rewarding. Never get upset and don't make any conscious attempt to be wiser to testify deliberately on cross-examination. Don't testify hurriedly any thing; and
23. not to forget that the defence counsel has nothing against you personally and he is only trying his best just to shatter the prosecution evidence. Hence a quiet, clear, calm and concise answer given pleasantly and in an impersonal manner can guarantee better results.

And finally, the banker should bear in mind that there are different types of defence lawyers with their own special behavioural tactics and operational approaches. Some may not indulge in the personal attacks on the banker and others may be explosive in their approach. A few may dramatise the entire cross-examination by gesticulations at the end of each question. They may make insulting remarks and may raise suggestive questions just to trap the banker. All these are part of the exercise and as such the banker may try to follow the following rules especially when he faces a cross-examination.

The rules are :

1. Be short in your answers.
2. Whenever possible, say 'yes or no'.
3. Be precise and specific in replies.
4. Think thrice before responding to questions.
5. Speak only the truth.
6. Don't get upset; be self-confident.
7. Don't become emotional.
8. Don't be overzealous or extra-zealous.
9. Think that you are answering questions before intelligent and educated people who are accustomed to this. Hence don't try to bluff or to be wiser.
10. Give respect and get the respect back.

Notes

1. Andre Evans, The Investigator in Court, from *Criminal and Civil Investigation Hand Book* by Joseph J. Grau, ed., New York, Mc Graw Hill Co., 1981.
2. *Ibid.*

References

Peper, J.P., *Basic Criminal Investigation,* California, State Department of Education, 1956.

Rhodes T.F.II. *Clues and Crimes : The Science of Investigation,* London, John Murray, 1963.

Weston, P.B. and Kennth Wells, *Criminal Investigation : Basic Perspectives,* New Jersey, Prentice Hall, Englewood Cliffs, 1970.

BIBLIOGRAPHY

Aggarwal, H.R., Jain, C.K., and Sehgal, Examination of Forged Currency Notes with Beta-ray Radiography, *C.B.I. Bulletin*, Vol. XIII, No.1, January, 1979.

Aggarwal, K.C. and A.K. Gupta, *A Quick Method for the Detection of Pencil Over-writings,* Police Research and Development, Quarter 1, 1972.

Anderson, N.L., Ball-point Pens and Ink, *Dyestuffs*, 41 (8) December, 1956.

Basalo, Martinez, J., The Examination of Typewritten Documents : Detection and Photography of Traces on Coloured Surfaces, *International Criminal Police Review*, No. 322, November, 1978.

Beviridge, W.I.B., *The Art of Scientific Investigation,* Random House, New York, 1957.

Bhalla, R.S., Bank Frauds– The Disease : Causes and Cure, *C.B.I. Bulletin*, Vol. XVIII, No. 4., April, 1984.

Bingham, W.V., and B.V. Moore, *How to Interview?* Harper & Brothers, New York, 1941.

Bonebreak, G.O., Fabricating Fingerprint Evidence, *Identification News*, Vol. 26, No. 10, 1976.

Bremen, Ulf Von, Invisible Ultra-Violet-Fluorscence, *Journal of Forensic Science*, July, 1965.

Chatterjee, S.K., Origin of Fingerprint Science and Its Development During Last 75 Years, *Journal of Indian Academy of Forensic Sciences*, Vol. 13, No. 1 January, 1974.

Chug, O.P., K.P. Singh and Ravi Dutt, Detection of Rubber Stamp Forgery in Documents, *C.B.I. Bulletin*, Vol., XIV, No. 3, March 1980.

Conway, J.V.P., *Fingerprints and Documents,* R.C. M.P. Seminar No. 6, 1965.

Deinstein, William, *Techniques for Crime Investigator,* Charles C. Thomas, Springfield, Illinois, 1974.

Dewan, Puri K.S., Tremors [Forged and Genuine], *International Criminal Police Review*, No. 282, No. 1974.

Durantaye, J.A.G. and Shewechuk, W., *Sequence of Writing and Folding in Documents,* R.C.M.P. Seminar, No. 6, 1965.

Durley, B.D., Safety Paper– U.S.A., *Journal of Police Science and Administration*, Vol. 7, No. 1, March, 1979.

Eiseman, James, S., *Elements of Investigative Techniques,* McKnight and McKnight, Bloomington, Illinois, 1949.

Fisher Jacob, *The Art of Dectection,* Carlton Press, New York, 1963.

Garg, S.N. *et.al.*, *Obliterations and Their Decipherment,* Police Research and Development, Quarter II, 1971.

Garg, S.N., Parasuramiah and K.P.C. Gandhi, *Invisble Writings and Their Devleopment,* Police Reserch and Development, Quarter IV, 1975.

Garrelt, Annette, *Interviewing : Its Principles and Methods,* Family Welfare Association of America, New York, 1942.

Ghosh, S.K., Crisp Spurious Currency, *C.B.I. Bulletin*, Vol. XIV, No. 11, Novermber, 1980.

Gross, E., David L. Sin and Almog Joseph, Transmitted Infrared Luminescence in Document Examination, *Journal of Forensic Science*, Vol. 25, No. 2, April, 1980.

Gupta, S.K. and Chowdhry. R., Decipherment of Obliterations by Chemical Methods, *Journal of the Indian Academy of Forensic Science*, Vol. 13, No. 1, January, 1974.

Harrison, Wilson, R., Erasures, *Methods of Forensic Science*, Vol. 3, 1964.

Houts, Marshall, *From Evidence to Proof*, Charles C. Thomas, Springfield, Illinois; 1956.

Johnes, Leland, *Scientific Investigation and Physical Evidence*, Charles C. Thomas, Springfield, 1959.

Kino, S.S. and M.D. G. Dabbs, The Use of Lycode Powders for the Detection of Erasures, *Journal of Forensic Science Society*, Vol. 19, No. 3, July, 1979.

Koopmans, K., Chemical Examination of Ink Dyes, *Archiv fur. Kriminologie*, Vol. 124, Parts 5,6, 1959.

Larson, John A., *Lying and Its Detection*; University of Chicago Press, Chicago, 1932.

Lfibers, Arthur, *The Investigator's Hand book*, Acro Publishing Co., New York, 1972.

Leslte, A.G. and Stimpson, T.A., Identification of Printout Devices, *Forensic Science International*, Vol. 19, No. l. Jan-Feb., 1982.

Macdonald, John M., *Burglary and Theft*, Charles C. Thomas. Springfield, Illinois, 1980.

Mangele, R. and J.M. Duff, Laser Detection of Latent Finger Prints—Treatment with Flourescers, *Journal of Forensic Science*, Vol. 24, No. l, 1979.

Martin, E., Watermarks on Paper: Their Value as Criminalistic Evidence, *International Criminal Police Review*, No. 150 Aug-Sep., 1961.

Mathur, J., *The Training of a Document Expert*, R.C.M.P. Seminar, No. 6, 1965.

Mehrotra, *Forgery by One's Own Finger Print : A Possibility*, Police Research and Development, Quarter III, 1983.

Mehrotra, V.K. and Sidhana, S.K., Non-Destructive Identification of Metalicions of Inks Used on Documents, *Journal of Forensic Science*, Vol. 9, No. 1, 1977.

Morton, S. E., How Does Crowding Affect Signatures, *Journal of Forensic Sciences*, Vol. 25, No. l, Jan. 1980.

Mulbar, H., *Interrogation*, Charles C. Thomas, Springfield, 1951.

Nag, N.K., Basak, N., and Mazumdar, T., The Role of Radiology in the Identification of Forged Notes, *Journal of Police Science and Administration*, Vol. 2, No. 3, September, 1974.

Nemeeck, J., A Deep Look into Typewriter Alignment, *Journal of Forensic Sciences*, Vol. 10, No. 1, January, 1965.

Nickolls, Lewis, C., *The Scientific Investigation of Crime*, Butterworth, London, 1956.

Paper, John, P., *Elements of Police Investigation*, California Peace Officers' Training Series, No. 25, California State Department of Education, Sacramento, California, 1964.

Poulantagaz, M.N., Handwriting as a Means for the Identification of Offenders, *Royal Canadian Movmed Police Gazettee*, Vol. 43, No. 5, 1981.

Purtell, D. J., *Carbon Papers and Carbon Copy Impressions*, R.C.M.P. Seminar, No. 6, 1965.

Ram Gupta, S., *Cumulative Effect of Multiple Variables in Hampering Handwriting Identification*, Police Research and Development, Quarter 1, 1972.

Rhodes, Henry T.F., *Clues and Crimes : The Science of Criminal Investigation*, John Murrey, London, 1963.

Rohilla, D. R., S.K. Dasgupta, S.K. Gupta and H.L, Bami, A Rapid Infra-Red Luminescence Method for Differentiation of Ink Writing, *Forensic Science International*, Vol. 15, No. 2, 1980.

Seksena, N.S., Special Squads for Economic Crimes, *Times of India*, No. 29, 1980.

Saudek, R., *Experiments with Handwriting*, George Allen and Unwin Ltd., London, 1928.

Sehgal, V.N., Bank Frauds and Their Detection by the Appucation of Scientific Methods, *C.B.T. Balletin*, Vol. XVII. No. 6, June, 1983.

Sharma, B.R., Problems of Proof in Questioned Documents [Scientific, Aspects], *C.B.I. Bulletin*, Vol. XVII, No. 3, March, 1983.

Sharma, K.N., Frauds in Financial Institutions, *C.B.l. Bulletin*, Vol. XIV, No. 7 July, 1980.

Singh, R.P., *Examination of Typewritten Documents*, Police Research and Development, Quater III, 1976.

Stedry, W.; Infra-red in Criminalistic, *Kriminalistik*, Vol. II, No. 1, January, 1957.

Vadackijmchery, James, *Crime, Law and Police Science*, Concept Publishing Company, New Delhi. (In Press).

Verma, N.C., The Way of the Counterfeiters, *C.B.I. Bulletin* Vol. XIV, No. 4, April, 1980.

Walls, Henry J., *Forensic Science : An Introduction to the Science of Crime Detection*, Praeger, New York, 1968.

Wilte, A.H., Examination and Identification of Inks, *Methods of Forensic Science*, Vol. 2, 1963.

INDEX

Additions ,103-104
Advances and Security measures, 175-76
Alignment, 35-39
Allegations,180
Alterations, 35, 94-100, 104-105, 122, 130, 172-74
Armed customers, 160
Arm movement, 26
Asoka Pillar, 147, 148
Autography, 140

B. C. S. systems, 116-118
Badgis, 161
Banfers, 161
Bankdrafts, 94
  issued by, 124-125
Bank employees, 169-70
Bank keys,164
Bank, law and crimes in, 170, 172, 183-84
Bank lockers and frauds, 178-79
Bank managers/Accountants and safety, 170-71
Bank notes, kind of, 137-138
Bogus demand drafts, 163
Bogus mail transfers, 162-63
Bogus traveller's cheques, 135-36
Burglary, 158-59, 161, 164-65
Business transactions, 72

Carbon guidelines,102
Carbon paper tracing, 76, 95
Cash and credit facility, 179-80
Cash vans, armed robbery of, 163-66
Cheating, 90-92
Cheque examination, 102
Cheque-leaf code, 121
Cheque-leaves, 115
  serial numbers transplantation of, 106-107
Cheque-writing machine, 94
Code system, 120
Commercial Banks, functioning of, 191
Committing crimes, 168, 176
  system help, 110-111
Committing forgery, 66-68, 83-74, 78-79
Committing theft, 184
Complex writing characteristics, 58
Composite forgeries, 85
Containing signature, 62
Corruption, 180, 183
Counterfeit coins, detecting method of, 152-56, 167
Counterfeit note, 142-43
Crimes in Banks, 169-70
Criminal Breach of Trust, 187
Criminal gangs, 160-61
Criminal investigation, 240
Criminal misappropriation of property, 186
Criminal prosecution, 221-22
Criminal trespass, 188
Currency notes, 137-39
  counterfeiting of, 150-151
Customers, criminal psychology, 195, 199-202, 204

Dacoity, 186
Dactylography, 1-2
Defence mechanisms, 195-200
Demand draft, 125, 130
Detoriated signature, 54-55
Discretionary authority, misuse of, 175
Disguised signature, 38
Document/cheques, examination of, 192-94
Draft Security Key (DSK) systems, 125, 130

Eliciting truths, indirect method of, 200
Erase guidelines, 80
Erased documents, 72
Erasures, 94, 98-99, 105
  ball-point pen inks, 96, 99-100
  deciphering of, 100-101
Exchange traces, 210
Extortion, 184

Fake coins, 155
Fake notes, 146
  simulated security thread, 143-144
  method use, 140-141
False documents, 67-68
False notes, 148-49
Fictitious account, 173
Fictitious names, 73-74

Finger prints, 1, 112, 169, 173, 211
equipment and materials use for, 14-15
examination of, 19-20
patterns, 7, 8
use of, 18, 19
First Investigation Report (FIR), 212, 215, 219-20
Fischhof method, detecting forgeries, 83-86
Fixed deposits and frauds, 177-78
Fool proof system, 180
Foot prints, 169, 211
Forged notes, detecting of, 81-84, 139
denomination of, 138
instructions to Bank, 150
legal provisions, 149-52
Forged paper money, 140
Forged signature, 32, 40-41, 73, 137-39
type of, 77
Forgeries, 70-71, 78-79, 209
law-relating to, 66-67, 70-71
methods of, 74-75
Forgery over genuine signature, 43-45
Forgery-proof signature, 55-56, 117-23
Formal signature, 52, 125
Frauds through clearance houses, 176-177
Freehand forgery, 43, 74-75
detecting of, 84, 90
Furrows, 2
tracks, 28

Genuine coins, 154-155
Genuine notes, 139-40, 146
comparisons of, 140
designs on, 149
photographies of, 144
Genuine retouching, 53-56, 87
Genuine signatures, 38
appreciation of, 62-67
characteristics of, 56-58
examination of, 45-46
general execution, 39-40
illustrations, 68-70
variations of, 53-54, 89
Ghosh, S.K., 180
Greedy employees, 173-75
Guided hand signatures, 55
Guioe lines, 79-80, 100, 102
Gum arabic, 95
Gymkhanas, 171

Hand-made notes, 140
Hand magnifiers, 192
Handwriting, characteristics of, 75-76
categories, 23, 40
pen position, 30-33, 46-47
shading in, 32-33, 47
size of, 28
slope or slant, 35-36
spacing, 36-37
speed of, 28, 29, 45-46
stroke impuls, 27
style characteristics, 24, 31-31, 48
terminology, 40-41
wrist movement, 26
Harrison, Wilson R., 25
Hiatus, 65
House-breaking, 188-89
Huge amount of money, withdrawls of, 162
Hypothecation and frauds, 178

Identification, 197-98
Illegal gratification, 173, 181
Illegible signature, 55
Imprisonment, 151
Indian money,
inks in notes and chemical tests, 149-50
shadow printing in, 144-45
stiching and stapling, 148
water marks in, 147-48
Informal signature, 52, 125
Infra-red radiation, 194
Inoperative accounts and Frauds, 179
Intoxication, 68

Left thumb impression, 16-17
Letters alignment, 34-35
form and formation, 37-38
relative positioning of, 89
size and proportion, 37-38
spacing, 36-37
Line quality, 29-30, 47
Litigation, 12
Loard's principle of exchange, 210-11
Locker-holders, pass-word, 178-79

Mahatma Gandhi, 148
Mail transfers, receiving branches, 131-32
Malyala Manorama, 144
Measuring apparatus, 193
Mechanical erasures, detection of, 96-98
Mischief, 187-88
Modern genuine coins, 193
Modus operandi, 158-59, 161, 167-68, 200

criminals, 159, 168-69, 170-171
Money transactions, 191
security in, 114-15
Moveable property, 70
MTS system, 131-32

New account holder, check list of, 113-14
New safety methods, 109,'30
Non-cognizable offences, 213

Obliteration, 105
Obtain clear impressions, 15
Offences committed, 213-14
Ornate signature, 55
Over sightness, 169
Over writing, 101-104

Paper money, numbering of, 141-42
obverse and reverse side printing, 138-39
Pass-word, 178-79
Perforation system, 127-136
Personal characteristics, 24-25
identification, 18
signature of customer, 20-21
Personation, 90-91
Petroleum ether, 97
Photographer's retouching desk, 119, 194-95
Physical evidence, types of, 212
Pick-pocket, 158
Pledged ornaments, 174
Police Museum, 143
Precautions, 16-17, 95-96, 111, 176, 209
against counterfeiting, 149
against forgery, 142
Precaution of Corruption Act, 180, 182
Professional criminals, 158, 159-60, 168, 200
Progress change, law of, 211
Projecting tracing, 76

Qualitative tests, 45-46
Quatlet's law, 126, 211
Quantitative characteristics, 25
Quantitative tests, 48-50
Questioning, direct method of, 200

Ramanujam, T., 162
Rationalization, 195-96.
Recruitment and crimes, faulty methods of, 180-81
Regression, 197
Reserve Bank of India, 142, 144-145, 148, 174
Ridge characteristics, 2-6, 12, 173-74
examination of, 17-18
Right Thumb impression, 16-17
Robery, 185
Rosethes, 149

Safe burglaries, 164-65
Scene inspection, principle of, 210-11
Schorles, 149
Security printing, 123-24, 130
Security watch in nights, 161-62
Signature, arrangement, 39-40
comparison of, 20-21, 41-42, 119-20
examination of, 65
forgery of, 72-90
identification, 58
pattern of, 53
types of, 54, 56
Simulated forgery, 73-74, 78
Sinatable viscosity, polyethylene glycols of, 96
Small amount, bank draft for, 171-72
Specimen signature, 42-43, 54
card, 112-13, 118-19, 122
points of, 65-66
Strangers to Bank, 159-60
Stolen cheque, precautions for, 123-24
Striking, 96
Surveillance, 179
Suspicious signature, 58

Telephonic message, 220
Temporary misappropriation, 175
Testimony, 222, 224-25
Theft, 184
Thumb impression, 1
errors in, 16
identification of, 12-14
Tolerance, 198
Tortureus, 225
Tracing paper process, 76-77
Traced forgery, 74-76, 77, 82-83
Transacting cheques, new method of, 21
Traveller's cheques, 134-36
Typescript, erasure of, 105-06

Ultraviolet (UV) lamps, 98-99, 193

Valuable security, 67-68, 70-71

Water marks, 130, 147-48
Withdrawal, 198
Word impulse, 27
Writing characteristics, 25-26, 45-46
variations in, 42
Writing/signature, style of, 31-32